# A CLASS A

## Learning the Lessons of Education in Post-Devolution Wales

# Welsh Academic Press – Education Series

**Series Editor**
Professor D Reynolds, Southampton Education School, University of Southampton

**Mission**
Education and educational systems are now a matter of political, public and professional debate as never before historically. This debate concerns the ways in which schools can be improved, the nature of the schools that societies will need in the future and the deficiencies of educational systems at present.

This series aims to make available to both the professional and general reader, books that explore policy, practice, debate and controversy in education from an international perspective, and from renowned international authorities who can review fields based upon substantial knowledge and experience.

These fields will include:

Educational policy;
Educational change and transformation;
Educational practice;
Educational governance and politics;
Special educational needs.

Additionally, whilst the series will be international in nature, a particular focus will also be given to Wales and the issues related to the Welsh educational system, including Welsh medium education, the future of Higher and Further education in Wales and the more general issues in Wales about how whole national systems can be 'turned around'. This will be compared and contrasted with similar systems and educational innovations globally.

Books will be research monographs, text book reviews of particular fields/areas of Education and specialist reviews in particular fields/areas.

**Submissions**
For further information about the series and for details on how to submit a publishing proposal, please visit out website: www.welsh-academic-press.com

# A CLASS APART

## Learning the Lessons of Education in Post-Devolution Wales

*Gareth Evans*

Welsh Academic Press

Published in Wales by Welsh Academic Press, an imprint of

Ashley Drake Publishing Ltd
PO Box 733
Cardiff
CF14 7ZY

www.welsh-academic-press.com

First Edition – 2015

ISBN
978-1-86057-123-7

© Ashley Drake Publishing Ltd 2015
Text © Gareth Evans 2015

British Library Cataloguing-in-Publication Data.
A CIP catalogue for this book is available from the British Library.

Typeset by Replika Press Pvt Ltd, India
Printed by Akcent Media, Czech Republic

# Contents

*For Jayne and Roger. First they had my back, now I have theirs.*

# List of Acronyms

| | |
|---|---|
| ACCAC | *Qualifications, Curriculum and Assessment Authority for Wales* |
| ACER | *Australian Council for Educational Research* |
| AM | *Assembly Member* |
| ASCL | *Association of School and College Leaders* |
| ATL | *Association of Teachers and Lecturers* |
| CBI | *Confederation of British Industry* |
| CDAP | *Child Development Assessment Profile* |
| CSSIW | *Care and Social Services Inspectorate Wales* |
| DCELLS | *Department for Children, Education, Lifelong Learning and Skills* |
| DfES | *Department for Education and Skills* |
| ELWa | *Education and Learning Wales* |
| EYDAF | *Early Years Development and Assessment Framework* |
| GCSE | *General Certificate of Secondary Education* |
| GTCW | *General Teaching Council for Wales* |
| HEFCW | *Higher Education Funding Council for Wales* |
| HEIs | *Higher Education Institutions* |
| HEPI | *Higher Education Policy Institute* |
| HESA | *Higher Education Statistics Agency* |
| HEW | *Higher Education Wales* |
| INSET | *In-Service Education for Teachers* |
| IWA | *Institute of Welsh Affairs* |
| JCQ | *Joint Council for Qualifications* |
| LNF | *Literacy and Numeracy Framework* |
| NAHT | *National Association of Head Teachers* |
| NASUWT | *National Association of Schoolmasters Union of Women Teachers* |
| NASS | *National Association of Small Schools* |
| NATFHE | *National Association of Teachers in Further and Higher Education* |
| NSP | *National Support Programme* |
| NUS | *National Union of Students* |
| NUT | *National Union of Teachers* |
| OECD | *Organisation for Economic Co-operation and Development* |
| PISA | *Programme for International Student Assessment* |

| | |
|---|---|
| *PLCs* | *Professional Learning Communities* |
| *QAA* | *Quality Assurance Agency* |
| *SATs* | *Standard Attainment Tests* |
| *SEF* | *School Effectiveness Framework* |
| *SEN* | *Special Educational Needs* |
| *SF* | *Skills Framework* |
| *SSU* | *School Standards Unit* |
| *SQA* | *Scottish Qualifications Authority* |
| *UCAC* | *Undeb Cenedlaethol Athrawon Cymru* |
| *UCAS* | *Universities and Colleges Admissions Service* |
| *UHOVI* | *Universities Heads of the Valleys Institute* |
| *UWIC* | *University of Wales Institute, Cardiff* |
| *WAO* | *Wales Audit Office* |
| *WESPs* | *Welsh in Education Strategic Plans* |
| *WISERD* | *Wales Institute of Social and Economic Research, Data and Methods* |
| *WJEC* | *Welsh Joint Education Committee* |
| *WLGA* | *Welsh Local Government Association* |

# Introduction

Wales has a proud history of educating its citizens. In the late nineteenth century, "the gwerin" – the common folk – became a symbol of Welsh national identity and the importance of a solid education was inherent long before the emergence of compulsory schooling. Wales was the nation whose love of learning and self-betterment led to impoverished miners investing money they could not afford to set up Welsh universities in the 1870s and 1880s. The need to up-skill and progress in the world through learning was well understood and parents strove to educate their children as best as possible. Education became a cultural institution in the way that religion, its places of worship and eisteddfodau had been for decades previous. It had a unifying effect and class differences became less prevalent. The gift of learning was available to all and schools became the focal point of their communities. It did not take devolution to focus hearts and minds.

In the years prior to and immediately following Wales' historic vote towards greater independence, the nation's education system was performing consistently above its UK rivals. Wales had proven itself capable of mixing with the very best and there was no reason why the advent of more powers would prevent further development. But hindsight is a wonderful thing and when Wales' charismatic and long-serving First Minister Rhodri Morgan stood down in 2009, his successor inherited an education system in turmoil. A rapid decline had seen Welsh teenagers go from achieving an above-average percentage of five A\*-C grades at GCSE to a percentage significantly below average. Wales was attracting fewer top grades at A-level and fewer top degrees at university. Key performance tables ranked Wales' basic skills among the poorest in the developed world and levels of literacy and numeracy were of grave concern. Not surprisingly, morale amongst teachers was at an all-time low.

The corrosion of Welsh education could scarcely have come at a worse time. The increasing malleability of cross-country borders had raised the stakes and world leaders were now benchmarking on an international stage; comparisons with nearest neighbours would no longer suffice. The Programme for International Student Assessment (PISA) was an important driver and what was once a leaning tower in Italy's west coast was now the talk of education ministries across the globe. Wales found itself at the bottom of the UK class but standards had been sliding for some time and no amount of change would revive Welsh fortunes overnight. The inquest had begun.

*A Class Apart* will look at why Wales' education system slipped so markedly and seek to answer some of the sector's most fundamental questions.

To do that, it will focus largely on the two key protagonists central to the drama. It will begin by considering the reign of long-serving and pioneering Education Minister Jane Davidson. Starting with schools and extending to universities, it will recount the major events taking place in the years immediately following devolution and seek to highlight those which define the nation's education system today. A trailblazer, Davidson had licence to do not what Wales did, but what Wales wanted to do next. An extended interview with Davidson will shed new light on her seven-year reign and scrutiny of the Welsh Government's cradle-to-grave learning strategy provides context for a new era under the man charged with bridging Wales' standards gap.

Leighton Andrews shared in Davidson's ambition, albeit his role was to put right what had gone so badly wrong before. His root and branch shake-up of education was more dramatic than any of his predecessors', but the seriousness of the situation demanded decisive action and a laissez-faire approach would have served only to quicken Wales' plight. With the evidence stacked against them, providers of education could no longer command the same levels of autonomy and drastic times called for drastic measures.

My own interest in Welsh education stems from my formative years in and around Cardiff. A product of Wales' education system, it became my job to report on it in December 2009 when I was appointed Education Correspondent for the *Western Mail*, the country's national newspaper. Given the timing of my appointment coincided with that of Andrews' as Education Minister, *A Class Apart* will major on his tenure and analyse closely the decisions taken during a time when Wales' schools, colleges and universities hit headlines like never before.

Devolution gave Wales an opportunity. It opened new doors and gave Welsh ministers freedom to break from the unilateral education system that had existed previously. Policymakers would consider developments in a number of countries and Scotland, Australia, Canada, New Zealand and Finland were all looked upon as possible trend setters. The emergence of Scandinavian nations, in particular, as powerhouses in education bred hope that success could be replicated on Welsh shores. But with opportunity came risk. *A Class Apart* will consider the effectiveness of policies introduced by the devolved administration and seek to determine whether they were right for Wales. It will assess the situation in which we find ourselves and plot a course for what has the potential to be a small, clever nation.

Many of the initiatives introduced in Wales were untried and untested in a UK context and while variations had been proven to work overseas, ministers had no way of telling whether policy would travel effectively. Wales was taking a giant step into the educational unknown but the emerging Welsh Assembly Government could be sure the decisions taken following devolution would resonate for years to come.

# 1

## The Times They Are-A Changing

## Wales forges its own educational course

*Setting the scene. A look at some of the early policy developments in Welsh education following devolution, with reference to Wales' 10 year plan and the inception of a revolutionary play-based pedagogy*

Prior to the creation of the National Assembly for Wales in 1999, the education systems of Wales and England were practically identical. While the Welsh Office had since the 1970s and 1980s enjoyed a certain amount of control over Wales' educational offer, its ability to dictate policy was minimal and only after the most marginal of "Yes" votes could the nation's people have a real and meaningful say over what went on in the classroom. At long last, Wales had licence to plough its own furrow and the new Welsh Assembly Government needed no invitation. The Department for Children, Education, Lifelong Learning and Skills (DCELLS) became a laboratory for change. Notwithstanding its comparatively small budget and lack of primary legislative powers, Wales developed its own distinctive policies that would define its education system for generations.

There remained parallel lines but with every passing year after devolution, Wales and England grew further apart. Education under Prime Minister Tony Blair's New Labour movement was ambitious but by no means a model and party colleagues in Wales took off in a markedly different direction. So what does Wales' bespoke education system look like and by what can we separate one from the other? Consider first that the ruling Welsh Assembly Government was in firm control of its own destiny and aside from teachers' pay and conditions, Assembly Members (AMs) had rule over every meaningful policy area.

A strong belief in community-led comprehensive education means there are no free schools or academies in Wales as there are across the border. A tripartite between Wales, England and Northern Ireland has seen qualifications shared across three of the four corners of the UK. With the exception of Scotland, which has its own well-established qualifications system, the rest of the home nations have retained faith in traditional GCSEs and A-levels. Hadrian's Wall is a far stronger buffer than Offa's Dyke but with greater autonomy to determine their own futures, Wales and Northern Ireland are growing in confidence and beginning to promulgate a genuine desire to pursue different exam routes.

Politically, Welsh Labour is a dominant force and has maintained a constant presence in government from the first plenary session of the Assembly, when AMs met to elect Presiding Officer Dafydd Elis-Thomas and inaugural First Secretary Alun Michael. Michael's sudden departure after barely eight months in office opened the door to Rhodri Morgan, who led a coalition with the Liberal Democrats in the First Assembly, a minority administration between 2003-2007 and a coalition with Plaid Cymru from then until 2011. Welsh Labour presides over a minority government in the Fourth Assembly. The Welsh language has been prevalent throughout and its equal status alongside English means Welsh-medium schools are increasingly popular. Indeed, the nation's determination to breed bilingualism and preserve Europe's oldest living language proves unequivocally that Welsh education is capable of rising from the ashes.

## Welsh-medium education

The first state-funded Welsh-medium primary school, Dewi Sant, opened in Llanelli in 1947. Since then, demand for Welsh-medium primary education has grown rapidly and by adapting in the latter half of the twentieth century the immersion techniques of countries like Canada, Wales has developed its own bespoke teaching methods. A boom in Welsh-medium education extended to the secondary and post-16 sectors, albeit at a slower rate. The first Welsh-medium state secondary school, Glan Clwyd, launched in Rhyl in 1956 and inaugural Welsh-medium qualifications were developed by the nation's exam board, the Welsh Joint Education Committee (WJEC), in the early 1960s. From those small acorns grew a new world of learning via Wales' mother tongue and the inclusion in 1988 of Welsh as a national curriculum subject marked an important milestone. By 2009, more than 400 qualifications were available through the medium of Welsh. Currently, Welsh is compulsory for all pupils in schools maintained by the state up to and including GCSE level (age 16). But while government intervention and significant financial investment has ensured the continuation of Wales' minority language – after Israel, it is considered only the second major nation to have done so – there remains work to be done. Statistics show the number of children who receive their education through the medium of Welsh decreases as they grow older and since devolution, successive Welsh-medium strategies have so far failed to deliver what they set out to achieve – that is, a distinctly bilingual Wales. According to a task and finish group commissioned to consider new ways of increasing the number of Welsh-speaking communities:

"The period following the Second World War was a key period in the history of Welsh education when Welsh was normalised as a medium of learning in the primary sector...To a large extent, in the secondary sector, it was simply a matter of 'lessons history, lessons geography, lessons English', as Dafydd Iwan once said. A positive change came about in the 1960s in some authorities under the enlightened leadership of elected members, education officers and senior school headteacher appointments. Developments were also facilitated by the Gittins report of 1967. Informal and gradual progress was confirmed in some of the relevant areas with local government reorganisation in 1974 and the formulation of education language policies in Gwynedd and Dyfed."[1] (Welsh Government, 2013)

The Welsh-medium Education Strategy was launched in 2010 and, building on the overview provided by the Iaith Pawb action plan in 2003, set in train the Assembly Government's long-term vision for the growth of the Welsh language in schools. Progress would be monitored via fixed five and 10-year targets, which proposed sharp rises in take-up. The strategy sought an increase of 9% in the proportion of primary age Year Two learners being assessed in Welsh by 2020 (the figure stood at 21% at the time of publication) and a 7% rise during the same period, from 16% in 2009 to 23% in 2020, at secondary Year Nine level. Local authorities, which retained democratic responsibility for the delivery of education, would be expected to agree their own targets as part of individual Welsh in Education Strategic Plans (WESPs). WESPs, submitted initially on a voluntary basis, would become statutory from April 2014.

A holistic approach to Welsh-medium education, the 2010 education strategy promised a lot but would ultimately be reliant upon the desire and commitment of local members to promote its expansion. Results of the 2011 Census showed that 19% of the population could speak Welsh (562,000 people). The figure was above the 18.7% recorded in the 1991 Census (508,100 people), but down on the 20.8% of Welsh speakers (582,400) noted in the 2001 Census a decade later. The nation's inspectorate makes no secret of the fact that pupils' progress in Welsh slows down as they progress through the education system. Despite having to learn the language for 13 years, very few pupils become fluent Welsh speakers after leaving school. The conversion rate between those who study and those who develop their skills into adulthood is painfully low and Wales has yet to find a way of linking the two systematically.

There is little doubt a fall in the proportion of people who could speak, write and understand Welsh was a blow to the Welsh Government's aspirations. But while the 2011 Census gave cause for reflection, the emergence of social media had at least offered a new platform through which the language could be nurtured. Allied to that, the increasing popularity of Welsh-medium schools are proof there is a thriving market of which parents continue to buy in. The key appears strengthening the teaching of Welsh in English-medium schools, a process which is currently far too tokenistic.

For all Wales' investment in its native language, it is important to note that the number of fluent Welsh speakers who migrate out of Wales is still considerably larger than the number of those who return. That inevitably impacts on overall figures although the struggle to preserve the Welsh language can be intrinsically linked to the closure, on mass, of so-called "small schools" in Wales. Given their important role as focal points of their rural communities, small schools – defined by the Audit Commission as having 90 pupils or less – are considered vital to the ongoing development of Welsh-medium education. They are structural facilitators and campaigners oppose their enforced closure on the basis that Welsh language provision in the locality will be diluted, bilingual families will be driven away and the traditional Welsh culture will be lost. They are good grounds with which to argue.

## Small schools

Other than maintaining a commitment to tackle surplus places, following devolution local authorities were allowed the freedom to administer their provision in the way they felt appropriate. As more and more people congregated around Wales' biggest towns and cities, not least because of the decline in agricultural and mining industries, it was rural schools that bore the brunt of falling pupil numbers. Councils across the country sought to reorganise their supply of school places and seldom did the Assembly Government, with its powers of intervention, choose to throw out what local members had proposed. It is therefore not surprising that the central administration, a self-confessed champion of the Welsh language, has been accused of reneging on its own pro-bilingual promise by assuming a predominantly hands-off approach. Iaith Pawb was explicit that the health and evolution of the Welsh language would be seriously threatened if it ceased to be a language with a strong presence in the community.

The School Standards and Organisation (Wales) Act 2013, which became law in the same year, set out proposals to strengthen school standards, enhance local determination and reduce complexity. It reformed the statutory process to provide a clearer path for school intervention and ensured decisions on reorganisation would be taken locally wherever possible. A subsequent School Organisation Code made clear the general principles and factors that should be taken into account by those bringing forward proposals to reconfigure school provision. The code was explicit that funding for education should be "cost effective" and where there were more than 10% surplus places in an area, local authorities should review the existing schools offer. It made it easier to close schools with fewer than 10 registered pupils and stated that: "Some spare places are necessary to enable schools to cope with fluctuations in numbers of pupils, but excessive numbers of unused places that could be removed mean that resources are tied up unproductively."[2] The document recommended that councils look to "recycle" assets from surplus school buildings and sites into the overall improvement of their schools estate, rather than allocate additional proceeds to projects outside the education portfolio. Given the onus on accountability at a local level, however, ministers would respect that financial implications were a matter for councillors.

Wales' education watchdog Estyn was asked to look at the viability of small schools and the quality of outcomes for pupils as part of its remit from the Assembly Government. A subsequent report, published in 2006, found that standards in small primary schools were about the same as larger schools, and there was no evidence to suggest that size was a factor in pupils' attainment. Nevertheless, it said leadership and management, staff development and curriculum planning tended to be weaker in small schools. "The smaller the school, the more challenging it often is for the teacher to match work to all pupils' learning needs," Estyn added. "This is because, in these schools, teachers have to teach pupils of widely different ages and stages of development in the same class."[3] Research commissioned by the Institute of Welsh Affairs (IWA) found in 2007 that the closure of small schools in Wales was "overwhelmingly beneficial" and the quality and standard of education improved when small schools merged into larger ones. Researchers interviewed teachers, pupils and parents at schools shut in Powys and Pembrokeshire to form an evidence-base. Professor David Reynolds, an academic who gained international recognition for his work on school effectiveness and improvement, said of the study:

"It is clear that the apocalyptic predictions about the impact of small school closures on the Welsh language and communities are not borne out by our sample. No parent or child thought the position of the language was worse after reorganisation. This is an extraordinary finding given the public debate on this issue."[4] (David Reynolds, 2007)

It was reported in 2014 that only a third of the total number of primary schools closed in the previous three years in Wales had been matched by new buildings opening. Figures released by government officials showed that, since 2011, a total of 123 primary schools had been shut, with just 42 schools opening – which equated to just under two-thirds of schools not being replaced. A total of 12 secondary schools were closed over the same period, with six new schools opened in their place. The National Association of Small Schools (NASS) warned in 2014 of a "growing threat" to small schools in Wales.

Whatever their impact on Wales' indigenous language, it is important to remember that small schools also serve an important social purpose. They are often the backbone of their rural communities; doubling as village halls and a meeting place for residents. The decline of post offices, chapels, banks and pubs has only served to magnify their worth but council spending cuts, borne largely out of the financial crisis in the late 2000s, make small schools more vulnerable than ever.

## The birth of a children's champion

Former First Minister Rhodri Morgan's "clear red water" is as prevalent in education as in any other government portfolio. Nowhere is divergence clearer than in the Welsh Government's vision for schools, colleges and universities. Policy has split and after an eternity of Westminster rule, Wales is going it alone on a number of key issues. One of the earliest and most anticipated deviations was the creation in 2001 of a Children's Commissioner. It was apt that Peter Clarke would start work on St David's Day following a series of interviews, including one with a panel of young people. A publicly-funded post, the Children's Commissioner would be responsible for protecting children's rights as set out in the Convention on the Rights of the Child. Clarke would hold the position until his death from cancer in 2007 and Keith Towler became Wales' second Children's Commissioner on March 1, 2008. Not for the first time, Wales was the trend-setter and although the idea of a Children's Commissioner was not immediately bought in England, its invention would soon catch the attention of the rest of the UK. Northern Ireland introduced its own adaptation in 2003 and Scotland's first Commissioner for Children and Young People assumed her position in April 2004. Following a lengthy campaign, England was last to follow suit in 2005.

# The Learning Country

Such is Wales' relative infancy as a devolved nation, many features of today's education system can be traced back to the turn of the last century. Initially, the role of Education Minister – or Education Secretary, as it was originally – was split into two. Upon creation of the Welsh Assembly Government, Newport West AM Rosemary Butler looked after pre-16 education while Lancastrian Tom Middlehurst, AM for Alyn and Deeside, presided over post-16 education. But neither was in a job for long and the roles merged in October 2000, when Jane Davidson was appointed Minister for Education, Lifelong Learning and Skills. A former drama teacher, Davidson entered politics in 1994 as a researcher for Cardiff West MP Rhodri Morgan and, five years later in 1999, was herself elected AM for Pontypridd. Described as one of the Assembly's "sexiest members", Davidson ruled with charm and eloquence and was known for establishing good working relationships with sector stakeholders. She remains the UK's longest-serving Education Minister and while her seven-year reign over Wales' schools ended in 2007, Davidson's footprints are prevalent within all facets of policy development. Without doubt, she is best remembered for carving out and nurturing the Welsh Assembly's own distinctive vision for education in Wales. She was not, it is fair to say, in the slightest bit fazed by setting out on a very different course to that being taken in England.

A history of school improvement in Wales starts in 2001 with the publication of the seminal Learning Country. Although added to and updated during the early 2000s, The Learning Country charted the Welsh Government's 10-year plan to transform education and lifelong learning in post-devolution Wales. It was the first comprehensive paving document for primary and secondary legislation in the field of education issued from the National Assembly. The Learning Country was holistic by nature and sought cradle-to-grave reform of education for all in Wales. Davidson said the nation was at "a turning point for education and lifelong learning" and The Learning Country would seek to "remove obstacles to effective teaching". She promised "excellence for all" and warned that failure to "heal the significant divisions in our society" was not an option. Davidson said:

"As the responsible minister, my vision for education and lifelong learning is that Wales should become internationally renowned as a Learning Country: a place which puts learners' interests first; offers wider access and opportunities for all; aspires to excellence across the board; and which will not settle for second best in making lifelong learning a reality. That means making the most of any opportunity that comes to hand to achieve excellent results and finding innovative and radical ways to create opportunities as well – whether they arise internationally, in the European Union, through the central government, or here in Wales."[5] (Jane Davidson, 2001)

The document remains as relevant now as it was during its inception. Davidson wrote in her foreword to The Learning Country that "our skills-base is relatively low" and above all, "success depends upon a rapid acceleration in lifting our knowledge and skills-base". It is a damning indictment of the Assembly Government in all its various guises that the same is almost certainly true today. It is striking that much of what Davidson argued as being of pressing concern at the turn of the new millennium, can be equally applicable now, more than a decade later. True, we have the benefit of hindsight and with it the virtue of knowing what works and what does not. But it is nevertheless a sad reflection on the state in which we find ourselves that we continue to entertain the same debate.

Davidson's tenure is characterised by "made in Wales" policies like the flagship Foundation Phase and Welsh Baccalaureate programmes. Both are considered shining lights of post-devolution Wales, and while tangible results have not yet come to the fore, there is an underlying respect for what Davidson and her department set out to achieve. The minister was ambitious and free from the shackles of Westminster, set out on a new course; devolution provided an opportunity to do things differently. Davidson used The Learning Country to set out her stall and wrote:

"We share key strategic goals with our colleagues in England – but we often need to take a different route to achieve them. We shall take our own policy direction where necessary, to get the best for Wales. It's right that we put local authorities, local communities and locally determined needs and priorities at the centre of the agenda for schools, for example. Our communities want excellent local comprehensive schools for all their children. Partnership on that front is at the heart of the way we do things in Wales."[6] (Jane Davidson, 2001)

The Learning Country sought to establish a firm capital expenditure programme, with the target of having all schools in good physical shape by 2010; provide nursery education to all children from the age of three; reduce all infant and junior classes to 30 pupils or less; develop a strategic policy for rural and small schools; and implement an all-age basic skills plan to better prepare the nation's youngest children for learning. Further along the scale, the Welsh Baccalaureate, designed to provide Wales' teenagers with a new breadth of experience, linked closely to the Learning Pathways

14-19 progression route and would develop into a trend-setter for others to follow.

But while invention had merits, pursuing a Wales-specific agenda so vehemently was also one of the great criticisms levelled against Davidson during her term in office. There was some doubt as to whether the Assembly Government was taking an alternative course for the sake of it, rather than doing so because the new course of action was proven to be best for the nation. South Wales East AM William Graham, the Conservative's education spokesman, said shortly before her resignation that Davidson had "attempted to make Wales different instead of making Wales best".[7] There is a suggestion that Davidson may have been better served mirroring her Labour colleagues in the UK Government, within which "education, education, education" was, of course, very much a priority. It is no coincidence that Sir Michael Barber and Robert Hill, both key figures in the Blair administration, would surface in Wales only after Davidson's resignation.

Like so many education ministers, Davidson vowed to put the interests of learners above all else, stressing that "standards, results and outcomes matter more than inputs"[8]. All sectors and providers, she argued, must set out to achieve stretching but realistic targets, share international best practice and set new benchmarks for quality assessment. She said barriers to learning had to be recognised and steadily overcome, and "the informed professional judgement of teachers, lecturers and trainers must be celebrated without prejudice to the disciplines of public accountability"[9]. A keen advocate of evidence in the policy-making process, Davidson would later attract criticism from MPs within her own party for taking a "consensual" approach, based on working too closely alongside professionals and trade unions rather than challenging them.

## Breaking the mould

One of Davidson's headline and most significant policy announcements regarded Standard Attainment Tests (SATs) and whether or not they had a future in Wales after devolution. SATs were introduced in stages from 1991 as a way of consistently assessing some of the UK's youngest pupils in the core subjects of English, maths and science. They were designed to make schools more accountable and provided valuable insight into children's strengths and weaknesses at an early age. Teachers could use SATs to compare how well their pupils were doing relative to their peers, and chart improvement across key stages.

To help support primary schools, The Learning Country vowed to "consider whether there is a continuing need to apply national testing arrangements for seven-year-olds (Key Stage 1) – given the very high degree to which pupils meet what is expected of them – and the possibility that the resources involved might be used differently to assist teachers to raise standards across the curriculum at that stage"[10]. True to form and following lengthy discussion with the sector, SATs were phased out by the Assembly Government from 2002. Testing at Key Stage 1 went first, followed by SATs at key stages 2 and 3 (years six and nine). Teachers in Wales had grown suspicious of their actual value and questioned whether testing pupils so young in their educational journey was a worthwhile exercise. There was a widely-held perception that SATs had run their course, but the decision to ditch external testing at seven and 11 would leave a weighty void. Finding a reliable substitute would be key and conscious of the void left by SATs, it was the Assembly's intention to strengthen teacher assessments as a way of monitoring pupil performance. The decision was based on thorough consideration of the negative aspects of testing and evidence that high-quality teacher assessment had a far greater impact on the quality of learning and learning outcomes.

Davidson is also credited with scrapping secondary school league tables, albeit that too won the sector's blessing. She explained her preference for sector-led performance data in The Learning Country:

> "Performance tables featuring information on individual schools were introduced at a time when there was relatively little information available to practitioners, or indeed to parents, about achievement. Ten years on, the situation is very different. There is much more data available, and practitioners are considerably more skilled in using it for the improvement of teaching and learning over time. It is essential that individual schools in Wales make performance information available to parents on a valid basis common to all. This is the information that teachers use year on year and they are best placed to put it into the broader context of the life of the school in their discussions with parents themselves."[11] (Jane Davidson, 2001)

Davidson's unashamed drive towards "communitarianism", that is the emphasising of community in the functioning of political life, was prevalent and in accordance with New Labour's rejection of the market-led ideology of the Conservative right. Davidson and her colleagues believed that government and industry had to work together to enhance the dynamism of the market, rather than potentially undermine it, and the profession was looked upon as an equal partner.

League tables were published annually in England and Wales from 1992 to 2001. They became popular with national and local media as a way of charting performance and stakeholders would call upon them to assess relative strengths and weaknesses. But league tables were also highly divisive and seen as creating unnecessary competition between schools. Pitting schools against each other could be counter-productive and facilitate friction between parents, lead to more calculated selection with regards pupil places, and fuel an uncomfortable rat race whereby staff deflect depending on their school's relative position. There was not, it is fair to say, a clamour to see them spared. But in stripping away SATs and league tables, Davidson had removed two important layers of accountability.

The Centre for Market and Public Organisation, based at the University of Bristol, considered the impact of performance tables on school effectiveness in its study published in October 2010. Researchers found "systematic, significant and robust evidence" that the abolition of league tables in Wales "markedly reduced school effectiveness" and the effect was concentrated in the schools in the lower 75% of the distribution of ability and poverty. The report acknowledged that the Assembly expected schools to publish performance data themselves – on individual websites and in prospectuses – but it questioned how many chose to divulge such information in practice. According to the centre, what schools made available to stakeholders largely depended on how well they had performed and what level of competition there was in their local area. Researchers said that, based on performance at GCSE level, "there was faster attainment growth in England than in Wales" after league tables were axed. They concluded:

"Our results suggest that school accountability policies hold promise for raising school performance, particularly for students in disadvantaged schools and neighbourhoods. If uniform national test results exist, publishing these in a locally comparative format appears to be an extremely cost-effective policy for raising attainment and reducing inequalities in attainment."[12] (University of Bristol, 2010)

The University of Bristol paper makes for compelling reading and provides the clearest indication that diminished scrutiny of performance data did not have the desired effect. Nevertheless, when the situation was redressed more than a decade later with school banding, it was met with near universal disapproval from within the sector which saw similarities with league tables. Former special adviser to the Assembly Government Dr Tim Williams revealed the administration's thinking in a blog in 2011. Williams was one of five educationalists appointed to review the structure of education services in Wales, under the leadership of long-time Neath Port Talbot education director Vivian Thomas. Serial college leader Wil Edmunds, Newport's director of education Dr Brett Pugh and retired headteacher Bethan Guilfoyle completed the team. A founding associate of Blair's Delivery

Unit in 2001, Williams had experience of working in both Westminster and Cardiff Bay and his recollection of how the review was established offers a fascinating insight into the vacuum identified by Welsh ministers. He wrote online:

"My committee colleagues were former or current heads of schools, colleges or education departments – all passionate about improving education and passionate about Wales; none of them satisfied with the system we have or the outcomes it is providing for Welsh kids. At the heart of our concerns was that Wales had a complacent education system which had little accountability in it – to parents, to governors, to the community, to the nation – for failure... We were particularly anxious that the Welsh get one thing: our record in terms of basic literacy and numeracy is poor and by UK, let alone international, standards we are letting our kids down. Something has to be done. Our report suggests reforms. We were delighted that it was well received by all political parties and indeed the unions, though I assure you that doesn't make it bland. I think it's just a report whose time has come because all buy the need for radical change."[13] (Tim Williams, 2011)

Professor David Hopkins, a former chief adviser on school standards to Westminster's Department for Education, said in 2008 that bringing back SATs and league tables would drive up Wales' GCSE results. Hopkins, Professor of Education at London University's Institute of Education, said testing at seven and 11 helped provide a framework for high standards. He said: "We very much know that the performance at seven correlates to success at 16. You need not necessarily publish them, but have a national assessment. The previous system was too harsh but Wales went too far the other way. Wales was too quick to abandon the accountability framework of tests and targets. That is one of the reasons that Wales did not perform as well in PISA as expected."[14]

Davidson invited Professor Richard Daugherty, an academic at Aberystwyth University, to undertake a review of national curriculum assessment arrangements for 11 and 14-year-olds in Wales. The study, published in 2004, complemented a wide-ranging review of the school curriculum that was being conducted by the Qualifications, Curriculum and Assessment Authority for Wales (ACCAC). Davidson said the subsequent reports were in absolute agreement on what should be aimed for in terms of appropriate assessment arrangements. She said in a cabinet statement:

"Both acknowledged that the current assessment arrangements have provided a means of measuring pupil attainment along a clear pathway and have improved teacher expertise in making judgements about those attainments. However, crucially, both Professor Daugherty and ACCAC acknowledge that the current statutory tests that form part of those arrangements put teachers under pressure to teach to the tests, do not help the transfer from primary to secondary school, narrow the scope of the curriculum, particularly during the final year of the primary phase – as Estyn has also regularly reported – and, subsequently have a negative effect on teaching and learning."[15] (Jane Davidson, 2004)

Davidson said there was clear evidence that change was needed if Wales was to get the best from its pupils, curriculum and teachers. As a result, she proposed to move away, over a four-year period, from the current testing regime to a system that was more geared to the pupil, that was focused more on skills and that put teacher assessment at its heart. Statutory teacher assessments at the end of key stages 2 and 3 would remain, but would be strengthened by new moderation and accreditation arrangements. ACCAC would be remitted to design systems and ensure that teacher assessments were robust and consistent. But it was not nearly as simple as Davidson made out and the reliance on teacher assessment was not accompanied by sufficient training and moderation, the like of which Daugherty had recommended. The onus on teachers themselves to pass judgement on pupil performance in the classroom called into question their reliability. There was no consistency in approach and with wild variations between assessment procedures, results could not be trusted. The process of assessing younger age children was effectively broken before it started and as Thomas noted in his review of education services in Wales:

"The moderation process for teacher assessment was never introduced and accredited status was not given to secondary schools. There are clear implications for the accuracy of these teacher assessments at key stages when there is no national system of moderation of teacher assessment. There is an urgent need for stringent national teacher moderation at the end of each stage of education."[16] (Vivian Thomas, 2011)

Thomas said moderation at both regional consortium and local authority level was required to help teachers understand key areas of under-attainment. But it was little wonder that problems had arisen when an aforementioned diagnostic test was never introduced and there was no national system for measuring literacy or numeracy skills. Thomas concluded that the introduction of tests in Year Five was essential if Wales was to improve standards. He said it was "unacceptable" that there was no national means of identifying and diagnosing deficiencies in key skills before pupils entered secondary school.

Incidentally, the mooted introduction of a skills-based assessment for every child at the age of nine was not forthcoming.

A subsequent study into teacher assessment at key stages 2 and 3 – published some years later in 2013 – confirmed ours was by no means a well-oiled machine. Researchers from the Australian Council for Educational Research (ACER) were tasked with providing insight into how teacher assessments were being conducted – and whether or not they were fit for purpose. Concluding, it said understanding of teacher assessments was "less than ideal" and the system being employed was "not fully in line with best practice". A survey of stakeholders found a quarter did not think current teacher assessment procedures were an effective use of resources and a third of schools, local authorities and cluster co-ordinators did not consider external moderation worthwhile. It highlighted a lack of confidence in the accuracy and reliability of teacher assessment. The ACER report concluded:

> "There is evidence that the face validity of the current system is already under threat because some schools have lost trust in the judgements made in the teacher assessment process. While face validity is not the only form of validity, it is important that those who need to operate the teacher assessment system should believe that its outcomes are valid. Without that confidence in the system, it will falter."[17] (ACER, 2013)

The system currently employed in Wales is one of social or consensus moderation, the most common form of moderation for school-based assessment systems. A quality assurance process that brings teachers together to review and discuss examples of pupils' work, it is based on a level of agreement about standards. But the interpretation and application of standards needs to be consistent within and across schools to ensure that work of comparable quality will be awarded the same grades. According to ACER, teachers' understanding of the system and how it should work was still low after four years of operation and national training of teachers across both the secondary and primary sectors was needed. Nevertheless, there was cause for optimism and researchers said Wales' teacher assessment system did have the main components of successful systems elsewhere in the world. It said the problems that needed to be fixed were well known by many in the system and what is more, they had ideas for how to solve them. But it warned that implementation was "an enormous task" and all parts "must be functioning smoothly" to produce effective educational outcomes. One suspects that without more rigorous moderation, teacher assessment in Wales will be forever doomed to fail.

Despite researchers' criticism, it is important to remember that the decision to ditch national tests for younger children in Wales was done with the sector's blessing. The Welsh Assembly cannot, therefore, be held solely responsible for stripping away an important level of school accountability. Education unions, for example, were incredibly supportive, citing the adverse impact of SATs on the breadth of the curriculum and their unnecessary strain on teachers and pupils. But getting rid of SATs was only going to work if the replacement teacher assessment system was suitably strengthened. Interestingly, the National Association of Schoolmasters Union of Women Teachers (NASUWT) voted at its annual conference in 2009 to take industrial action if the Westminster Government decided to follow Wales' lead. It said replacing SATs with teacher assessment would create more work and bureaucracy for teachers. Furthermore, members in Wales told NASUWT that their workload had risen uncontrollably as a result of the Assembly's decision to do away with statutory testing.

While Wales was busy forging a new identity, post-devolution education was no less prevalent across the border and, under the stewardship of Education Secretary David Blunkett, England was busy reforming its own schools system. The emphasis there was on prescription, as was demonstrated by national numeracy and literacy strategies and in their secondary school equivalent, the Key Stage 3 strategy. But by imposing rigid lesson formats and teaching methods, the Westminster Government had at least shown its teachers what it wanted. And England was not alone, countries like Cuba – one of the world's great education reformers – ensured all of its teachers were well versed in gathering data and solving problems. Teacher training in Cuba was rigorous and all those wanting to enter the profession were subject to an active pedagogy that focused on how to teach the national curriculum. Once they had graduated from state-run training institutions, teachers were held responsible for their performance through intensive monitoring and evaluation. It may not have been the perfect model, but it worked and Davidson, who instigated high-level talks with Cuban ministers after a family holiday to the island in 2001, had seen for herself the benefits. Summing up what devolution meant for Wales, Reynolds, an adviser to education ministries across the world, wrote:

"The English national strategies that gave all their teachers the foundations and bodies of knowledge that they needed and which built 'capacity' were not implemented here. Instead, we trusted the profession to deliver and only tried the very simple to resource them... We preferred – stupidly – to leave the profession to reinvent the wheel in its exhausted state of midnight oil burning, rather than give it the wheels that clearly worked across the world."[18] (David Reynolds, 2011)

According to Reynolds, most industrial societies in the 2000s changed systems but in so doing, scaled up innovation and tried out new methods of delivery. He said Wales had committed a cardinal sin by allowing the producers of the system to have the freedom to run it. Most countries moved beyond trying to correct the "supply" of education and moved, he argued, to "demand" side policies that put pressure on the suppliers of education. Wales did not. Parents, he maintained, should have been given the freedom to vote with their feet. The availability of school performance data – on a far more structured basis than was actually provided – would have opened a market for compulsory education, with parental choice the determining factor.

## Foundation Phase

Regardless of their success, it is to Davidson's credit that many initiatives introduced in the early part of devolution remain a feature of today's education system. For the most part, their longevity is testament to the high regard in which they are held. The Foundation Phase is, perhaps, the highlight and personifies all that was good about Davidson's foray into the wider education world. Designed to meet the developmental needs of all children, the Foundation Phase was based on the concept of "learning through play" and was a product of world-leading Scandinavian countries. Launched on a statutory basis in 2008 following a successful pilot, it marked a radical departure from traditional classroom practice and delayed formal learning until Key Stage 2. Its introduction was met with almost universal approval and was based on research that showed children did not begin to benefit from extensive formal teaching until the age of six or seven. It combined what was called early years' education (for three to five-year-olds) and Key Stage 1 (five to seven-year-olds) of the national curriculum and sought to reduce inequalities in social and educational outcomes by focusing on the formative stages of a child's development.

Children were given time to develop their speaking, listening, reading and writing skills in more relaxed environments and so the Foundation Phase put greater emphasis on teaching assistants, whose role would become increasingly prevalent as the programme developed. Rhodri Morgan hailed the £170m scheme as his proudest achievement in government and the "most momentous change to education in Wales since devolution", but not everyone bought into the new play-based approach. Traditionalists questioned the informal style of learning and there were concerns over the programme's financial sustainability. A radical overhaul of early years' education in Wales would not come cheap and schools had to recruit extra staff for the prescribed pupil-teacher ratios (of 1:8 for children aged three to five and 1:15 for those aged five to seven). The fact that support staff accounted for roughly 44% of the total school workforce in Wales in 2013 was an unintended consequence. As well as investing in people, schools would also invest in new buildings, outdoor facilities and equipment.

Given its relative infancy, we have yet to see the fledgling Foundation Phase translate into tangible results and it will be some time before a thorough analysis of its impact can be undertaken. But while there is promise in abundance, the early signs are not overwhelmingly good. An independent review of the Foundation Phase conducted in 2013 unearthed "varying interpretations and attitudes" towards the initiative that appeared to influence practice within classrooms. The study found that the attitude of headteachers and senior management was "pivotal" to the extent to which the Foundation Phase had been adopted in schools and the emergence of contradictory policies had "diluted" its impact. The first in a series of reports evaluating the implementation and impact of the Foundation Phase, it also warned that key aspects had been "misinterpreted" by practitioners and successful delivery varied between local authorities.

Researchers from the Wales Institute of Social and Economic Research, Data and Methods (WISERD), based at Cardiff University, were appointed to undertake a three-year evaluation of the policy in July 2011. Writing in their first annual report, commissioned by the Welsh Government, WISERD researchers reported "a mixed picture" of the Foundation Phase and said the way in which it had been interpreted by various professionals was significant. In particular, they reported that "play" – a defining factor of the Foundation Phase – had been taken out of context. Furthermore, researchers suggested the skills, training and qualifications of newly qualified teachers and teaching and learning assistants was not always up to scratch, albeit they were crucial to the programme's successful implementation. Concluding, WISERD said the Foundation Phase had made a significant impact but it had placed an additional burden on teachers, particularly in the management of other adults in the classroom.

Designated "Foundation Phase Advisers" considered "contradictory or moderating educational policies" an issue and an accompanying report on pupil outcomes unearthed a "persistence of inequalities" between youngsters from different backgrounds. It said the introduction of the Foundation Phase had not managed to bridge the equality gap and pupils eligible for free school meals – a measure of poverty – and those with Special Educational Needs (SEN) remained the most disadvantaged. In fact, deficiencies in SEN provision often went unnoticed and the nation's failure to sufficiently accommodate all of its children remains a major issue in Wales. Notwithstanding the government's desire to give every pupil the best possible start in life, there is a suggestion schools do not have the resources available to fund and tailor bespoke teaching for the most vulnerable.

Figures released in 2013 showed that almost one in four pupils in Wales had SEN. According to the annual schools census, there were 103,599 pupils requiring specialist support in Welsh classrooms. A breakdown of SEN showed there were 29,243 pupils with moderate learning difficulties – defined by policymakers as those attaining well below expected levels, despite intervention – and 9,161 suffering from dyslexia. A further 13,825 had speech, language and communication issues while 13,596 suffered behavioural, emotional and social difficulties. According to government guidelines, children had SEN if they had a learning difficulty which called for special educational provision to be made for them. Children could have a learning difficulty if they had a "significantly greater difficulty in learning" than the majority of pupils of the same age; or had a disability which hindered them from making use of educational facilities of a kind generally provided within a local authority. Nevertheless, a review published by England's education watchdog Ofsted in 2010 suggested that teachers may have wrongly labelled thousands of children as having SEN. It recommended, somewhat controversially, that schools should refrain from putting children into category, when all they needed was better teaching and pastoral support. Wales' inspectorate, Estyn, has not been quite so forthright.

WISERD's research provided the clearest picture of Foundation Phase performance since its inception. But it was not the first negative critique and Estyn warned two years earlier in 2011 that a lack of understanding from teachers was hampering success. It said the Foundation Phase had split opinion and some staff were not convinced about its educational value, with children in up to 40% of schools administering the initiative not learning as much as they should be. In a minority of cases, it said children were not being offered challenging enough opportunities to develop and practice their key skills and many teachers did not know enough about the Foundation Phase to ensure effective implementation. The reports were a blow to the legions who thought Wales' early years' offer was the answer to all the nation's education woes. They were a reminder that no one policy would be enough to lift the schools system from its stupor.

# Notes

1.   Welsh Government. (2013). Increasing the Number of Communities Where Welsh is the Main Language. Report of the Task and Finish Group. p 22.
2.   Welsh Government. (2013). School Organisation Code. p 10.
3.   Estyn. (2006). Small Primary Schools in Wales. p 3.
4.   Reynolds, David. (2007). Western Mail. November 7.
5.   Davidson, Jane. (2001). The Learning Country, National Assembly for Wales. p 1.
6.   Davidson, Jane. (2001). The Learning Country, National Assembly for Wales. p 2.
7.   Graham, William. (2007). Times Educational Supplement. April 27.

8.   Davidson, Jane. (2001). The Learning Country, National Assembly for Wales. p 10.
9.   Davidson, Jane. (2001). The Learning Country, National Assembly for Wales. p 11.
10.  Davidson, Jane. (2001). The Learning Country, National Assembly for Wales. p 19.
11.  Davidson, Jane. (2001). The Learning Country, National Assembly for Wales. p 35.
12.  The Centre for Market and Public Organisation; University of Bristol. (2010). A Natural Experiment in School Accountability: The Impact of School Performance Information on Pupil Progress and Sorting. p 23.
13.  Williams, Tim. (2011). How to Restructure a Nation's Education Services. Tim Williams: View from Down Under.
14.  Hopkins, David. (2008). Western Mail. January 14.
15.  Davidson, Jane. (2004). Welsh Assembly Government. July 13.
16.  Thomas, Vivian. (2011). The Structure of Education Services in Wales. p 36.
17.  Australian Council for Educational Research. (2013). An Investigation Into Key Stages 2 and 3 Teacher Assessment in Wales. p xiv.
18.  Reynolds, David. (2011). Western Mail. October 7.

# 2

# Measuring Success

## Mixed reviews for education policy

*Judging what works and what does not; using written and anecdotal evidence to assess early progress. Includes a reflection on the impact of poverty and funding on attainment*

While the jury on the Foundation Phase is still out, we know for certain that plans to make all school buildings "fit for purpose" by 2010 was one Learning Country commitment that fell spectacularly short of the mark. In fact, it became clear relatively soon after the Welsh Assembly set its target that breathing new life into Wales' stock would take a lot longer than anticipated. Davidson said in 2006 that a "range of unforeseen factors"[1] – including asbestos and the introduction of the Foundation Phase, given its reliance on more indoor and outdoor space – would make the government's goal difficult to achieve. Teacher testimonies cited damp and draughty classrooms, leaking roofs, inadequate playgrounds, outside toilets, dry rot and falling masonry. True, the Assembly Government had invested heavily in school buildings, but it was nowhere near enough. Research conducted by the Welsh Local Government Association (WLGA) found an average of £190,000 was being spent on repairs and maintenance at every English school in 2005-06, compared with just £90,000 in Wales. The gulf in capital spending was perfectly encapsulated by Brian Lightman, general secretary of the Association of School and College Leaders (ASCL), in 2011. When asked, he said the "dilapidated state" of many Welsh schools was a serious issue and the worst secondary school buildings in England were better than the majority in Wales. Better funding, he argued, would vastly improve working conditions for teachers, improve support for pupils and help develop the next generation of school leaders. Lightman said:

"If you go into a school in England you notice some very stark differences. The first difference is in the premises. Whenever I go into a school that hasn't been rebuilt and I meet the head, the head is invariably apologetic for the state of their buildings. And I invariably have to reply that if you had buildings like those in Wales, you would be very happy."[2] (Brian Lightman, 2011)

Lightman, a former headteacher in Wales, said formula capital funding, allocated to state schools in England by the Department for Education, had allowed heads to improve facilities. He said schools across the border were more secure and had access to a better pool of resources, including business managers. A mainstay of England's education system, business managers were given a strategic mandate to oversee the day-to-day running of their schools which, in turn, removed a significant weight from the burden of headteachers. Lightman's observation, a decade after the Assembly's promise to improve education's infrastructure, was damning. And he was not alone; I have since come across two senior consultants working for the devolved administration in Cardiff Bay who were of exactly the same opinion. One, with whom I visited a school in the Welsh capital, simply said: "You wouldn't get schools like this in England." Before they had even time to put pen to paper in the classroom, the conditions in which pupils were working in Wales was said to be holding them back. How could children in Wales compete with their peers in other parts of the UK if their school environment was so clearly lacking? This was not a level playing field and children in Wales were being held back through no fault of their own. Overall, the facilities available to Welsh pupils were far inferior to those available across the border and a former director of capital development was in no doubt as to who was responsible.

Martin Lipson, who was brought into Wales to lead what became known as the 21st Century Schools programme, accused the Welsh Government of having an "endemic" inability to see policies through in the wake of its decision to scale back funding. He said the public did not realise the extent of the problem Welsh schools faced and expecting councils to source 50% of funding for new builds – up from the 30% quoted initially – was unfair. While the majority of earmarked capital projects would indeed come to fruition, the change meant they were likely to take much longer to complete. Work would start later and be spread over a longer period as a result of councils having to find a larger contribution than was first envisaged. Lipson, who led the programme for two years from 2009, said shortly after leaving in 2011 that the Welsh Government was guilty of "flitting from one priority to the other". He added: "There is a chaos of policies and a lack of continuity – these are fundamental issues that in my view have to be addressed." A qualified architect, Lipson's stock in school improvement stemmed from his time working alongside the Department for Education in Westminster. Under Tony Blair's Labour Government, he helped implement the Building Schools for the Future programme, which ran for six years after its introduction in 2004. "I worked there with five ministers in succession," said Lipson. "But they didn't waver in their commitment to something important that had been started. That's the difference as far as I can see."[3]

## Learning Pathways

As part of its 10-year vision for Wales' education system, the Welsh Assembly made a commitment to transforming 14-19 provision – an area that, historically, had lacked focus and direction. Its goal, that 95% of young people by the age of 25 would be ready for high skilled employment or higher education by 2015, was by no means unassailable. Learning Pathways 14-19 was designed to transform young people's options and opportunities through local networks of providers. It would seek to extend choice and flexibility, while securing individually tailored learning pathways to meet learners' needs. Learning Pathways would also strive to provide access to personal support and impartial careers advice. A balance of formal learning, wider choice, flexibility and a learning core of the skills, understanding and experiences that all 14 to 19-year-olds need was designed to help lift the proportion of Welsh teenagers with higher level qualifications. In so doing, it would seek to reduce the number of 16 to 18-year-olds not in education, employment or training (NEET). Its work in practice, however, is open to debate. While there are undoubtedly fewer young people in Wales leaving school without recognised qualifications, the extent to which Learning Pathways has impacted directly on learner outcomes is not clear. According to Davidson, the key to the Assembly's approach was "choice". She added:

> "We want to move away from a one-size-fits-all approach, where achieving anything other than good academic qualifications is often seen as less useful or prestigious. We want our young people to be able to choose Learning Pathways that best suit them – mixing and matching vocational, academic and occupational qualifications and experience."[4]
> (Jane Davidson, 2004)

The Assembly wanted to extend learning beyond the school or college gates to include other opportunities and experiences which enable young people to develop and apply a wider range of essential skills. It sought to break from tradition and assumptions about what particular types of qualification ought to be taken and when. Learning Pathways was designed to stretch expectations and remove barriers between academic and vocational routes through education. Crucially, it also provided a vehicle for the flagship Welsh Baccalaureate qualification.

## *Welsh Baccalaureate*

The Welsh Baccalaureate was introduced in pilot centres in September 2003 to provide broader experiences than traditional learning programmes, thus meeting the diverse needs of young people in Wales. It combined personal development with mainstream GCSEs and has grown steadily in popularity since its inception. In 2014, the Welsh Baccalaureate was being taken at more than 230 centres by around 65,000 learners in Wales. An overarching qualification, it incorporated academic and vocational options and a compulsory core of four components: key skills; Wales, Europe and the world; work-related education; and personal and social education. The Welsh Baccalaureate is currently available at Foundation, Intermediate and Advanced level – equivalent to a grade 'A' at A-level – but while uptake is increasing, rising numbers can be deceptive. In some schools, the Welsh Baccalaureate is less an "option" and more a necessity, with teenagers required to sit the qualification alongside their mainstream studies. Its validity amongst universities is not guaranteed and it does not carry the same credence everywhere.

A report published by Estyn in 2012 found parts of Wales' flagship Welsh Baccalaureate were not being taught well enough and standards varied between schools. It said many teachers spent more time completing paperwork than they did improving pupils' skills. In some cases, Estyn said more able students were not being challenged enough because teachers did not plan sufficiently for the needs of every ability. Not for the first time in Wales, meaningful evaluation was an issue and only a minority of schools employed a manageable tracking and monitoring system. But the inspectorate was not without hope and praised the Welsh Baccalaureate's potential and general benefit to students. Indeed, it said the wide range of standards being achieved on the Advanced level qualification suggested that grading the qualification would provide a fairer reflection of the range of student outcomes. Its wish became reality a year later.

The core of the Advanced level Welsh Baccalaureate was broken down into grades from its existing pass/fail model for courses starting in September 2013. But further research into the qualification's impact, published earlier that year, offered a less than ringing endorsement. A study by Cardiff University found students with a Welsh Baccalaureate qualification were less likely to achieve a "good" degree at university. It uncovered evidence to suggest the Wales-specific qualification had a possible "detrimental" effect on students once they had progressed into higher education. Experts said students with the Welsh Baccalaureate appeared not to succeed as well in university as those without the qualification, due to the "inflationary nature" of its 120-point tariff on their actual attainment. But WISERD maintained there was strong evidence to suggest the Welsh Baccalaureate was "enormously valuable" in helping students to enter higher education.

WISERD gave three reasons as to why the Welsh Baccalaureate could boost participation in higher education: First, the qualification was seen to give relatively low achieving students an opportunity to get an award that would help them get a place in university. The second was its ability to increase the range of higher education opportunities on offer, usually in terms of the number of universities to which students could consider applying. A third positive related to the way in which the qualification could give students more confidence that they might get accepted, especially if taken as a "back-up" alongside traditional A-levels. In its report on the relationship between the Welsh Baccalaureate and higher education, WISERD said:

> "Critically, low achieving students appear to have the most to gain from having the Welsh Bacc in terms of university participation. Although overall levels of higher education participation for relatively high-achieving students do not appear to be affected by having the Welsh Bacc, it does confer some advantage in terms of entry to Russell Group universities."[5] (WISERD, 2013)

The report identified three main areas in which the Welsh Baccalaureate could be improved: by focusing more on its promotion and delivery within centres; by making it more challenging, in terms of skills and knowledge; and by tailoring more the qualification to the particular needs of its students. WISERD, which was contracted to undertake the research between June and November 2012, said overall response to the qualification had been mixed and despite its general positive benefits on university participation, "there was also an awareness of its limitations". The study found support for the introduction of grading, but felt that unless there were changes to the content and delivery of the Welsh Baccalaureate, it may have limited benefits.

## School Effectiveness Framework

The School Effectiveness Framework (SEF) represented the Welsh Government's long overdue attempt at school reform, focusing primarily on standards of teaching and learning. It came about as a direct consequence of Wales' poor PISA performance in 2006 and was designed to raise pupil attainment and wellbeing. The SEF was underpinned by five core themes

– bilingualism, support, equality, high-performance culture and the more innocuous "systems thinking". As its title suggests, the SEF provided an overarching framework that involved schools, local authorities and the Assembly Government working in partnership to lift the system via a process of tri-level reform. It involved practitioners sharing best practice and the notion of reducing wild variations within and between schools was a good one. But variation is an endemic that remains rife in our education system today and the SEF's impact was therefore limited.

The Assembly communicated its ideas through an SEF "pizza" diagram. Slices included teaching and learning; leadership, working with others; groups to share good practice; supporting one another; and improving and taking responsibility. Schools were encouraged to report on how pupils had been involved in each piece of the pizza, so as to share best practice and achievements with others. Sounds simple, but as with so many other facets of education policy, the pizza was easier to construct than it was to digest. In fact, the assertion by policymakers that "the framework will only work... if it is owned by staff and leadership teams, local authorities and the Assembly Government" was pertinent. Guidance on the SEF stated that:

"Schools do not exist in isolation. They operate within a local context (with its own history and complexities) that is constantly changing. The people within a school community – and the way they interact with one another – are the most important factor in the way the school works. However, it is vital that schools are viewed not just as systems within themselves, but as part of the wider educational system of Wales. Successful tri-level reform requires systems thinking."[6] (Welsh Assembly Government, 2008)

Professional Learning Communities (PLCs) were a key component of the SEF and were established to promote sharing and facilitate staff development. They would see schools cluster together into groups that in turn would devise their own bespoke ways to improve performance. Systems leaders would offer challenge and support but, in reality, PLCs would only served to muddy waters further. PLCs were not given a strong enough steer and poor implementation conspired against them. Critics spoke of a lack of direction and it appeared nobody ever quite knew what they were supposed to be doing.

## Tackling deprivation

A flagship early years' scheme designed to improve performance in Wales' most deprived areas, Flying Start is said to be making "a tangible difference" to many high-need families. Providing the right conditions for children even before they have started school is considered essential to their long-term development and Flying Start prided itself on free quality childcare, parenting support, an enhanced health visitor service and help for early language development. It took a holistic approach and was targeted in areas with high numbers of children claiming free school meals. Flying Start was unveiled by Davidson in 2005 with the intention of decreasing the number of people in Wales with low skills, thereby reducing levels of income inequality. A study commissioned by the Welsh Government and conducted by independent researchers Ipsos Mori included 60 in-depth interviews with parents receiving Flying Start services in five local authorities. Published in 2013, it said high-need families had varying issues including poor health and housing, depression, limited or no qualifications and a lack of access to employment opportunities. According to the report:

"Evidence shows that Flying Start services are making a tangible difference to the lives of many high-need parents... The key to this difference is usually the health visitor, whose access to the family home can allow for an effective, family-centred approach. Where health visitors had frequent contact and strong relationships with high-need families they were instrumental in helping them access other Flying Start services and the wider services the family may need. They do this by providing information but also motivating parents to take up services where otherwise they would not. Where there was an absence of strong encouragement from a trusted health visitor, many parents did not take up services they might benefit from, such as parenting programmes."[7] (Ipsos Mori, 2013)

The evaluation found there were often difficulties engaging parents and support programmes were not being accessed by all families who would benefit from them. Researchers said the capacity of health visitors to increase demand for parenting programmes could be better used in some areas and fathers were often sidelined by a "heavily mother-focussed approach". But early language development was frequently cited as a marked benefit by parents who said their children were talking more often and clearly, had an improved vocabulary and had more of an opportunity to practice their Welsh. Parents reported that their children had learned a range of literacy and numeracy skills such as counting, reciting the alphabet and naming colours. Breaking the link between poverty and attainment is a notoriously tough nut to crack but in Flying Start, the Welsh Government had found a way of making at least partial inroads. Professor David Egan, special adviser to Davidson in the latter years of her rule of education, describes deprivation as the great "fault line" running through Wales' education system. Unless it is addressed, he warns, standards will never reach their optimum level. Egan wrote in 2012:

> "There is a very strong association between coming from a relatively disadvantaged background and low levels of educational achievement. This is not a new phenomenon for it has always been a feature of the education system in Wales. Although over time school students in Wales have improved their educational standards, the gap between relatively privileged and disadvantaged students has persisted and is probably growing. Whilst some countries are making progress in narrowing this 'poverty gap,' Wales is not currently one of them."[8] (David Egan, 2012)

Like Flying Start, Communities First was part of the Assembly Government's attempt to tackle widespread poverty in Wales. Launched in 2000, it was an area-based regeneration strategy that used the Welsh index of multiple deprivation to identify the parts of Wales that were considered most in need. Communities assumed a crucial self-improving role and helped determine what interventions were used to stimulate regeneration. Six areas for potential intervention were identified by the Assembly, including education and training, and while major gaps in achievement continue to exist between Communities First areas and the rest of Wales, positive strides have been made. An evaluation of the programme commissioned by the Welsh Government and published in 2011 identified that the average attainment of students in designated areas had improved at a greater rate than in non-Community First areas, particularly for 15-year-olds, where there had been an improvement equivalent to half a GCSE grade.

But the issue of poverty is no quick fix and you felt sure a national strategy encompassing all sectors would be required to make tangible difference. Education has an important role to play but it is by no means the sole vehicle for change. Children are said to spend just 12% of their waking time in school and it is the outstanding 88% that is hardest to refine. The onus is more often than not on parents, peer groups and the communities in which we live to help nurture child development. Education is not an island removed from society – and there is no room for complacency. Teachers cannot work in isolation and schools can only do so much. Regardless of ministerial preference, breaking the link between poverty and attainment will be far easier said that done and there is a perception that genuine appetite for serious action on the agenda has yet to emerge. To a certain extent, there is still a blank canvas from which to work.

A school serving one of Wales' most deprived communities proved in June 2014 that poverty need not get in the way of a good education. In a remarkable inspection report, Herbert Thompson Primary School's current performance and prospects for improvement were deemed "excellent" and Estyn rated everything – from the Cardiff school's standards and teaching to its leadership and wellbeing – the highest level possible. The term "value-added" has become increasingly popular in the education fraternity, albeit it is difficult to quantify. But the way in which Herbert Thompson transformed pupils – who entered school with skill levels well below those expected for their age – into top performers rightly constituted excellent practice.

In an age of increased collaboration, it is no surprise that Herbert Thompson is a school in hot demand. Teachers from across Wales have been to visit and the school's latest plaudits will doubtless win a host of new admirers. But for Wales' perennial underachievers, Herbert Thompson's report will make for uncomfortable reading. At the time of its inspection, around half of Herbert Thompson's 460 pupils were entitled to free school meals and no fewer than 45% had additional learning needs. Allied to that, 10% of pupils were on the child protection register, with an extra 16% on the school concern register. Based in Ely, which features heavily on the Child Poverty Map of the UK, Herbert Thompson is a school with its fair share of challenges but while the impact of deprivation is a factor, poverty should never be used as an excuse.

# Paying the price of education

The Welsh Government has something of a chequered past when it comes to education. Suffice to say, not every initiative has come up trumps since devolution and few have yet translated into tangible results. True, the administration is still relatively young and newfangled policies will take time to bear fruit. Some are so far removed and so radically different from those of yesteryear, that we may have to wait a while before their impact can be properly measured. The flagship Foundation Phase is a prime example and we know that the early years' revolution is by no means the finished article. We do have much to be proud of in Wales and over the past 15 years stakeholders have pioneered some truly distinct education initiatives. But while devolution created a wealth of opportunity, a newfound freedom also had its drawbacks.

Funding has long been a contentious issue and the correlation in Wales between money and performance is regularly touted by critics, who point to a growing annual spend shortfall between pupils in Wales and England. The supporting figures are startling. According to The Learning Country, the average budgeted spend per pupil in Wales in 2000-01 was more than every region of England except London and the metropolitan authorities of the West Midlands and the North West. At the last count in 2009-10, Wales lagged £604 per pupil behind those in England – a figure verified by

Welsh Government statisticians. Regardless of the actual impact of funding on performance, the fact that pupils in Wales went from being better to considerably worse off, does not reflect well on the devolved administration. Whatever its settlement from Westminster, the Welsh Government and, in turn, local authorities – for it is they who are responsible for siphoning off central funds – have seemingly starved schools of cash relative to their peers across the border. It can also be said that underfunding of schools in Wales has stymied innovation and hampered the kind of technological developments that have been made elsewhere in the world.

In the absence of up-to-date comparative funding levels, the following table compiled by the Trinity Mirror Data Unit includes a projection of what each nation spends on education. It is based on official data compiled by government officials and uses a forecast formula of average trends to predict latest gaps in expenditure. The emergence of academies and a rise in the number of schools in England breaking from local government control has prevented officials from drawing definitive conclusions.

**Table 1 Local Authority Education Budgets Per Pupil 1999-2014:**
**Wales and England Comparison**

| Year | Wales | England | Difference |
|---|---|---|---|
| 2013-14* | £6,676 | £7,533 | £857 |
| 2012-13* | £6,393 | £7,187 | £794 |
| 2011-12* | £6,114 | £6,839 | £725 |
| 2010-11* | £5,829 | £6,476 | £647 |
| 2009-10 | £5,595 | £6,200 | £604 |
| 2008-09 | £5,282 | £5,814 | £532 |
| 2007-08 | £5,004 | £5,478 | £474 |
| 2006-07 | £4,706 | £5,123 | £417 |
| 2005-06 | £4,459 | £4,817 | £359 |
| 2004-05 | £4,178 | £4,419 | £241 |
| 2003-04 | £3,955 | £4,128 | £173 |
| 2002-03 | £3,562 | £3,735 | £174 |
| 2001-02 | £3,372 | £3,432 | £61 |
| 2000-01 | £3,092 | £3,123 | £31 |
| 1999-00 | £2,868 | £2,926 | £58 |

SOURCE: Welsh Government 1999-2010
(* Projection based on forecast formula)

Evidence suggests funding on its own does not always bring about the desired educational results. Countries including Finland and New Zealand spend considerably less on education yet perform better in PISA, while, closer to home, authorities such as Blaenau Gwent splash out the most for very little return. Funding is not the sole issue but schools are unlikely to be disadvantaged by more resources. Extra money can only help in the quest to raise standards and whether it be additional teaching assistants or classroom aids, a school's wish-list is never complete. That said, Wales remains one of the highest spenders on education in the Organisation for Economic Co-operation and Development (OECD) and figures show there is not a particularly strong relationship between levels of expenditure and PISA performance. The OECD points to the USA – which spends more than $100,000 (£64,000) per student by the time they reach PISA age – and Poland, which spends $40,000 (£26,000) but performs to a similar same level. In the space of 10 years between 2000 and 2009, expenditure per student on average across OECD countries went up by 25% in real terms, yet there was no improvement on average across countries in performance. So throwing more money at education is not necessarily the answer and there is truth in the assertion that it is not how much you have but what you do with it that is most important.

# Notes

1.    Davidson, Jane. (2006). Times Educational Supplement. July 7.
2.    Lightman, Brian. (2011). Western Mail. June 14.
3.    Lipson, Martin. (2011). Western Mail. July 19.
4.    Davidson, Jane. (2004). Learning Pathways 14-19 Guidance, National Assembly for Wales.
5.    WISERD. (2013). Relationships Between the Welsh Baccalaureate Advanced Diploma and Higher Education. p iii.
6.    Welsh Assembly Government. (2008). School Effectiveness Framework: Building Effective Learning Communities Together. p 6.
7.    Ipsos Mori. (2013). Flying Start Qualitative Research with High Need Families. p 88.
8.    Egan, David. (2012). Communities, families and Schools Togther: A Route to Reducing the Impact of Poverty on Educational Achievement in Schools Across Wales. Save the Children. p 4.

# 3

# Trading Places

## The start of a white-knuckle ride for education in Wales

*International comparators shine a light on skills deficiencies before a sea of change in Welsh education. A new minister, Chief Inspector and Director General of Education heralds a new era*

Davidson's underlying goal was for Wales to develop and own one of the best education systems in the world. She wanted Wales to be a learning country, where high quality, lifelong learning provided the skills people required to prosper. PISA alone would suggest she failed. The world's biggest education survey, PISA is designed to study how different countries are performing against one another. Compiled every three years, it has grown in stature and is considered the best gauge of international school performance. Suffice to say, education systems can rise or fall by their PISA results.

The OECD developed PISA in response to member countries' demands for regular and reliable data on the knowledge and skills of their students and the overall performance of their education systems. The OECD began work on PISA in the mid-1990s and it was officially launched in 1997, with the first survey taking place in 2000. PISA benefits from its worldwide scope and its regularity; more than 60 countries and economies regularly take part and the survey allows policymakers to track their progress in meeting key learning goals. It is also the only international education survey to measure the knowledge and skills of 15-year-olds, an age at which students in most countries are nearing the end of their compulsory time in school.

Rather than examine the mastery of specific school curricula, PISA looks at students' ability to apply knowledge and skills in key subject areas and to analyse, reason and communicate effectively as they examine, interpret and solve problems. PISA measures student performance in reading, maths and science as well as asking students about their motivations, beliefs about themselves and learning strategies. PISA is forever growing and with its burgeoning reputation as an important economic benchmark, it is already established as one of the world's premier advisory tools. In total, 43 countries took part in PISA in 2000, 41 in 2003, 58 in 2006, 65 in 2009, 65 in 2012 and there are currently 71 signed up to participate in 2015.

PISA allows countries to compare best practice and to drive improvements appropriate for their own school systems. Logistically, schools in each country are randomly selected by the international contractor for participation in PISA. At these schools, the test is given to students who are aged between 15 years and three months and 16 years and two months at the time of the test, rather than to students in a specific year of school. The selection of schools and students is kept as inclusive as possible, so that the sample of students comes from a broad range of backgrounds and abilities. Crucially, PISA is not designed to test how well a student has mastered a school's specific curriculum. The tests themselves, which will be entirely electronically administered in the coming years, are made up of both multiple-choice questions and questions requiring students to construct their own responses. Participating students are given two hours to complete.

## A rude awakening to PISA

Wales came late to the PISA party and entered in its own right for the first time in 2006, rather than as part of the UK as it had previously. Davidson had become frustrated by the tendency for Wales to be compared only with England. It was a competition she felt Wales could not win and, with that in mind, sought to broaden Welsh horizons and compete on a more international stage. But there were risks involved and in entering PISA, Wales would ultimately benchmark its education system against many other nations. Wales would look, for the first time, beyond the confines of the British Isles and pits its wits against countries as far afield as Singapore and New Zealand. It was a landmark step for education in Wales but not everyone in the Assembly Government was convinced entering PISA was the right thing to do. First Minister Rhodri Morgan, for example, took some persuading and was not immediately sold on the idea. It was ironic that Davidson herself would not be in post long enough to see Wales' first tranche through.

The 2006 PISA results – published in 2007 a year after they were sat – came as a disappointment to Wales and its new Education Minister, Vale of Glamorgan AM Jane Hutt. Welsh teenagers were performing worse than their counterparts in every other part of Britain. Wales was marginally above average for science, but below average for reading and maths. The PISA league tables showed Welsh secondary pupils trailing behind more than 33 other countries, including Lithuania and Latvia, in maths. They ranked desperately low in reading and behind the likes of Slovenia, Estonia and Poland. Overall, Wales took 504 points in science (OECD average 496), 484 points in maths (average 494) and 480 points in reading (average 488). It meant Wales ranked 30th for reading, 34th for maths and and 22nd for science out of the participating 58 nations.

David Reynolds, a PISA partisan, described the scores as "shocking" and worthy of a national debate. Suffice to say, he got what he wanted although the Assembly Government stood defiant, maintaining that its education policies were on the right track. In reality, the results were an eye-opener for a system seen by many to be coasting. According to PISA, 22 countries did "significantly better" than Wales in maths and 16 "significantly better" in reading. This was not the educational utopia Davidson and her allies had led us to believe. All was not well and the veil on standards had been lifted. Reflecting, OECD secretary-general Angel Gurria said the PISA research should be used to help governments improve education policies. "In today's competitive global economy, quality education is one of the most valuable assets that a society and an individual can have," he said. "PISA is much more than just a ranking. It is about how well individual education systems are equipping their young people for the world of tomorrow. It tells countries where their strengths and weaknesses lie."[1] Hutt's reaction was more restrained. PISA, she said, was "an episode on our journey, not a starting point" and the report gave Wales a valuable snapshot of where it stood on the international stage. Her defiance is encapsulated in the following statement:

"We have already set the tone and direction of travel for education policy in Wales and we have learnt from evidence and practice in other countries in developing our policies... My overarching priority is to secure better outcomes for all learners, not just to score highly in PISA rankings – not that we do not recognise the importance of PISA as a yardstick against which we can measure our progress. The real benefits of the PISA assessments will come, not from the headline figures and league table rankings, but from the detailed analysis of strengths and weaknesses and what more we can learn from the best and most effective practice internationally, that we will explore closely over the coming months."[2] (Jane Hutt, 2007)

Anna Brychan, director of the National Association of Head Teachers (NAHT) Cymru, assumed a much firmer disposition. She said the figures had to be taken seriously and the Assembly Government must be "absolutely rigorous" in analysing what the results could tell Wales about the way it was developing and implementing educational change[3]. Wales' Director General of Education Steve Marshall was under no illusions as to the level of challenge in hand. It was his firm belief that improved PISA results would take time and he warned that it could take within three to 15 years for Wales to better its position. Marshall urged patience and said critics should back reforms including Flying Start and the Foundation Phase.[4]

There are many within the system who consider Marshall to have been the nation's best-performing Director General of Education, despite the relatively short period in which he held the post. Brought in by Davidson in 2006, his two-year tenure was extremely productive and Marshall is fondly remembered as one of the great education reformers of his generation. Prior to his arrival in Wales, Marshall was chief executive of the Department of Education and Children's Services in the Government of South Australia, where he believed that learning and care was at the heart of all that the department did and it could only be fully effective if all parts of the system worked together. Marshall's appointment was considered a real coup for the emerging Assembly Government, but his work to instil newfound rigour and demand into the system was impeded by Davidson's exit and a subsequent change in minister. He was headhunted to go to Canada shortly after and was appointed Deputy Minister of the Ministry of Education in Ontario prior to his untimely death in 2010.

Given Wales' proud tradition of holding education in high regard, PISA was undoubtedly a huge disappointment. On reflection, there is every chance Marshall had been right to call for calm in the face of such self-deprecation but the baying public – and parents, in particular – were always going to demand green shoots of recovery well within his generous 15-year timeframe. Then again, Wales had no divine right to slot in smoothly near the standards summit. The PISA rankings of 2006 provided Wales with a good assessment of where it was going wrong, and where it needed to improve. Question was, how would it respond?

To a certain extent, PISA was a step into the unknown and nobody really knew what to expect. As disappointing as Wales' inaugural PISA scores were, policymakers would have to wait until 2009 to have something to compare against. Only then would the Assembly Government be able to benchmark its PISA performance, albeit the administration would do so under a different Education Minister. Unlike her predecessor, Hutt's two year reign of education in Wales, from 2007 to 2009, can be considered largely uneventful. The man chosen to replace her would ensure the next phase of Welsh education's evolution was anything but.

# Introducing Leighton Andrews

The appointment of Leighton Andrews as Education Minister in December 2009 was described by Elaine Edwards, general secretary of Welsh teachers' union Undeb Cenedlaethol Athrawon Cymru (UCAC), as "the beginning of a white-knuckle ride for education in Wales"[5]. But it was a rollercoaster the nation's schools system desperately needed. There can be no finer definition and over the next three and a half years, Andrews would leave no stone unturned in pursuit of improved educational standards. He had his own inimitable style that was not to everyone's liking, but he was, arguably, exactly what Wales needed.

Andrews was first elected as AM for Rhondda in May 2003, winning back the seat for Labour from Plaid Cymru. A self-made man, Andrews had built and sold two businesses and was once head of public affairs at the BBC in London, which would explain his clever knack for a headline. But Andrews was not a one-party politician and was an active Liberal in the 1980s. At the age of 29, he stood as the SDP-Liberal Alliance candidate for Gillingham in the 1987 General Election, coming second to Conservative James Couchman with a 30% share of the vote. In fact, his defection to Labour in the mid 1990s would come as a huge surprise to many. Former Liberal MP and philosopher Michael Meadowcroft said Andrews' decision to leave the party was so improbable, to believe it would have been akin to emulating Lewis Carroll's White Queen who "sometimes believed as many as six impossible things before breakfast". Andrews, he stressed, was the "solid, dependable comrade whose Liberal instincts and libertarian heart could always be trusted"[6].

Frontline politics took a back seat for Andrews after his defeat in 1987 and his professional career took precedence. He left the BBC in 1996 to set up his own public affairs consultancy which, initially based in Westminster, would later expand into Cardiff. Andrews' homecoming – he was born in the Welsh capital and went to school in Barry – would herald the beginning of a new chapter in his political life. Not surprisingly, Andrews had banished all memory of his Liberal past upon joining the Labour Party. But some diehard Labourites, like veteran Newport West MP Paul Flynn, were by no means willing to forgive and forget. In his book, Dragons Led By Poodles, Flynn described Andrews as "oleaginous, accommodating, feline, [and an] apprentice shape-shifter"[7]. Coincidentally, the fact Andrews – a long-time follower of Cardiff City Football Club – had been a keen supporter of his local football team while campaigning in Gillingham, had not gone unnoticed either. To split one's allegiance is no more the done thing in sport as it is in politics.

Immediately prior to his election as Rhondda AM, Andrews was a visiting lecturer at Cardiff University's School of Journalism. He played a significant part in Wales' decision to vote "Yes" in 1997, having been co-founder of the

Yes for Wales campaign in the referendum on devolution. Closer to home, Andrews is revered for his support of Burberry workers in Treorchy. The battle to save more than 300 jobs ended in vain as the clothing factory closed, but his impassioned campaign ensured a better redundancy deal for staff. Following his re-election to the Assembly in May 2007, Andrews joined the Cabinet as Deputy Minister for Social Justice and Public Service Delivery and, when the new coalition government was formed two months later, Andrews was appointed Deputy Minister for Regeneration. In December 2009, Andrews was brought in by new First Minister Carwyn Jones, whom he had supported as campaign manager following Rhodri Morgan's resignation, as Minister for Children, Education and Lifelong Learning. His meteoric rise from relative obscurity is an interesting one. Aside from junior Cabinet roles, Andrews had spent much of his political life as an AM on the backbenches. But after finding his feet and masterminding Jones' leadership campaign, Andrews was seen to have earned his place at the top table. Truth is, he had his eye on the education brief for some time prior to his appointment and assuming Jones was successful in his bid to become First Minister, Andrews was nailed on to land the job he wanted.

Plucked from the fringes of the Assembly, Andrews was not one of Wales' better known AMs – neither had he the sort of colourful personality that has earned the adulation of the media in the past. In fact, I remember vividly one of the first official press releases emanating from government after his appointment referring to the new Education Minister as "Layton". His was seemingly not a name on the tip of the department's tongue. No, this was not a man whom, on face value, you would have expected to leave quite so big a mark. Andrews enjoyed a relatively quiet first year in charge of Wales' education system and spent the first three months after his appointment swotting up on his new brief. Andrews had not gone in cold as is often the case with new ministers, and was already familiar with the inner workings of the education system after studying in the months prior to his promotion. He would become known for being studious and forensic in his research. Not withstanding his workman-like ethic, it would become apparent to Andrews that Wales' education system was not the Garden of Eden so many had assumed. Michael Barber, one of the minister's core advisers, would later reflect on "a politician who had the courage to act, even if some sacred cows would need to be slaughtered along the way".[8] A retrospective piece by Dr Philip Dixon, director of the Association of Teachers and Lecturers (ATL) Cymru, would encapsulate perfectly a noticeable change in tack.

"From the start it was clear that Leighton was going to be different to his predecessors. Gone were the mumsy muddle of Jane Hutt and the patrician *hauteur* of Jane Davidson. Instead we were presented with a man who knew his own mind. He had already done a lot of background research and had his own views about the state of Welsh education. And they weren't very complimentary."[9] (Philip Dixon, 2013)

There were no significant policy announcements in 2010 and although the minister was still finding his feet, the sector itself withstood considerable change. A series of high-profile resignations saw the arrival of two new names to the top of the education tree in Wales. The first saw Chief Inspector of Education and Training Dr Bill Maxwell return home to his native Scotland, where he succeeded Professor Graham Donaldson in a similar role. Maxwell was replaced by Ann Keane.

## The changing face of Welsh education

Boasting a wealth of experience in the education sector, Keane had worked for Her Majesty's Inspectorate since 1984. A former strategic director and head of directorate at Estyn, her previous responsibilities included the inspection of early years, primary, secondary, special and independent school provision. Following her appointment, Keane said she was looking forward to building on the legacy of her predecessor. "Bill was a strong leader and we all shared his vision for the future," she said. "He was a very easy Chief Inspector to work with and I can honestly say that I never disagreed with his direction of travel. He really carried us with him and allowed us to initiate ideas." In his last annual report, Maxwell had said pupils from less wealthy backgrounds and ethnic minorities were the most likely not to fulfil their potential. Keane said breaking down the achievements of different groups of learners was a way of monitoring the situation.

Wales' new Chief Inspector was born in Carmarthen and attended Llanboidy and Llandovery primary schools before progressing onto Ystalyfera and Llandysul grammar schools. Having read English literature and art at Aberystwyth University, Keane attended the London School of Economics, where she gained a post-graduate qualification in social administration, and completed a master's degree in art history at University College London. She began her professional life as a teacher, holding posts at Merthyr Tydfil Technical College and Canterbury College of Art among others. Initially, Keane landed the top job at Estyn on an interim basis until her long-term appointment was confirmed a few months later. A conscientious and articulate operator, Keane was a popular choice.

The second big change of 2010 saw the revolving door of DCELLS spin open again and the Director General of Education in Wales announce his intention to step down from the role. Professor David Hawker cited personal reasons for leaving DCELLS though his resignation came as no great surprise given his increasingly fractious relationship with the new minister, with whom he clashed regularly. The former teacher was to take up a secondment with the Department for Education in London, where he would lead the UK Government's review of arms-length bodies in the education and children's sectors. In a letter to colleagues in July, Hawker said he would be relocating to Sussex to be closer to his family and that the decision to leave had not been easy. He said: "The two years I have spent here with WAG (Welsh Assembly Government) have been challenging, absorbing and for the most part, immensely enjoyable. It has been a privilege working with partners across Wales in taking forward a demanding and exciting policy agenda in the education, training and children's sectors."[10]

Hawker, formerly deputy chief executive and director of children's services at Westminster Council, had been made director of DCELLS in August 2008. But despite his relatively fleeting stay in Wales, Hawker's 30 years' experience in the English education system made him a good sounding board for the sort of initiatives being implemented by the Assembly Government. In a speech to London's Institute of Education, Hawker said of Wales:

> "By comparison with England, it is really quite small, accounting for about 5% of the UK population. There are talented people on a par with the best in England, but there are fewer of them. Budgets are proportionately smaller, so Wales has to be smarter in what it tries to do. It can't compete with England – nor indeed should it – in terms of the number and scope of its initiatives. It has a fraction of the number of people to dream them up and take them forward. So it has to concentrate on a small number which are proven to work."[11] (David Hawker, 2009)

It was an interesting observation and Hawker had acknowledged the issues arising from Wales' size and population relative to others. His suggestion that Wales should prioritise and focus its attention on key areas would resonate strongly in the coming years.

Hawker, it is fair to say, did not leave a huge impression on the Welsh education department. He failed to elicit the wholehearted support of the civil service and many found his past association with the Bugbrooke Jesus Fellowship, an evangelical Christian group for which he was a spokesman in the 1980s, difficult to comprehend. Hawker retired from the Westminster Government in 2011 to concentrate on his consultancy work.

Hawker's successor would be the fifth appointed to the position of Director General in five years and Cardiff Central AM Jenny Randerson, the Liberal Democrat education spokeswoman, was among several concerned by his sudden resignation after just two years in post. "The high turnover of director generals in the education department suggests that all is not well," she said. "With rising child poverty levels and a high number of young people not in education, employment or training, Wales can ill afford this revolving door."[12]

Following Hawker's departure in September 2010, experienced civil servant Dr Emyr Roberts slid into the hot seat from the Department for Public Services and Local Government. A North Walian, Roberts was brought up in Benllech, Anglesey, and attended Ysgol Syr Thomas Jones, Amlwch. He had a degree from Reading University, a PhD from Aberystwyth University and began his career in the National Farmers' Union. To many, Roberts' appointment represented a steadying of the ship. DCELLS, it is fair to say, had undergone considerable upheaval since its merger with five formerly separate education bodies in 2006. Dissolving the likes of ACCAC and post-16 agency Education and Learning Wales (ELWa) was never going to be straightforward and the modified Assembly department had yet to settle down. The role of director had become something of a poisoned chalice but with a Welsh Office record stretching back to 1991, Roberts stood a good chance of outlasting his predecessors.

Splitting the two appointments was the publication of a report into how funding in Wales was allocated to schools, colleges and universities. According to PriceWaterhouseCoopers, just 44% of a budget of more than £4bn was spent on teaching. A review into the cost of administering education in Wales identified opportunities to transfer resources from administration to the delivery of frontline services. It revealed that around a third (32%) of annual education expenditure was spent on support services, such as service management and financial administration. The report estimated that a 2% shift in spending away from behind-the-scenes services into the frontline would equate to a cash injection of £83m. Collaboration was a key theme, with the possibility of so-called cluster schools sharing the cost of support services to improve internal efficiency. Responding to the review, Andrews stressed the importance of reducing bureaucracy and "streamlining" the education system to make it "lean and effective" for the benefit of learners. He said:

> "I have made it clear that I want to ensure more funding reaches the education frontline – our schools, colleges and universities. Much has already been done across the public sector in Wales, specifically within education to deliver efficiencies and improve services to achieve the highest possible standards of education and training. This review suggests some practical ideas and opportunities, laying strong foundations for action. We now require a step change to take these forward with purpose and urgency, with all organisations involved in the delivery of education having a crucial part to play."[13] (Leighton Andrews, 2010)

The report would add fuel to the minister's fire and provide an evidence-base from which he could attack the seemingly lax delegation of council money into frontline services. Andrews would later secure a commitment from local authorities to increase delegation levels by 5% within two years and 10% within four years. At the time, school funding delegation rates were set at around 75%, which meant almost £600m was being stashed by local authorities. It was the beginning of a long-running battle between central and local government, which would remain a nagging thorn in the minister's side for the duration of his tenure. But if his first year in office was to be largely uneventful, the next 12 months would see Andrews mark his arrival on the political stage. Everything was about to change and in December 2010, two major educational events would demand a proactive response from the Welsh Government. More importantly, it would give Andrews opportunity to cut his teeth as a Cabinet minister.

## A rise in tuition fees

Former oil tycoon Lord John Browne raised eyebrows by suggesting in October 2010 that the cap on university tuition fees be lifted. His widespread report into higher education was the most radical since World War II but given the devolution settlement, reviewed financial support for students in England only. In reality, of course, the implications of his findings would be felt much further afield and impact directly on Welsh students and institutions. A joint study by the National Union of Students (NUS) and HSBC earlier in the year found that two thirds of students would have turned their backs on higher education had fees been raised to £7,000. The advent of higher fees could, of course, price poorer students out of the market and make elite universities out of reach for the nation's top achievers. With graduate unemployment at its highest for two decades, higher education had scarcely been so unappealing.

When Browne opened the door for universities to set their own tuition levels, Welsh students were seemingly resigned to their fate. Such is the cross-border nature of the education sector, proposed changes to the system in England were certain to be felt in Wales. Browne had spoken and the talked about trebling of tuition fees from in the region of £3,000 to a ceiling of £9,000 was soon to become reality for thousands of prospective learners. But in a remarkable about-turn, Andrews delivered on his promise to protect Welsh students and proved beyond all doubt that there was another, uniquely Welsh way. The equation was simple – although difficult for the other UK governments, England especially, to comprehend.

The Assembly Government's radical plan to spare students in Wales a rise in tuition fees sent shock waves through the entire higher education establishment. In practice, it meant universities in Wales would be allowed to charge up to £9,000 a year in fees, provided they could demonstrate a commitment to widening access and other strategic objectives. But in a surprise twist, the additional cost would be met by the Assembly Government, and Welsh students who went to university in 2012-13 would be no worse off than if they had gone to university the previous year. The income repayment threshold for student loans would rise from £15,000 to £21,000 and part-time students would be entitled to a tuition fee loan depending on the intensity of their course. Andrews said the arrangements Wales had put in place "were both fair, equitable and sustainable". The teaching grant for Welsh universities would be top-sliced by 35% to pay for the subsidy but Andrews was adamant the income of Welsh Higher Education Institutions (HEIs) would be at least the same in real terms in 2016-17 as it would be in 2012-13. The formula was reliant on additional revenue being made from the 24,000 English students studying in Wales, who were exempt from Assembly Government protection and would pay their fees in full. At the time, about 16,000 Welsh undergraduates studied across the border, but Andrews said the cost to English students would help mitigate money spent on Welsh-domiciled students wherever in the UK they chose to study. He added:

> "The state cannot shirk its responsibility to intervene to secure inclusion and to build community cohesion. This is a 'Made in Wales' policy which demonstrates the benefits of devolution. We are preserving the principle that the state will subsidise higher education and maintain opportunities for all. Should Parliament refuse to endorse the proposals of the UK coalition Government, then we will rejoice and develop an alternative approach."[14] (Leighton Andrews, 2010)

And rejoice the minister did. The Welsh Government's tuition fee policy announced Andrews on the UK stage and set the tone for a combative relationship with Westminster. But not everyone was appeased by the minister's philanthropy and in times of austerity, vice-chancellors bemoaned what they said was in the region of £50m being lost to institutions outside of Wales. Possible alternatives included supporting Welsh students who chose to study in Wales only, or means-testing students to provide for those who needed financial aid the most. There remains a strong argument to suggest students from more affluent backgrounds should not be entitled to the same subsidy as those who find affording the cost of their own tuition more of a struggle. Not surprisingly, the policy represented a significant win for NUS Wales. But given its responsibility to all students, the union's joy at securing relief for Welsh-domiciled learners was tempered by disappointment for its non-Welsh members, whom they also represent.

From a near impossible situation, Andrews had scored an unlikely victory. By shouldering a rise in fees, he had shifted the onus back onto Westminster and ensured Welsh students were not short-changed. There was no dispensation for undergraduates from England, but the Assembly Government had honoured its pledge to support its own learners financially. The decision would ensure students from all backgrounds were given the opportunity to prolong their education, and heap more pressure on the creaking Westminster coalition to find its own credible solution. Andrews dangled an alternative in front of UK Education Secretary Michael Gove who, amid growing strain, chose not to bite. If nothing else, the policy was a sure vote winner with an Assembly election around the corner.

# Notes

1.   Gurria, Angel. (2007). Western Mail. December 5.
2.   Hutt, Jane. (2007). Western Mail. December 5.
3.   Brychan, Anna. (2007). Western Mail. December 5.
4.   Marshall, Steve. (2008). Western Mail. January 17.
5.   Edwards, Elaine. (2011). Western Mail. December 29.
6.   Meadowcroft, Michael. (2003). What's He Doing There? Michael Meadowcroft and Liz Bee.
7.   Flynn, Paul. (1999). Dragons Led By Poodles; The Inside Story of a New Labour Stitch-Up. p 16.
8.   Barber, Michael. (2014). Foreword, Ministering to Education. p ix.
9.   Dixon, Philip. (2013). Click On Wales. Leighton Andrews' Assault on Systemic Failure. June 28.
10.   Hawker, David. (2010). Western Mail. July 27.
11.   Hawker, David. (2009). Institute of Education, University of London. May 14.
12.   Randerson, Jenny. (2010). Western Mail. July 27.
13.   Andrews, Leighton. (2010). Western Mail. May 20.
14.   Andrews, Leighton. (2010). Western Mail. December 1.

# 4

# Wales' Leaning Tower

## A wake-up call to a complacent system

*A turning point for Welsh education. Andrews responds to PISA and policymakers plot a revival. But there are skeletons in the closet and no-one, least not the civil service, escapes unscathed*

Never before have international benchmarks meant so much. Success hinges on a successful PISA showing and education systems can live or die by their performance on the world stage. And so it proved in 2010. Of the 65 countries taking part in the 2009 study – the results of which were published a year later – Wales ranked 38th for reading, 40th for maths and 30th for science. The paltry return was painfully below expectations. It meant Wales again ranked the lowest of all the home nations and alongside countries like Luxembourg, Slovenia and Israel in the ultimate test of key skills. That's not to say Wales had automatic licence to sit pretty above some of the OECD's most impoverished nations. Far from it. But the subsequent outpouring of negativity proved critical. There is much evidence linking education and skills to economic growth and PISA's prominence makes favourable performance essential. The OECD's director of education and skills Andreas Schleicher, who devised PISA and is considered one of the world's most influential educationalists, is adamant that "your education today is your economy tomorrow". His message has been circulated across the globe.

The publication of PISA results in December 2010 was arguably the most significant event of Andrews' entire three and a half years as minister. In fact, his response can be considered a turning point for Welsh education, post-devolution. But sector leaders had seen it coming. Results were leaked well before publication on December 7 and critics had a good steer on where Wales would rank in the international scale. Nevertheless, when PISA was made official, education experts blamed a "whole system failure" for Wales' slide down the school rankings. Pinning his colours to the mast, Andrews said everyone in the sector should be "alarmed" by Welsh scores. "These results have made it clear that schools in Wales are simply not delivering well enough for students at all levels of ability," he said. "There can be no alibis and no excuses. Countries with less money spent on education have done better than Wales. Schools, local authorities and ourselves as Government need to look honestly at these results and accept responsibility for them."[1]

Wales scored 472 for maths, below Latvia, Lithuania and the OECD average of 496. Figures for reading (476) were also desperately low and while science remained the nation's best discipline, Wales' tally (496) was still five points below the international average. All three scores were lower than those recorded in 2006. The OECD found that Welsh 15-year-olds had difficulty in summarising information and in general performed lower on assessments of continuous text which demanded age-commensurate attainment in reading comprehension, reading "stamina" and an ability to infer, interpret and summarise information. Andrews' response to the results left nothing to the imagination. He said on the day of publication:

> "This can only be described as a systemic failure – we all share responsibility for this and we must equally share in the difficult task of turning things around. The young people of Wales have the same potential as young people across the world. We need to refocus on higher standards, set our ambitions and expectations high and look for improvement in every aspect of our system. We need to address this as a matter of absolute urgency. It requires honesty, leadership and a new approach to accountability."[2] (Leighton Andrews, 2010)

Inevitably, Andrews was asked why Wales had performed so poorly despite a decade of devolved Labour rule. He said: "We have introduced a number of new initiatives and we have responded in many ways. The profession wanted to see us abolish SATs and league tables – and we have. Results are improving overall year-on-year and there are fewer students leaving school without qualifications. Notwithstanding that fact, what we clearly now need to do is identify that we are not performing as well as we should be. Some countries are bypassing us and they shouldn't be." It seemed strange that the under-fire minister should, of all things, refer back to SATs and league tables. Had Andrews identified the problem? Did the stripping away of two important performance measures – both still readily available in England – contribute in some way to Wales' sorry plight? Could that missing layer of accountability really impact on Welsh scores? The coming months and years would be telling.

Andrews promised to outline the Assembly Government's response to PISA in a major speech in February 2011, determining that there were "a whole series of things I want to debate with the rest of the education world first". In the meantime, those involved in Welsh education would engage in a national debate on what had gone wrong and what was needed to rectify the situation. Outsiders were less than gushing in their praise and disparaging headlines in the London-based media added to a cacophony of dissenting voices. The implication was that Wales' continued substandard performance was dragging the rest of the UK down. The potential damage to Wales' reputation and economy – for the two are intrinsically linked – would cause considerable concern. Closer to home, critics pointed to Scotland's stability in the rankings as a yardstick and proof countries as small as Wales were at least capable of maintaining current performance.

Scotland fared similar in 2009 to what it did in 2006 in all three subject areas, following declines in previous years. It was above the OECD average in reading and science, and similar to the OECD average in maths. Philip Dixon said Scotland's performance proved devolution was not to blame for Wales' poor record of achievement. "We'd be better looking to Scotland and learning from them about how to run a high performing, co-operative education system than across the way to England where competition and conflict are not delivering the goods," he said. "This is not the time for finger pointing or blame shifting. It would be a mistake to look for one single cause; the results point to a whole system failure."[3] Gareth Jones, secretary of ASCL Cymru, said the results were a "wake-up call" but should not be taken out of context. "The PISA results should be considered carefully, but there is an urgent need to identify what other strategies are essential to improvement," he said. "Welsh education policy is still in its early days. New strategies will take time to feed through into the achievements of 15-year-olds."[4]

As is the correlation between testing and results, PISA had been sat in Wales shortly before Andrews' appointment. The lag allowed the Welsh Government time to consider its position. Knowing PISA to be bad news, Andrews could either acknowledge Wales' scores and pass them off as one of many performance indicators or, as was the case, use PISA as a driver for change. It was a bold move and by placing such strong emphasis on PISA improvement, he had made a rod for his own back. Whatever his plan of attack, failure to meet the required standard was bound to reflect badly on him. Nevertheless, it is worth noting that PISA was growing in popularity and participation. More countries took part than ever before in 2009 and once involved in the study, it would have been very difficult to turn a blind eye to its findings. If the gun was loaded, PISA gave Andrews licence to pull the trigger. Archaic standards required radical solutions; this was not about rogue schools or indifferent authorities and the dearth of key skills ran much deeper. Andrews was duty-bound to stop the rot and Welsh education was at a crossroads.

A week before the minister's grandstand response to PISA, Wales' new Chief Inspector compounded matters by delivering her first annual report. Hers was a chilling assessment and Keane warned children in Wales were being left further behind their counterparts across Europe because the pace of improvement in Welsh schools was too slow. In addition to reporting on 2009-10, Keane looked back at progress over the previous six years during which Estyn had inspected all providers of education and training in Wales. The document found that many pupils' literacy and numeracy levels were not being fully developed. Crucially, it appeared to back up conclusions PISA had drawn just a few months earlier.

Keane said that since 2004, Estyn had judged provision to be good with outstanding features in only 8% of all maintained schools. She said assessment was inconsistent and "not robust enough", making it difficult to identify gaps in basic skills and plan support in a consistent way. "Yes, we have made some improvements, but we haven't progressed enough and our own report shows that," she said.[5] The Chief Inspector warned there was a need to "face facts" and added: "There are challenges we need to tackle before education in Wales can rival the best in the world." Keane used the report to set out her stall:

> "First, evidence over the last six years shows that systems to track learners' progress throughout their education are not good enough. Different kinds of assessment measure performance in different ways and sometimes, at the end of primary school for instance, assessments are just not robust enough. This makes it difficult to identify gaps in basic skills and to plan support in a consistent way. Second, developing literacy and numeracy skills is also a challenge. There are still far too many learners of all ages and ability level whose skills are not being developed fully... Third, we also need better training for leaders and education professionals which will help them to be more confident in creating new opportunities for joint working. We need to champion and foster an environment of creativity and innovation in the classroom."[6] (Ann Keane, 2011)

Keane's report coincided with the end of the Assembly's 10-year Learning Country strategy. But it was not a ringing endorsement and while overall standards of education and training in Wales were considered to have been maintained or improved since 2004, Keane warned that improvement had been slow, particularly in schools. Standards, she said, were not as good as they should be in more than 30% of maintained schools and standards in very few schools and providers were consistently outstanding. The proportion of more able pupils achieving above expected levels had generally fallen between 2004 and 2010. Literacy, she said, was an important shortcoming and pupils were not developing their writing skills well enough at any key stage.

> "In summary, schools and other providers have made progress since 2004 and they have responded positively to the challenges we set in the last two annual reports. But too many aspects of provision are not good enough yet."[7] (Ann Keane, 2011)

At first glance, Keane's assessment appeared a fair one. Her observations resonated with those of other sector leaders and her criticisms of leadership and key skills, in particular, would remain an underlying feature. Nevertheless, a decade after The Learning Country, Wales would have surely hoped for better.

## A call to arms

As expected, the minister opened a collective eye on standards in February 2011 during a grandstand speech at the National Museum's Reardon Smith Theatre. It was there that Andrews first shattered the perception that all was well in Welsh education and if the sector had been lulled into a false sense of security, it was his job to provide a dose of reality. Coincidentally, Andrews had delayed his response to PISA – the results having been published a full two months earlier – deliberately so as to give the profession time to reflect on the nation's scores. But having spent the festive season mulling over his response, the minister made good his promise to counter December's verdict, albeit the nation's foremost educationalists, gathered together in the same room, were seldom given so much food for thought. Andrews' speech was met with eerie silence and upon leaving the lecture theatre that day, stakeholders would have been under no illusions as to what was expected of them. Everyone had been responsible for breaking Wales' education system – and everyone was responsible for putting it back together. Dixon, who chaired the day's event, said of the meeting:

> "Within months of taking office he set out his stall in a lecture – Teaching Makes a Difference – that I was privileged to chair at the National Museum. It was a tour de force. The great and the good of Welsh education were gathered and our collective responsibility exposed. PISA showed that we were under performing and by extension

failing to give our children the requisite skills for life... Only the head-bangers denied it. The atmosphere was akin to the headteacher telling the sixth-form that he was disappointed in their conduct. We left rather sheepishly, realising that we had all played a part in what was labelled 'systemic failure'."[8] (Philip Dixon, 2013)

Geraint Talfan Davies, chairman of the IWA, made a similar assessment. He recalled: "The large lecture theatre was packed to capacity. As I walked in, a leading figure in local government alongside me gaped as he saw the assembled throng and whispered: 'It's just amazing how many people will turn out for a bollocking.'"[9]

In a drawing of the battle lines, Andrews told an eclectic mix of teachers, trade unionists and civil servants that Wales could, and must, do better. It was a time for reflection, to take stock and to gauge what the Welsh Government and the profession had achieved – but so too was it opportunity to put forward his vision. Andrews said:

> "In Wales over the decade of devolution we have implemented many of the changes the profession wanted to see. We have worked with the profession. We don't have league tables. We abolished SATs. We introduced the Foundation Phase. We created a skill-based curriculum. We have avoided many of the antagonistic competitive features of the English system. We do not have academies. We will not have Michael Gove's so-called free schools. We have maintained faith in the comprehensive model of education. As I said to Michael Gove last year, one of the advantages of devolution is that is allows England to be a laboratory for experiments. But if we believe in the comprehensive model in Wales, then we have to make sure that it delivers for all our children."[10] (Leighton Andrews, 2011)

Reading between the lines, Andrews appeared frustrated that the Welsh Government's willingness to work in partnership with the sector had not paid dividends. Put simply, Wales' unique approach to educational development had to translate into results to justify the very different path being taken. Andrews said PISA was a "highly respected and robust measure of the relative performance of education systems" and Wales' results could not be argued away or excused.

> "We need to face up to the harsh truth: the education system in Wales is not delivering the outcomes that our young people need and deserve... I look to the whole sector to support the actions necessary to bring about sustained, positive change. PISA, I am afraid, is a wake-up call to a

complacent system. There are no alibis and no excuses. It is evidence of systemic failure. But, as I always say, never waste a crisis."[11] (Leighton Andrews, 2011)

Andrews, meticulous in his preparation, outlined a radical five-year plan to improve standards in Welsh schools. The introduction of a national school grading system to ensure minimum standards set the cat amongst the pigeons and was among 20 actions unveiled before stakeholders in Cardiff. If The Learning Country was Davidson's paving document, this was Andrews' paving speech. He said improving performance was essential, with fewer initiatives and better implementation of existing practice key to success. Moving forward, no school would pass inspections unless it could show its governing body had discussed performance data and set in place actions to improve. Accountability, it seemed, transcended well beyond the confines of the profession. Andrews said schools would be graded annually on their ability to reach certain targets, and those falling short of the mark would be closed. He revealed plans to revise teacher training to become a two-year master's course. In future, there would be a statutory requirement on all qualifying teachers to be trained in literacy and numeracy and one INSET (In-Service Education for Teachers) day a year would be dedicated to staff assessments. New national reading and numeracy tests would be developed to ensure fewer pupils fell behind expected levels and seek to arrest some of the headline shortcomings causing concern within Estyn. Testing pupils as young as five, however, would remain the subject of considerable consternation.

Outside The Learning Country, Andrews' 20 point plan represented the most radical raft of education proposals ever introduced in Wales. Welsh education's equivalent to the Ten Commandments, they included the development of a School Standards Unit (SSU). The unit was launched in May 2011 under the leadership of Dr Brett Pugh, who had been seconded from his role as director of education at Newport Council – widely regarded one of Wales' best performing education authorities. The SSU would be responsible for formulating the Welsh Government's school grading system, to be published for the first time in December 2011. Andrews was typically brutal in his assessment of Wales' education system, now known to be lagging behind the rest of the home nations in all key disciplines. He said:

"Ours is not a good system aiming to become great. Ours is a fair system aiming to become good. And that requires honesty and clarity from all involved. For systems moving from fair to good there has to be a significant amount of central input to ensure standards are being upheld. School systems moving from good to great can afford to free up their systems."[12] (Leighton Andrews, 2011)

Like a teacher to an unruly pupil, Andrews' tenure began with a cracking of the whip. But the parallels did not go unnoticed and the profession took umbrage. The need for improvement was accepted – the minister's tone was not. Teachers were not used to being told what to do and seldom were they told they were doing badly. Andrews' approach was far more prescriptive than that of his predecessors and his speech was not one to warm the hearts of his workforce. He accused Wales of being "too cosy" and said there had been "a reluctance to rock the boat". Andrews continued:

> "Fortunately, a reluctance to tell it like it is has never been one of my problems. We have assumed that things were going well, so we have designed systems intended to move us from the good to the great. In fact, we have to move our system from the not-so-good to the good. We are complacent – complacency kills aspiration. We have not articulated stretching targets, nor have we provided parents with the confidence and expectation that things can and should be better."[13] (Leighton Andrews, 2011)

After the disappointment of PISA and a rude awakening from Wales' inspectorate, the minister's announcement was never going to be pretty. Andrews had more than enough ammunition to wield his heavy axe over a "complacent" system struggling to meet the needs of Welsh learners. He called for honesty, leadership and a new approach to accountability. The search for alibis, he said, was a continuous distraction. But while sector leaders shared in his analysis, the speech marked the beginning of a rocky relationship with the wider teaching fraternity. Despite his efforts, it was a relationship the minister would never fully reconcile. Andrews pointed to the breaking down of education authorities in the 1990s as a contributing factor to Wales' downturn in educational performance. Increased learner choice, he argued, was not necessarily a good thing. To ensure key skills were learned properly, the sector would need to go back to basics.

> "The doctrine of learner choice which has underpinned much of educational thinking over the last 20 years has been bought, to my mind, at the cost of quality and rigour."[14] (Leighton Andrews, 2011)

There was no grey area and delegates left knowing exactly what Andrews expected of them. The minister was honest in his assessment: "We did not fare as well as we would have liked in the 2006 PISA assessments and we all hoped that our policies would have yielded improvements by the 2009 assessments. Sadly, we know now that is not the case. The 2009 figures painted an even more disappointing picture of our educational performance and progress."

# A department in turmoil

In delivering his call to arms, Andrews gave one of the few real insights into his thoughts on Labour's 12 years in devolved government. Not one to mix his words, he branded his own department fragmented and implementation of policy weak.

> "We have a department which saw several quangos merged with it in 2006. I do not know if those mergers were ever culturally integrated. I do know that a single departmental culture has yet to emerge. My impression as a minister is of a department that has been culturally and geographically fragmented without a clear focus... Historically, civil servants have been strong on policy design, but less good at policy implementation and embedding."[15] (Leighton Andrews, 2011)

It was a remarkable admission. If the sector had to shoulder responsibility, so too did DCELLS. No-one was free from accountability and the department itself was suffering from chronic instability. A constant shuffling of senior management was not conducive to that of a well-oiled machine. There were splits in the camp and reports of factions between subsidiaries. Civil servants were overly protective, joint working was limited and a complete team ethic had yet to be developed. The net result was a strategic plan lacking in fluidity. For the system to work, policy had to flow; schools and higher education had to work together, for example, and it was in everyone's best interests to know what the other was doing. Andrews would later recall sitting in two meetings on literacy, held on the same day with two completely different teams. It has been suggested, on more than one occasion, that DCELLS lacked direction and it was not uncommon for officials to flit randomly from one meeting to another. According to Gary Brace, long-time chief executive of the General Teaching Council for Wales (GTCW): "There were too many instances where policymaking was left to officials who were unprepared to consult genuinely and respond to those with relevant experience, or who were too prone to jump to decisions at the behest of the loudest political voice, or who simply were not up to the job."[16] It is, perhaps, little wonder that the department fell so woefully short on implementation.

The 2011 Vivian Thomas report on the structure of education services in Wales highlighted deficiencies in the Department for Education perfectly. Thomas warned there was a "significant gap in the national accountability framework for education in Wales" and problems ran deep. He said there was a "distinct lack of clarity in terms of mission or outcomes" and silos within DCELLS had operated individually with little understanding of the bigger picture. According to Thomas, limited use had been made of educationalists with immediate and direct experience of schools, colleges and further education institutions. It seemed that even where the department had the expertise, it was incapable of utilising it effectively. But Thomas saw light at the end of the tunnel:

> "We are hopeful that, under the management of a new Director General, DCELLS will coordinate itself better, seek the help of experienced educators and become a department that can lead educational development in Wales over the next period of years and add significant value to everything that Welsh educationalists do. It is some way from that clarity, coordination and role at this point."[17] (Vivian Thomas, 2011)

Thomas said the perception of stakeholders was that there was a need for change and that during his deliberations with colleges, the quality and capability of DCELLS staff in understanding present day further education was often questioned. He said the quality of many staff was seen to be too low for the job and as one college leader put it: "The further one is from DCELLS, the better we perform"[18]. This was hardly a ringing endorsement:

> "It has been argued that there is a lack of knowledge in DCELLS relating to a real understanding of what happens at local authority level, let alone at school level and there may be a lack of engagement and effective communication with the teaching profession. That does not come as a surprise since out of 710 employees only two permanent employees have experience of working in schools, colleges or local authorities during the past five years."[19] (Vivian Thomas, 2011)

Thomas said it was "perfectly clear" that DCELLS did not in 2011 have the capacity to properly hold local authorities and others to account. He warned that if urgent steps were not taken, "we could well enter a downward spiral in terms of performance". The report recommended that the education department be reorganised to ensure clarity of function and accountability. Responding, Andrews was by no means dismissive and said everyone with an interest in improving education in Wales should read Thomas' report.

The origins of the department's inadequacies can be traced back to Rhodri Morgan's bonfire of the quangos in 2006, following a decision by AMs to abolish ELWa and ACCAC. In fact, the First Minister met with strong opposition prior to their dissolution, with management within the qualifications body, in particular, warning that experienced officials would be lost. Fears became reality when some of ACCAC's most respected staff were poached by rival organisations and those formerly employed by ELWa were appointed to senior regulatory and qualifications roles within the new-look Welsh Assembly department. Their limited experience in the field would hamper early progress. Allied to staffing issues, there was a feeling that the decision to bring ACCAC into the Assembly's direct control could create problems, given policymakers would have dual rule over both qualifications and their regulation. The apparent conflict of interest was not lost on critics and the move would resonate strongly during the infamous GCSE grading fiascos of 2012 and 2014. There is also a feeling that the incorporation of ELWa and ACCAC into the department gave fledgling civil servants too much to do and relationships were not easy to forge. Responding to questions about a perceived gap in curriculum expertise and direction following the abolition of ACCAC, WJEC chief executive Gareth Pierce told AMs in May 2014 that: "It seems as if the Welsh Government and WJEC are holding hands around a hole, and the hole is ACCAC."[20] His analogy was not without substance and perfectly encapsulated the situation in which Wales found itself. There would be a high turnover of staff under Andrews and with every passing Director General came subtle structural change that caused further disruption and delay. Deficiencies within the newly-renamed Department for Education and Skills (DfES replaced DCELLS in May 2011) were a badly-kept secret and while there was improvement under Andrews, the self-fulfilling mindset had not been eradicated. The Welsh Government was unlikely to build anything tangible while it was still putting out fires from within.

The inspectorate also attracted criticism and Andrews was scathing of its failure to properly support and challenge. He said there had been a "complacency about judgements" and Estyn's inspection framework had only recently become "fit for purpose". With an Assembly election around the corner, Andrews' speech added fuel to the fire that the Welsh Labour Government, in all it various guises, had failed to properly educate the nation's children. But, at the same time, it served as a sure statement of intent and proved unequivocally that Andrews was more than willing to roll up his sleeves. Turning the good ship education around would, as the minister suggested, not be easy – but past lessons had to be learned. He said:

"There is a formidable agenda ahead of us in respect of schools alone. There will, in future, be no hiding place for poor performance. In my department, performance will drive every aspect of what we are doing. There will be a single focus. We will raise standards. We will provide opportunities for all to learn to the best of their ability. Our young people deserve better. And I believe that we can deliver."[21] (Leighton Andrews, 2011)

Concluding, Andrews threw down the gauntlet and challenged Wales to be in the top 20 of school systems measured in the PISA tests of 2015. In hindsight, Andrews would regret setting the bar quite so high. Wales was, after all, starting at a very low point and the increase in participating countries alone would make his top 20 aspiration all the more difficult to achieve. Consider then that in drafting his post-PISA plan, Andrews had initially wanted to land a place in the world's top 20% – which amounted to Wales having one of the top dozen education systems. There is a fine line between ambition and recklessness and while expectations should be suitably high, Andrews was rightly talked down. But for one rogue adviser, the minister would have been shackled to a PISA plan that was quite clearly insurmountable.

One of the minister's closest allies, David Reynolds, said meeting Wales' top 20 target would be difficult, but failure to do so could have "economic consequences". Given PISA's growing reputation as a global benchmark for performance, he said prosperous nations would be less likely to invest in Wales if its education system was considered sub-standard. There was a precedent and Chile, albeit not known for its educational prowess, rose 39 points in the PISA rankings from 2000 to 2009. But could we seriously expect lightening to strike twice? Reynolds explained the extent of Wales' challenge:

> "The PISA mean is about 500 [points]. We (Wales), on mathematics for example, are on about 480. To be a top 20 country we probably need 520, which means we've got to go from 480 to 520 and we've got to do it in only five years – which are the five years post-2011 when the minister made his speech. The only other country in the world that's ever gone 40 points upwards is Chile – and it took Chile 10 years to do it."[22] (David Reynolds, 2012)

It was a sobering assessment of the state of play. With every best will in the world, it appeared that Wales would still fall well short of its PISA target.

## A PISA backlash

PISA had become big news but while the sector had been shocked into action, there remained those deeply sceptical of its validity. To this day, many believe Andrews made a mountain out of a mole hill with PISA and NASUWT, in particular, was vocal in its disapproval. Rex Phillips, NASUWT Wales organiser, accused the Welsh Government of "misusing" PISA data for its own purposes and described the minister's 20 points as a "cynical" attempt to push forward his agenda for change. And the union was not alone. Other critics questioned whether Andrews had created a crisis for his own personal gain.

Experts called for a more balanced view of Wales' schools following the publication of a study by London's Institute of Education that claimed England – which performed far better than Wales by comparison – had been harshly treated and evidence of a decline in standards across the border could not be justified. In his analysis of English pupils' scores, Dr John Jerrim unearthed problems with missing data, survey procedures and the target population. He said the fact there were more participating countries in 2009 than when PISA launched in 2000 could have something to do with England's slide down the rankings. Jerrim added that the introduction of poorer performing nations into the fray would impact on scores more generally. He said: "The fact that Welsh schools did not take part in the PISA 2000 study hence means that the average PISA maths test score for England in that year is likely to be higher than in the other survey waves."

And there were other issues. "Perhaps the most important is the month when children sat the PISA test moved from between March and May (in PISA 2000 and 2003) to roughly five months earlier in PISA 2006 and 2009," he said. "England had special dispensation to make this change and although it was for good reason (PISA clashed with GCSE exam preparation) it may have had unintended consequences."[23] Jerrim was not alone in his analyses and Professor Gareth Rees, an expert on Welsh education based at Cardiff University, made clear his reservations. Rees said Wales was right to join PISA but there were fundamental questions about how data was collated. "PISA is an important study but, as with any set of results, we've got to interpret them sensitively," he said. "The notion is that, between 2006 and 2009, there has been a deterioration but you can't conclude that from those results because each measurement is based on different pupils. We shouldn't conclude that because the PISA results have gone down that everything is terrible in the Welsh education system and that the system is deteriorating."[24] Not withstanding its confidence in individual assessments, the OECD itself has reservations with regards country-to-country comparisons. It writes on its website:

"Any assessment of the skills of people, whether it is a high school exam, a driving test, or an international sample–based assessment like PISA, will have some uncertainty – because the results depend on the tasks that are chosen for the assessment, on variations of the ways in which the assessment was administered, the fact that the assessment is sample-based or even on the disposition of the person taking the test on the day of the assessment."[25] (OECD)

The fact that most of the world's foremost economies choose to volunteer their time and money so readily on PISA gives the survey considerable credence.

But there are important caveats and PISA has yet to win the hearts and minds of teachers. The profession is not convinced by PISA's credentials and without the buy-in of key stakeholders, it is hard to imagine any of the home nations challenging world leaders. In the classroom at least, Wales' approach to PISA is far more casual than, say, that of South Korea, where it is not uncommon for children to be clapped into their exams as if representing their country on the rugby field. PISA is taken far more seriously in many front-running East Asian territories, where a lot of tuition takes place outside of school surroundings. In those particular circumstances, it is harder to gauge the value-added impact of the education system itself but it could well be that extra-curricular activities are a contributory factor to success.

So PISA was not the be all and end all as far as educationalists were concerned, albeit those who questioned its validity would attract the acerbic tag of "PISA denier". An argument often levelled at policymakers is their supposed tendency to use PISA for their own purposes and, courtesy of NASUWT in particular, Wales appeared no exception. Governments were often accused of stretching PISA too far and using results as a driver for change that was not justified. But working in Andrews' favour was the fact that all evidence pointed to the same dreary conclusion. Estyn was consistently scathing of key skills and Wales' cumulative GCSE and A-level results had been languishing well below those in England and Northern Ireland for some time. In 10 years, Welsh teenagers had gone from achieving an above average percentage of five A*-C grades at GCSE to a percentage significantly below average.

One of the first things Andrews did in response to PISA was to integrate PISA tests into school assessments at 15. Schools would be asked to work with their Year Eight and Nine students ahead of the next round of tests in 2012. A PISA crash-course, past papers would be made available to all secondaries. Then again, "teaching to the test" was taboo in some circles and inherent shortcomings would not go away overnight. As the Chief Inspector suggested, if pupils could not decipher the questions, how could they be expected return the best answers? Wales needed to go back to basics and the nation's lack of key skills was a serious hindrance. PISA was the main driver – but it was by no means the only one.

Wales' slide down the school world rankings were, in educational terms, earth-shattering. This was not supposed to happen and after the rude awakening of PISA 2006, failure to improve at all was nothing short of catastrophic. Andrews called for collective responsibility and for the sector to pull together in what were undoubtedly testing times for Welsh education. Accountability in the nation's schools was key and, amid accusations the Welsh Government had taken its eye off the ball, Andrews was duty bound to tighten his grip. Brace conceded that PISA "had changed the whole atmosphere among education professionals and policymakers". The 2010 results, he said, made clear "that we in Wales have a much bigger task on our hands than we realised". Brace concluded:

> "While no-one is suggesting that the performance of teachers in Wales is the main cause of these uncomfortable results, it must certainly be a key part of the effort to put things right."[26] (Gary Brace, 2011)

According to Brace, this was not a profession intent on deflecting criticism; more a sector prepared to pitch in for the greater good. He said the PISA figures were "something of a shock to the system" and while Wales had assumed progress was being made, the results were a "reality check on what actually needs to be done". As a former teacher and GTCW chief executive since the body's inception in 2000, Brace's view was not to be ignored.

Another teachers' leader, however, took a very different view. Much to the minister's frustration, NASUWT general secretary Chris Keates would draw comparison between Andrews and his Conservative nemesis, Michael Gove. Two months after the grandstand post-PISA speech, Keates said there were "frightening similarities" between Andrews and Gove – and the Cabinet front-runners had a lot in common despite their political and geographical divide. She said Andrews used the same rhetoric and convergence of policies and, given the growing animosity between the Welsh and UK governments, it was not a comparison of which either party would have been particularly fond. Keates accused Andrews of "alienating" and "demoralising" teachers in the wake of PISA's disappointing report into educational standards. She said:

> "One of the key things at the moment that Leighton Andrews is doing, is misusing international data in order to justify a change in the way schools are operating. That is exactly the same thing that the coalition Government in Westminster is doing and the end result is a punitive regime for teachers. Clearly, we have no objection to data being used to inform, but we're using it selectively and reusing it in the wrong way to drive change. PISA changed things and we've heard the same rhetoric in Wales as we've been getting in the coalition in Westminster."[27] (Chris Keates, 2011)

Keates, the face of NASUWT since 2004, said politicians were using PISA as a "shield" for failed policies and warned against ranking countries which had little in common. She opposed wholesale structural change and said that workforce reform was crucial to raising standards and addressing spiralling teacher workloads. Lo and behold, one issue that remains patently unresolved in Wales is that of supply and what happens when teachers are absent from school. The issue cannot be underestimated and is well worth considering given its clear impact on performance.

## Teacher supply cover

A report published in 2013 provided ample evidence and found that pupil progress in Wales' schools was being hampered by teacher absence and an increasing number of lessons being covered by supply agencies. A team from Estyn and the Wales Audit Office (WAO) visited 23 primary and secondary schools and reported a growing reliance on supply teachers and cover staff. They said that just under 10% of lessons in Wales were covered by temporary teachers and pupils' education was suffering as a result. Maintained schools in Wales spent around £54m on classroom supply cover for teachers who were absent in 2011-12. Reasons for absence included sickness, training, attending meetings and work associated with curriculum development.

According to the WAO, whose report focused on value for money and effectiveness, expenditure on supply cover had risen by 7% since 2008-09, with teacher absence impacting on pupils across the ability range. It said less able pupils were less likely to receive the support they needed, and middle ability and more able pupils were likely to make less progress than they should because the work being set was not challenging enough. The WAO said there was scope to reduce teachers' sickness absence and while improvements had been made, the average of seven days' sickness absence per teacher in Wales was well above the 4.5 average recorded in England. It estimated that if the level could be limited to that of England, schools in Wales could reduce the number of days requiring cover by around 60,000, saving more than £9m a year in cover costs. The WAO also raised serious wellbeing issues, namely that not all schools in Wales ensured safeguarding procedures were in place for temporary staff. Where supply staff were recruited from a local authority pool or recruitment agency, it said in most instances schools relied on the local authority or agency concerned to carry out pre-employment checks. But according to the WAO, not all schools were aware of all the checks that should be carried out, and schools did not always keep records that checks had been completed.

Estyn's report, which considered more the impact of teacher absence on learners, found that pupils made less progress when their usual class teacher was absent and their behaviour was often worse. Inspectors said teaching by supply staff not employed by a school was often less effective because they did not know enough about the needs of the pupils they taught. Due to the short-term nature of their work, Estyn said it was difficult for temporary staff to establish effective working relationships with learners, who did not have the same regard for supply teachers as they did for their usual teachers. Estyn concluded:

"Generally, morale among supply staff working through recruitment agencies is low. They work in challenging circumstances and in many cases are not paid in line with the teachers' main pay scale. A minority of schools say that cost is the most important factor when covering for teacher absence. They compare prices between recruitment agencies and negotiate a price where the supply teacher may earn less than half the equivalent teachers' daily rate. In a few secondary schools, cover supervisors are recruited to cover short-term absence rather than supply teachers, as this is cheaper."[28] (Estyn, 2013)

But the issue had not developed overnight and critics had long argued the need for a structured and more formulaic approach to teacher supply. Regrettably, there was little in either the WAO or Estyn report that stakeholders had not seen before.

# Notes

1.  Andrews, Leighton. (2010). Western Mail. December 8.
2.  Andrews, Leighton. (2010). Western Mail. December 8.
3.  Dixon, Philip. (2010). Western Mail. December 8.
4.  Jones, Gareth. (2010). Western Mail. December 8.
5.  Keane, Ann. (2009-10). Estyn Annual Report. p 1.
6.  Keane, Ann. (2011). Western Mail. (2011). January 25.
7.  Keane, Ann. (2009-10). Estyn Annual Report. p 5.
8.  Dixon, Philip. (2013). Click On Wales. Leighton Andrews' Assault on Systemic Failure. June 28.
9.  Davies, Geraint Talfan. (2013). Click On Wales. Welsh Government Loses Incisive Education Minister. June 26.
10. Andrews, Leighton. (2011). Teaching Makes a Difference. February 2.
11. Andrews, Leighton. (2011). Teaching Makes a Difference. February 2.
12. Andrews, Leighton. (2011). Teaching Makes a Difference. February 2.
13. Andrews, Leighton. (2011). Teaching Makes a Difference. February 2.
14. Andrews, Leighton. (2011). Teaching Makes a Difference. February 2.
15. Andrews, Leighton. (2011). Teaching Makes a Difference. February 2.
16. Brace, Gary. (2014). Western Mail. December 6.
17. Thomas, Vivian. (2011). The Structure of Education Services in Wales. p 12.
18. Thomas, Vivian. (2011). The Structure of Education Services in Wales. p 60.
19. Thomas, Vivian. (2011). The Structure of Education Services in Wales. p 120.
20. Pierce, Gareth (2014). National Assembly for Wales. Children, Young People and Education Committee, Transcript. May 7.
21. Andrews, Leighton. (2011). Teaching Makes a Difference. February 2.
22. Reynolds, David. (2012). Western Mail. December 13.

23.　Jerrim, John. (2011). England's "Plummeting" PISA Test Scores Between 2000 and 2009: Is the Performance of Our Secondary School Pupils Really in Relative Decline?

24.　Rees, Gareth. (2012). Western Mail. January 7.

25.　OECD. PISA FAQ. Technical Questions. www.oecd.org/pisa/aboutpisa/

26.　Brace, Gary. (2011). Western Mail. January 6.

27.　Keates, Chris. (2011). Western Mail. April 8.

28.　Estyn. (2013). The Impact of Teacher Absence. p 5.

# 5

# Reform Gathers Speed

## Collective responsibility for a sector in shock

*Regional consortia are kicked into gear as the minister toughens his stance on local authority education services. School improvement becomes king but talk of teacher mutiny prompts a change in tack*

Andrews spoke of his "unfinished business" after retaining the education brief in First Minister Carwyn Jones' Cabinet reshuffle of May 2011. A strong personality with a reputation for getting things done, Andrews had been tipped to become the next Minister for Business, Enterprise and Technology. It was a train of thought that would not go away and such was the minister's perceived talent, his future within the Cabinet would remain subject to considerable speculation as long as he was in it. Although Andrews had been in post a little over a year, his impact was plain for all to see and the wider education sector was delighted to see him return to the fold after his comfortable re-election as AM for Rhondda. Andrews continued in the education brief, for the time being at least, and with so much in the pipeline, stakeholders were keen for continuity. A change in minister, three months after the unveiling of a revolutionary 20-point plan, would have surely hampered progress further. Andrews had drawn up his way forward; he had to now see it through and with the surety of a full term in government, would have time to turn things around. But he knew that he too would ultimately be judged by his results.

Speaking shortly after his re-appointment, the minister said he had got what he wanted and was looking forward to "getting on with the job" as quickly as possible. It is true, Andrews had made almost as many enemies as he had friends during his short time in office. But whatever your own personal disposition, his re-appointment was met with near universal approval from a sector desperate for stability. The minister said:

"Our manifesto was very clear on the things we want to do and was largely based on the speech I gave in February. We have a very full agenda but there will be other challenges that we face no doubt during the course of the next few years. I have enjoyed my first 18 months in the education sector as minister, however, I think there is a lot more to be done."[1] (Leighton Andrews, 2011)

Andrews made clear exactly what needed to be done – and, indeed, what had been done – at his second major address on school standards at Cardiff University, a month after his re-appointment. In a speech hosted by the IWA, Andrews reported on the delivery of his 20-point plan and set the wheels of change firmly in motion. He put meat on the bones of his schools strategy and began by justifying his radical reform of education, which he said had undergone "the most rigorous consultation exercise that we have in Wales – namely a Welsh General Election". Andrews said the results of the poll – a landslide win for Welsh Labour, albeit short of an overall majority – had given the party a "clear mandate" to drive forward his agenda.

## Speech to Cardiff University

Headline news saw Andrews give Wales' 22 local authorities a year to deliver a "radical set of shared services" to improve performance in the nation's schools. He said regional partnership working was the answer to addressing the "systemic failure" in Welsh education and gave local authorities until September 2012 to conform to a more stringent regional agenda. Failure to comply would trigger a reduction in government funding. The minister said he had been given assurances from all council leaders that education was their number one priority and a "radical overhaul" was needed. The nation's councils were already divided into four regional consortia – South-East Wales, North Wales, Central South Wales and South West and Mid Wales – but their work in practice was questionable. Andrews was adamant there would be "no opting out of the regional working agenda". He said:

"There is an unacceptable amount of underperformance in both our primary and secondary schools across Wales. They require immediate and specialist support and challenge on top of the current assistance they receive from their local authorities... I want partners to work together to stand up to challenges and insist on improvement. Should I sense that progress is not fast enough or worse that people are 'playing at collaboration' with the forlorn hope that somehow I will not trouble them, they are deluding themselves."[2] (Leighton Andrews, 2011)

Andrews had made no secret of his desire to reduce the number of local authorities in Wales and he threatened to test local government to ensure they had "made good on their promises" to delegate more funding to schools, share services and improve standards. Failure to do so, he said, could see "more radical restructuring of education delivery on a regional basis". Andrews, not afraid of pursuing "a different route" if consortia did not deliver, had ratcheted up the pressure on local government. His warning was clear: If they chose not to conform, he would make them.

The speech included an update on his department's new SSU, developed to "end complacency" and support the work of local authorities in Wales. By collecting and analysing data, Andrews said the SSU was building a shared understanding of historical performance, trends, patterns, benchmarks and what excellence looked like. From this baseline, the SSU would be able to identify irregularities early and intervene to ensure problems were swiftly addressed. Capacity was always the likely sticking point and the SSU would only be as good as its relationships with consortia and local authorities. Nonetheless, it would serve a valuable purpose and was a belated addition to Wales' school support structure. Andrews said:

> "The unit will need to operate quickly and end complacency. It will also be honest and engage to build strong lasting relationships. It must be viewed by directors of education as helping to strengthen their role in challenging and supporting schools. It will create a culture of continuous learning from the bottom up. It will support our efforts to improve performance across the whole system."[3] (Leighton Andrews, 2011)

There was, among other things, fleeting reference to the Foundation Phase and plans for a new national baseline assessment of each child's development needs upon entry. Meanwhile, the introduction of a national school grading system – first announced in February and criticised by many as akin to league tables – had since been downgraded to a banding system. Andrews said a national system for the categorisation of schools would use data to identify strengths and weaknesses and provide "real time" monitoring alongside Estyn's inspection cycle. Grading, he said, sounded more judgemental than banding. "We are not trying to create league tables. But clearly, we expect local education authorities to identify challenges facing their schools," he added.

Andrews said all primary and secondary schools in Wales would know the band in which they were placed during the autumn term. It would become apparent, though, that with up to a third of Welsh primaries too small to be banded, the plans would require further analysis. Outlining his approach, Andrews said it was not possible to produce a "statistically robust and objective measure" for 30% of the nation's smallest schools. He alluded to the possible pitfalls of grouping infant and junior schools, plus schools with resource bases for children with SEN under the same criteria. There were around 150 infant or junior-only schools in Wales at the time, which accounted for roughly 10% of the nation's 1,435 primaries. Nevertheless, Andrews dismissed suggestions there would be a "two-tier" banding system and maintained the vast majority of pupils would be included in the process. Initially, primary schools were to be given their provisional bands before Easter 2012, with final bandings distributed some time in the summer term. But under pressure from the sector, the minister agreed to delay the introduction of primary school banding until September 2014.

Whatever you made of the minister's progress report, PISA remained the underlying driver. Bespoke workshops were held with local authority advisers and action was being taken to make the current bank of PISA tests widely available to secondary schools. The Welsh Government, it seemed, had at long last woken up to what David Reynolds called "tactics". Preparing Welsh pupils for what would be put in front of them in November the following year seemed obvious, if simplistic. It would not, on its own, provide the long-term solution to Wales' education woes, but it was a decent place from which to start. A national reading and numeracy test would be administered annually through key stages 2 and 3 to supplement the assault on key skills.

As with earlier in the year, teachers, lecturers, academics and union officials descended on the capital as if Welsh education's answer to Mecca. But after a significant build-up, many left disappointed. Yes, Andrews updated on the work being undertaken to deliver school reform. But progress had been slow and five months after the minister's radical call to arms, little had happened. Time, as we were so often reminded, was of the essence and given the dire situation Wales' education system found itself in, more immediate action was needed. Compared with Andrews' grandstand speech in February, when sense of urgency was palpable and the entire sector left looking over its shoulder, the summer came and went without so much as a whimper. If the sector had been roused by his speech to the National Museum, its new energy had been wasted. The time to strike had passed and Andrews had let the attention of the workforce slip through his fingers. Small strides were being taken, yet in the midst of an election campaign and with a referendum on extending Wales' law-making powers pending, the Welsh Government had seemingly lost sight of the need to press ahead with educational reform.

## A history of underachievement

Andrews ended 2011 by giving what equated to his biggest admission of guilt. The minister accepted a portion of blame for school standards by accepting the Welsh Government had taken its "eye off the ball" following the devolution of power to Wales. In a surprise confession, Andrews conceded that the administration had not done enough when it came to accountability in schools. But he was not alone and the season of goodwill – and reflection – extended beyond Christmas when Plaid Cymru's education spokesman Simon Thomas admitted his party did not do enough to address failures in Welsh education during its four years in coalition. Thomas, AM for Mid and West Wales, said there was something intrinsic within Wales' education system that was not delivering for young people and Plaid had to accept "at least partial responsibility" for the difficulties in which it found itself. The sector had been blighted by a series of damaging reports into standards and there was little to show for a decade of devolution, he said.

> "We (Plaid Cymru) are in a slightly semi-detached position where we can see that there are failures and we accept that we were in government for four years and we should have addressed those failures. But actually, we can show the things that we did do to try and address those failures. Maybe they weren't enough, in which case when we are critical of Leighton or the Welsh Government, we're critical of ourselves."[4]
> (Simon Thomas, 2012)

Welsh Labour was by no means alone in nurturing the nation's substandard education system and Thomas was right to shoulder some of the blame for its failings. Nevertheless, his assertion that Wales' education system had been allowed to "coast" and the buck stopped with Labour – as the dominant party – was a fair one. He bemoaned the "cosy relationship" between central and local government and criticised what he called "vested interests" within teaching unions about the type of education system employed in Wales. But problems were systemic and it was not just school standards that were causing concern. Further up the scale, Wales was attracting fewer top grades at A-level and producing fewer top degrees at the nation's HEIs. The trend has continued over time.

**Table 2 Percentage of first degree students obtaining**
**First and Upper Second honours**

| Location of HEI | 2008-09 | 2009-10 | 2010-11 | 2011-12 | 2012-13 |
|---|---|---|---|---|---|
| England | 62 | 62 | 64 | 66 | 68 |
| Wales | 58 | 58 | 60 | 61 | 63 |
| Scotland | 69 | 69 | 70 | 72 | 72 |
| N Ireland | 63 | 66 | 68 | 65 | 69 |

SOURCE: Higher Education Statistics Agency (HESA)

Concerns were compounded by evidence that showed the cream of Welsh students were choosing to study at universities in England. Figures published in 2014 provided the clearest indication that Wales' best young brains were being lost to HEIs across the border. They also highlighted the apparent gulf in stature that existed between Welsh universities and their English counterparts. A table based on average tariff points – the system employed by the Universities and Colleges Admissions Service (UCAS) which assigns points to qualifications to calculate entry into higher education – revealed a marked difference in the grades students needed in Wales and England. Welsh-domiciled learners had accumulated, on average, 317 tariff points to study in Wales in 2012-13, compared with the 375 points required by those going to university in England. It meant that, on average, Welsh students needed 58 more points to study in England than they required in Wales – and the gap was widening.

In 2010-11, the difference stood at 53 points – Welsh students needing 294 points for Welsh universities and 347 points for those in England – and a year earlier, average scores were 285 and 337 (a gap of just 52 points). In 2011-12, the gap had risen to 57 points, with English universities yielding an average tariff score of 362 points and Welsh universities 305 points. A breakdown by institution in 2012-13 painted a mixed picture, with five universities in Wales accepting students from England at a higher tariff rate. Cardiff University, a member of the prestigious Russell Group, accepted an average of 433 points from English students but just 421 points from Welsh students. The average tariff score for Welsh students at all Russell Group institutions was 435. By comparison, the average point score obtained by Welsh-domiciled learners studying at Oxbridge was 571 in 2012-13 – up from 549 a year earlier.

## *An olive branch for teachers*

For Andrews and DfES, 2012 was a year spent largely on the attack. School standards took a back seat as the heat on Wales' universities intensified and Andrews would prove beyond all reasonable doubt that there was a uniquely Welsh alternative to the fight for supremacy being fought in Westminster over GCSEs and A-levels. It was a frenetic period for Wales' Education Minister and a number of long-running battles drew to their conclusion. Mounting speculation that Andrews was to swap seats in a Cabinet reshuffle gave heed to the idea he was settling scores before moving on.

Andrews' rousing Teaching Makes a Difference speech to the National Museum had set the cat amongst the pigeons and it was time now to let the sector and his officials grapple with the demands of his 20 point plan. Wales' education system had been woken from its stupor and the Welsh Government was conscious of knocking practitioners into submission. In his next major address in March 2012, the minister championed the crucial role of parents and teachers in raising educational standards. "There is a thirst for learning in the profession," he said. "Working together, learning together; we can make a difference." His speech at Cardiff's All Nations Centre set sector tongues wagging. It wasn't so much the content as the marked change in delivery. "To build the Learning Country, we must have a government that is prepared to learn as well. And to listen," said Andrews. "I have a reputation for speaking bluntly. But I welcome people speaking bluntly back to me." Andrews knew that keeping the profession on-side was essential and any hint of a revolt would be detrimental to the nation's foremost education need. A surprise U-turn on two very unpopular policies – primary school banding and pupil assessment profiles – was a guaranteed winner in the popularity stakes. Andrews told the conference:

> "Let's be clear. We made a mistake with the Child Development Assessment Profile (CDAP) for the Foundation Phase. We asked the profile to deliver too many things. It probably happened too early in the term. It didn't track effectively to the key outcomes we want to measure... I have asked my department to learn the lessons of this experience."[5] (Leighton Andrews, 2012)

And you do not doubt that he did. CDAPs were an embarrassment to both Andrews and the Welsh Government and were indicative of the Department for Education's long and notorious record of poor implementation. If he had not already, Andrews had now seen for himself the limitations of central government and the civil service in Wales.

CDAPs were designed to help teachers gauge children's ability and plan each child's learning from their first day at primary school. But their demise less than six months after inception spoke volumes. Introduced across Wales in September 2011, CDAPs would be used to inform how far a child had made progress through the Foundation Phase and were a replacement to the 12 accredited baseline assessment schemes being employed in Welsh schools. But their work in practice was very different and unions argued that the "bureaucratic burden" being placed on teachers detracted from their time spent teaching children. Getting new starters – as young as three – settled into their new surroundings is often a challenge in itself and it was no surprise that CDAPs were considered needlessly draining, with teachers required to identify and record up to 114 types of behaviour within the first six weeks of a child starting school. A child's ability to appreciate humour and whether or not they showed care for a favourite toy and could jump with two feet together off the floor were some of the more peculiar areas requiring attention. According to the Assembly Government's guidelines on CDAPs:

> "The deliberate and more flexible grasp of spoken language required to make and understand a joke requires an increasing vocabulary and awareness of different meanings in conversation. This capability will be revealed during the day in all provision areas in children's conversations with each other and with adults. Adults should listen to children's discussions for use of jokes and humour. Wordplay may be encouraged."[6] (Welsh Assembly Government, 2011)

It seemed laughable that when faced with a chronic dearth in key skills, Wales should be worrying about pupils' ability to raise a smile. But there was a more serious side to CDAPs. One union said the demands were so great, many members had been reduced to tears and were on the verge of resigning. A report commissioned by Andrews and published less than a year after implementation provided a stinging critique of the assessment tool. In her "rapid review", Professor Iram Siraj-Blatchford, an expert at the London Institute of Education, said CDAPs "lacked clarity of core purpose" and asked too much of the profession. She said there were too many descriptors for an initial baseline assessment and some of those earmarked by officials were "not necessarily the correct ones". Siraj-Blatchford concluded that the ability of teachers to not compromise their teaching for six weeks during CDAP development could prove "a very tall order". She said considerable thought should be given as to whether "there should be a complete re-think/re-write". Either way, it was back to the drawing board. CDAPs were ill-conceived and without sufficient input from Foundation Phase teachers, were seemingly always doomed to fail. Although an overarching baseline assessment tool had been universally welcomed, the minister's subsequent decision to scrap CDAPs guaranteed their place in the Welsh Department for Education's hall of shame. But it could not say it wasn't warned and future success would hinge on meaningful consultation with those on the ground.

The scrapping of CDAPs just a few months after their introduction raised fresh questions over the department's ability to see through major policy initiatives. A lot of time and energy had been wasted on a tool that teachers wanted, but had little say in developing. The void left by CDAPs would be filled 18 months later by the Early Years Development and Assessment Framework (EYDAF). Piloting had been due to start in September 2014 but it was announced in March of that year that the new on-entry assessment tool would instead be introduced on a statutory basis from September 2015. The school system will doubtless hope that those commissioned to deliver the EYDAF get right what the Assembly Government got so horribly wrong.

The launch of CDAPs was an object lesson in how not to develop policy – a remarkable achievement given they were intended to deliver what schools and policymakers had agreed was needed. Making it easy for teachers to teach is a basic premise that will almost always ring true.

Andrews told delegates at the All Nations Centre that Wales laid claim to a number of schools displaying best practice in their field. He acknowledged the plethora of good work going on in Wales but recognised that variation between schools was an ongoing issue. The problem, he put it, was that "although we have some of the best practice here in Wales, we are not very good at sharing that. And even when we do – it is not on a systematic basis but through random acts of kindness." The largely impressive Learning Wales website – developed and administered by DfES – would provide a portal through which best practice could be disseminated more widely. Andrews said Wales could make a difference by working together:

> "Innovation in IT. Detailed use of data to break the deprivation and attainment link. Genuine parent and governor involvement. Proper individualised plans for pupils falling behind. This is what our best teachers are doing in Wales today to improve the Wales of tomorrow; world-class teaching giving Wales' children the best start in life – no matter where they are born, or what school they attend. Our challenge now, which we must meet together, is to turn best practice into normal practice. I am confident we can do just that."[7] (Leighton Andrews, 2012)

Overall, Andrews' address was welcomed by unions, who noted a "significantly different"[8] tone from the minister's first call to arms a year earlier. It was no coincidence that Andrews was noticeably upbeat and keen to retain the ear of teachers. For the most part he succeeded, but it would be a lasting regret that not everyone bought into his drive to raise standards. Despite his best efforts, the damage for some had already been done. Bridges had been irreparably burned in February 2011 and Andrews would never properly win back large swathes of the profession. His honesty had come at a price.

Now considered a heavyweight politician, Andrews' stock had risen markedly by the time he stood before sector leaders at the All Nations Centre. I recall his sleek chauffer-driven saloon waiting, engine running, no more than a few feet from the building's entrance. In the realms of Welsh politics at least, Andrews had become something of a celebrity. So frequent were his appearances on radio, television and in the national press, there would not have been many in Wales who did not know who he was and what he did. The same, of course, could scarcely be said of others Cabinet ministers at the time. Andrews' newfound fame would hold him in good stead come the summer, when he would face one of the most challenging periods of his tenure.

# Notes

1.    Andrews, Leighton. (2011). Western Mail. May 19.
2.    Andrews, Leighton. (2011). Raising School Standards. June 29.
3.    Andrews, Leighton. (2011). Raising School Standards. June 29.
4.    Thomas, Simon. (2012). Western Mail. January 12.
5.    Andrews, Leighton. (2012). Teaching Makes a Difference: One Year On. All Nations Centre, Cardiff. March 8.
6.    Welsh Assembly Government. (2011). Foundation Phase Child Development Assessment Profile. P 47.
7.    Andrews, Leighton. (2012). Teaching Makes a Difference: One Year On. All Nations Centre, Cardiff. March 8.
8.    Brychan, Anna. (2012). Western Mail. March 8.

# 6

## The Qualifications Quandary

### Shifting boundaries signal the end of three-country regulation

*A headache all of their own making. Cross-border relations sour and irreparable damage is done as pupils fall foul of exam regulators. Government intervention papers over cracks in qualifications system*

Andrews announced himself on the UK stage by sparing Welsh students the brunt of a trebling of tuition fees. But if that made-in-Wales alternative attracted its fair share of headlines, the GCSE grading fiasco had near-monopoly over newspapers in late summer 2012. A brewing row over the year's GCSE English language scores ignited in August when teachers across Britain raised concerns that exams had been marked too harshly. Alarm bells were raised when the proportion of those achieving the crucial A\*-C benchmark in Wales fell sharply to 57.4% from 61.3%. Andrews ordered an inquest into the marks, with regulatory officials not satisfied such a noticeable slide was possible. From there, the Welsh Government's grip on exam regulation was severely tested but Andrews won cross-border plaudits for ordering WJEC to re-grade the subject. It was the year's big UK education story and once again, Andrews had, publicly at least, come out of a potentially tricky situation smelling of roses.

Regulators in Wales, England and Northern Ireland have an obligation to rule by consensus with regards qualifications – a single set of standards across the UK (excluding Scotland, which has its own exams system) ensures portability and respect. But on this occasion, England's exam regulator Ofqual had pulled rank. Although WJEC accounted for 95% of GCSE English language entries in Wales, the Welsh exam board was popular across the border and its work in England was far more significant. Overall, more than 70% of WJEC English language candidates were from England and it was on that basis that Ofqual commanded the strongest voice in negotiations. A report commissioned by Andrews and published by Welsh Government officials in September 2012 found that Ofqual's insistence on using new methodology to award grades led to candidates from Wales being awarded lower marks than would normally be expected. It said that Ofqual had "early in 2012" insisted on using Key Stage 2 predictors – specific to pupils in England – to determine expected outcomes.

Officials said they had expressed "serious concerns" that Welsh results could be determined by prior achievement in England, but it was "hard to justify continued resistance" when there were more students sitting WJEC's English language exam across the border. Subsequently, the Welsh Government said it reluctantly agreed a "compromise" with Ofqual so as to guarantee results were published on time. Andrews, who as minister doubled as head of exam regulation in Wales, said pupils had suffered an "apparent injustice" and demanded grade boundaries were shifted in the interests of fairness. Overall, 2,386 Welsh pupils were given improved GCSE English language scores by WJEC – with 1,202 students seeing their scores rise from a D to a C. Few qualifications are as important in later life but Andrews' decision to re-grade tainted papers fell foul of Ofqual, which maintained initial grades were fair and should have remained as they were. In Wales, the apportion of blame fell at the door of the education department's Qualifications and Learning Division. The Welsh Government's investigation into GCSE English language concluded that:

> "In hindsight, and in the light of the evidence which has subsequently become available, this compromise was, in our judgement, an inappropriate solution to accept on behalf of candidates in Wales."[1] (Welsh Government, 2012)

Andrews maintained Ofqual's intention to use Key Stage 2 data as the defining factor to set grade boundaries only became apparent late in the day during "final rounds of conversations" between regulators. Recalling the events that led to the debacle, he said:

> "What I found out at the end of July, was that there might be an issue with GCSE English. They (Ofqual) suddenly got into the position that Key Stage 2 predictors should be the determinant – not just a factor you take into account – so it's at that stage it becomes a major issue. Ofqual itself, during that process of negotiation you have in a three-country regulatory system, suddenly becomes a lot more demanding I think, in respect of the use of Key Stage 2 predictors."[2] (Leighton Andrews, 2012)

Andrews maintained that he could not have intervened earlier in the year owing to a lack of evidence, and the only time he could have stepped in was after results had been made available. The Welsh Government was adamant that "at no point" in their early discussions with Ofqual did officials think that the use of Key Stage 2 predictors would "have any significant impact on the outcomes for candidates in Wales". Andrews said:

> "I thought my officials behaved in the only way they could within the three-country system. The only alternative to this would be that the minister is involved at every stage of a conversation between our officials and the other regulators. I don't believe that's sensible within the system that we have and I think it is right that the minister only gets involved at moments when there is a need for a fundamental decision... I'm not sure what my officials could have done differently at all."[3] (Leighton Andrews, 2012)

In England, it became apparent that grade boundaries had been changed halfway through the school year, with students sitting exams in June facing a tougher task to get top marks. Ofqual maintained there was no suggestion of malpractice, yet conceded assessments marked in January were done so "generously" and the revelations had had a "serious impact on perceptions of fairness". In a startling offensive, Ofqual accused teachers of playing a part in their students' misfortune. It said evidence of "over-marking" in some English secondary schools meant grade boundaries had to be raised. Together, Gove and Ofqual's chief regulator Glenys Stacey maintained there was no reason to follow Wales' lead and re-grade GCSE English language papers in England. In fact, they blamed the Welsh Government for jumping the gun and "meddling" in a process supposedly free of political interference. Ofqual's chairwoman Amanda Spielman would later accuse the Welsh Government of finding it difficult to accept a "clear divergence" in performance between candidates in Wales and England. Stacey would respond to the strength of feeling and sense of injustice by offering students who sat exams in the summer the opportunity to re-sit in November.

## Failing the GCSE test

While it was quite plausible that Andrews was not party to exchanges between regulators earlier in 2012, it is inconceivable that his officials were in no way culpable. In the Welsh Government's report into GCSE English, there was reference to regulators in Wales agreeing an "inappropriate solution" to a problem of comparability. It said Ofqual's insistence on using Key Stage 2 predictions to project GCSE performance – and the disregard of data relevant to maintaining comparable outcomes for Welsh candidates – had impacted on final scores. While GCSEs and A-levels are uniform across both countries, testing at Key Stage 2 is externally marked across the border. Pupils in Wales, meanwhile, are subject to locally-moderated teacher assessments at the end of the Foundation Phase, Key Stage 2 and Key Stage 3. Regardless of known flaws with teacher assessment in Wales, officials were not comparing like with like. The removal of external tests (SATs) this side of Offa's Dyke put paid to that.

Welsh Government officials, apparently without the minister's knowing, recognised there were potential issues but "reluctantly agreed to accept this amendment". Could they have been flagged sooner and the post-results fiasco avoided? Quite possibly. Andrews, who claimed to have more of a watching brief over regulatory issues, may well have taken a different view had he known about Ofqual's decision to ride roughshod. Nevertheless, he said the net result was "unfair" and it was "not right that hundreds of our learners should have to live with the consequences of having been awarded what, in all likelihood, is the wrong GCSE grade". Following his decision to order WJEC to re-grade, Andrews attracted support from the most unusual of sources and even Conservative-led councils in England broke ranks in support of the Welsh approach. But Andrews was not out of the woods yet.

The minister came under increasing pressure after it emerged he met with regulatory officials from the Welsh Government's Qualifications and Learning Division 24 times between October 10, 2011, and August 22, 2012. Data released under the Freedom of Information Act revealed Andrews spent nearly 20 hours discussing regulation and qualifications in the academic year leading up to the fiasco. Critics questioned why issues surrounding the summer's scores were not addressed sooner, given the "ample opportunity" Andrews had to seek answers. Conservative Shadow Education Minister Angela Burns said it was "inconceivable" that Andrews could be unaware of the planned changes to GCSE grading and called on the minister to "come clean" about what he knew in the weeks and months leading up to his decision to re-grade tainted WJEC papers.

Giving evidence to the Assembly's Children and Young People Committee, Ofqual's acting director of standards Cath Jadhav said the Welsh Government had sent an e-mail supporting the use of Key Stage 2 predictors "fairly quickly" after its meeting with UK regulators on March 14. Freedom of Information data showed Andrews met with his officials a number of times – on March 27; April 12; April 23; April 30; May 1; May 9; and May 30 – in the immediate aftermath of their talks with Ofqual. An e-mail exchange between Jadhav and Cassy Taylor, Wales' head of general qualifications regulation, revealed Welsh officials first considered changes in methodology – which led to students in Wales receiving lower grades – as far back as January 13. But in written evidence to the Assembly's Children and Young People Committee, Andrews said it was seven months later – on August 15 – that he was made aware of the Welsh Government's decision to approve the changes.

**Table 3 Meetings between Leighton Andrews and officials from the Welsh Government's Qualifications and Learning Division, October 2011-August 2012**

| Date | Time | Date | Time |
|------|------|------|------|
| October 10, 2011 | 17:00-17:30 | April 30, 2012 | 15:00-15:45 |
| October 19, 2011 | 11:00-12.30 | April 30, 2012 | 15:45-16:30 |
| December 12, 2011 | 11:15-12:00 | May 1, 2012 | 10:30-11:00 |
| January 16, 2012 | 11:30-12:00 | May 9, 2012 | 13:30-14:30 |
| January 16, 2012 | 12:30-13:00 | May 30, 2012 | 11:00-11:30 |
| January 18, 2012 | 11:00-12:30 | June 18, 2012 | 14:00-14:30 |
| February 21, 2012 | 10:30-11:00 | June 21, 2012 | 16:00-16:30 |
| March 5, 2012 | 10:00-11:00 | July 11, 2012 | 10:00-11:00 |
| March 27, 2012 | 10:30-11:00 | July 18, 2012 | 11:00-12:30 |
| April 12, 2012 | 11:30-13:00 | July 30, 2012 | 10:00-10:30 |
| April 12, 2012 | 14:00-14:30 | August 15, 2012 | 12:30-14:00 |
| April 23, 2012 | 15:30-16:00 | August 22, 2012 | 11:30-12:30 |

SOURCE: Welsh Government

It is unclear what, if not Key Stage 2 predictors, Andrews and his officials talked about during their 24 meetings. For whatever reason, Andrews was not told about changes induced by Ofqual and, if nothing else, you felt sure he could have been briefed on possible ramifications sooner. When questioned on the issue by the Children and Young People Committee, the minister maintained the right course of action had been taken. Andrews hit back at criticism of his handing of the GCSE grading fiasco and told AMs that he was only alerted to the possibility of results being down by WJEC chief executive Gareth Pierce during "a previously scheduled meeting on other matters" on July 30. Later, on August 15, Andrews said he was briefed by officials "on the events of the previous week in relation to GCSE English language... [who] explained how it had been necessary to agree a compromise". Andrews said it only became apparent that the change in methodology had impacted on Welsh scores after results had been published. He told the committee:

"After I became involved in this, after July 30, the question for me was whether I should intervene and, if so, what would be the implication of my intervening. It was a question that I had to think about in early August, but it would have been the same in July, April, March or January. If I were to intervene at that stage, it would, essentially, mean that I would be saying that the setting of grade boundaries in Wales would be done on a different basis from the setting of grade boundaries in England."[4] (Leighton Andrews, 2012)

Andrews said he would have been "crucified in the media and indeed by members" if he had intervened sooner and broken from the existing three-way regulatory system without supporting evidence. He added that he would have faced the same predicament regardless of whether he had been made aware of the situation in August or January. When asked about his role as regulator in Wales, Andrews said: "It's our view that ministers should be brought into regulatory issues when there is a fundamental issue... otherwise, you would essentially have ministers involved at every stage, every time there is a meeting with regulators." Andrews maintained he only became involved in regulatory issues in "exceptional circumstances", adding: "I think it is entirely right that the overwhelming bulk of this work is done by regulatory officials."

Truth is, the Welsh Government did an extremely good job of diverting attention from its own misdemeanours to those more obviously pertaining to Ofqual. Across the border, fallout from the summer's grading catastrophe was incessant and like a red rag to a bull for educational commentators. Scrutiny in Wales, it is fair to say, was a lot more sparing. But if Andrews and his officials had got off lightly in the immediate aftermath of the fiasco, the Children and Young People Committee gave rival politicians the perfect opportunity to land their blows. That was their chance to interrogate the minister and make clear the Welsh Government's role was less than passing. It was not often that the shields came down and Andrews was left exposed in the full glare of the public. The Conservatives, Liberal Democrats and Plaid Cymru were doubtless champing at the prospect. But the chance to rock the normally bullish minister onto the back foot went begging.

So what were the charges? Firstly, it seems patently obvious that there was someone within the Qualifications and Learning Division holding a bomb. They helped construct it; they helped deliver it; and, only after it blew up in August, did they take steps to clean it up. Andrews' guilt was less obvious. But as regulator in chief, he was caught with his finger off the pulse – an allegation that was seldom levelled against him. Nevertheless, Andrews did not get the grilling at the Children and Young People Committee that his department deserved. Plaid's Simon Thomas probed the hardest but softer questioning from Labour AMs cushioned the blow and Andrews left Committee Room One of the National Assembly almost unscathed. Andrews had no doubt swotted up on all things GCSE English language during his half-term break, just a short while before, and like a boxer before his next bout, would have been properly prepared, well-drilled and wanting to land the first punch. But he need not have bothered.

Writing in 2014, Andrews suggested Ofqual knew well the negative impact use of the Key Stage 2 predictor would have on Wales. He described the board's admission that "predictions can only ever be used for candidates in England" as "devastating" and accused Ofqual of "driving a process of grade deflation in its approach to exam regulation". Whilst that may well be the case, Ofqual's motives and supposed disregard for Welsh learners is largely irrelevant. I took the view – as did all three opposition parties – that it was more appropriate to challenge Andrews as to why officials had accepted the use of Key Stage 2 predictors, knowing them to be incompatible. The former minister made reference to my having "taken this line" in his book, Ministering to Education. He added: "I was not involved in any decision to accept the Key Stage 2 predictor and nor did I accept that my officials had made an error."[5] Suffice to say, I have not wavered from my view.

Taylor told the Children and Young People Committee in November 2012 that Welsh officials "would never support the use of one sole indicator to determine grade boundaries" and using Key Stage 2 predictors was "untried and untested"[6]. Regardless of its supposed reluctance, the fact Key Stage 2 predictors were still considered by the Welsh Government to be fit for purpose did not reflect well. Neither did the fact Andrews was unaware of the possible pitfalls before it was too late.

## Breaking the code

Andrews' next fight would prove far more testing and after emerging from skirmishes over university tuition fees and GCSE English language with a certain amount of favour, it is not yet clear where Wales stands with regards qualifications more generally. That said, the Welsh Government has at least built upon solid foundations and a report into how schools and colleges examine children in Wales was published in November 2012 amid almost universal praise from interested parties. It is not often you get consensus in any walk of education policy, but the groundswell of support for the Welsh Government's review of qualifications boded well for the future.

In a major divergence from educational policy in England, the review board recommended retaining both A-levels and GCSEs despite Westminster's concerns over a tainted exam brand. It also proposed the creation of a Scottish-style single body to regulate, accredit and award exams in Wales. Some of its 42 recommendations were more radical than others but all were well-informed and therein lay its biggest strength. The review sought contributions from a broad and varied cross-section of educationalists, as well as business leaders. Schools, colleges and universities participated in the debate and every facet of learning was represented. For that alone, the Welsh Government won justified plaudits. Teachers and lecturers object when initiatives are imposed upon them without fear or favour, but the review of qualifications in Wales was nothing if not thorough and the inclusive approach taken by ministers was in stark contrast to that preferred by their near-neighbours.

In England, Gove had taken a much more parochial view of qualifications delivery. A shake-up of qualifications across the border was designed to drive up standards, with tougher exams and less modular work to match the education system championed in countries like Sweden. Gove was concerned that England's existing offer was not rigorous enough and believed changes would prevent schools choosing what they perceived to be the easiest test papers to inflate results. First there was a mooted return to O-Levels, then a new English Baccalaureate Certificate (EBacc), before a much-maligned return to GCSEs. Either way, qualifications in their traditional form would be developed and designed to reduce reliance on coursework and focus more on stringent end-of-year exams. Within the sector, the underlying perception was that policymakers made decisions and then teachers were asked, belatedly, how best to implement.

Today, the issue of qualifications is by no means resolved and there are two very different approaches on the table. Unlike in England, reaction in Wales – from politicians, trade unions and frontline teaching staff was overwhelmingly positive. There was a startling show of support for the Welsh Government's review and its recommendations. But it was not without its limitations and, notwithstanding its inclusivity, the make-up of the review panel was interesting. Given its designs to be world-class, membership was for the most part limited to names made-in-Wales. Familiar faces included Nick Bennett, principal of Gower College Swansea; Arwyn Watkins, chief executive of the National Training Federation for Wales; and Professor John Hughes, vice-chancellor of Bangor University. Granted, Hughes was a Northern Irishman, but he had a vested interest in his adopted homeland and, at that time, was chairman of umbrella body Higher Education Wales (HEW). Huw Evans, the report's author, boasted his own long history in Welsh education and was principal of what is now Coleg Llandrillo Cymru for more than two decades. That is not to suggest Wales wanted a big noise in England deciding its qualifications fate, but the critical eye of a recognised "outsider" would have given the report's findings yet more credence. Coincidentally, a review that claims to be completely independent is not with its attributed four "Welsh Government board members", including the soon-to-be head of qualifications, Kate Crabtree.

Speaking in December 2012, shortly after the report's publication, Evans said his panel had scoured the globe in pursuit of greatness. The University of Warwick was commissioned to look at qualifications systems across the world and it considered structures employed in countries as far afield as Australia and New Zealand. Board members left no stone unturned and visited Denmark and Scotland to see for themselves examples of overarching qualifications frameworks in action. Notably, Evans said the report's raft of proposals should be implemented in full and failure to do so would run the risk of "weakening the overall package". He told an education conference in Cardiff that "cherry picking" certain recommendations over others would detract from what the review was designed to achieve. It was a curious statement given the sector had scarcely had time to digest his team's findings. The feeling was compounded when Andrews announced – just a week after the report's publication and a month ahead of schedule (the Welsh Government had been due to respond in January) – the creation of "Qualifications Wales".

A new arms-length body, Qualifications Wales would award and regulate all qualifications aside from degrees, with far-reaching implications. As well as removing regulatory functions from the Welsh Government, it called into question the future of WJEC. Part-owned by each of Wales' 22 local authorities, WJEC provided around 80% of GCSE and 70% of the nation's A-level entries overall. And so while the decision to introduce Qualifications Wales was no great quandary, the minister's timing was. There were two possible reasons as to why Andrews jumped the gun. First, ditching exam regulation from his long list of responsibilities would surely have been a weight off the minister's shoulders given the furore of the GCSE grading fiasco. And on that basis, the sooner he was rid, the better. Second, the overarching Qualifications Wales was a natural place to set the ball rolling. Logistically, exam reform needs a vehicle from which to operate. Ensuring confidence in Wales' exams system would be key moving forward and, with so much cross-border flow, portability of qualifications was essential.

Responding to the minister's announcement, WJEC said it was "very surprised" by the timescale given a due diligence review had yet to be conducted. It said there were "several complex and fundamental issues which a review will need to address" and it was possible closer scrutiny could uncover "insurmountable difficulties in respect of the current plans for Qualifications Wales". It was not the first time WJEC had felt its nose out of joint by decisions taken in Cardiff Bay. The GCSE grading fiasco raised the stakes and frayed relations between the Welsh Government and WJEC officials were pushed to the limit. Meanwhile, Andrews himself had become increasingly antagonistic, making reference in the Senedd to WJEC's part in the infamous *Telegraph* seminar expose. WJEC hit the headlines for all the wrong reasons in December 2011 when it was alleged that examiners had been advising teachers attending seminars on how to boost GCSE and A-level results. Undercover *Telegraph* reporters attended 13 seminars run by exam boards, during which teachers were "routinely" given information about upcoming questions and areas of the syllabus teachers should focus on. WJEC suspended two of its history examiners and conducted its own inquiry into the allegations. It did nothing for the board's integrity. Pierce responded to Andrews' broadside in kind with a provocative essay on Qualifications Wales. Of real concern was that festering animosity between both parties might impinge on the bigger picture. Political pandering and commercial interests aside, it was imperative learners' interests were placed at the heart of any structural change and key players owed it to future generations to get qualifications reform right.

A model similar to that employed by the Scottish Qualifications Authority (SQA), which is responsible for developing, accrediting, assessing and certificating all Scottish qualifications aside from degrees, appeared the Welsh Government's preferred option. The SQA aimed to provide a "learning ladder" for students and was different to the systems being employed elsewhere in the UK, where a range of organisations offered the same qualification and schools could choose between awarding bodies. So with its mind's eye fixed, the more pressing concern was implementation and how the Welsh Government plotted the new qualifications scene in practice. Figures obtained using the Freedom of Information Act revealed there were 37 people employed in the Welsh Government's Qualifications and Learning Division in late 2012. It sounded a lot, but when you considered the department had played more than a passing role in the summer's GCSE grade war, there were concerns it would not be enough.

As well as leaving unassuming pupils short-changed, the 2012 grading fiasco also served to destabilise the GCSE brand itself. One thing appeared certain – the days of a three-way system involving England, Wales and Northern Ireland appeared numbered. Regardless of what course it chose, there were always going to be repercussions and the Welsh Government would need to be on its guard. If there was a split, officials would have to ensure qualifications in Wales were not regarded as somehow subservient to those being dished out in England. Would employers think less of Wales-specific GCSEs and would Welsh students be disadvantaged before putting pen to paper? The questions remain as pertinent now and an overhaul of qualifications on the scale of that being proposed in Wales – and England, for that matter – brings with it both opportunity and risk.

Andrews maintained the Welsh Government's belief in GCSEs and a system introduced in 1986 was buoyed by strong stakeholder support. He had the confidence Gove lacked and it was the latter who had chosen to break free from a model shared by England, Wales and Northern Ireland. Andrews was not fazed by the possibility of Wales ploughing its own furrow, and said pupils and parents should have confidence in Welsh exams. He bemoaned a longstanding "inferiority complex" and met with Northern Ireland Education Minister John O'Dowd to discuss a possible bipartite between the two nations.

The GCSE grading fiasco took a final twist with the appearance of Andrews before a Westminster committee. Four months after AMs had been given opportunity to quiz the minister, Andrews was invited into the bowels of Parliament to take questions from the cross-party Commons Education Select Committee, which was only fair given criticisms levelled by his Tory counterpart at an earlier hearing. It was during a meeting of the same committee in September 2012 that Gove described the Welsh Government's decision to re-grade tainted papers as "irresponsible and mistaken". His attack attracted widespread media coverage as Westminster grappled with the surprise precedent set in Wales and the implications for students in England. Yet when Andrews hit back in March 2013, describing comments made by his English adversary as "inconsistent, inflammatory and uncharacteristically ignorant", the London-based press fell silent. Newspaper coverage was confined to a mere four paragraphs and Andrews was not paid his dues. Make no mistake, his was a very assured performance on one of the biggest educational stages.

Try as they might, MPs landed no significant punches and Andrews articulated well the difficulties faced by his department under pressure from Ofqual. Committee chairman, Conservative MP Graham Stuart, was most combative and suggested papers were re-graded in Wales because Welsh pupils were "falling behind" those across the border. Responding, Andrews told members his officials' "sober and serious" report had made clear outcomes for students in Wales were "unsafe" and action was taken to "deal with that unfairness". A lot had been said about who was responsible for what and while three-country regulation continued for the time being in its current form, relations would remain strained. But the ability of home nations to agree terms appeared incumbent on Gove, who had been less than forthcoming with the devolved administrations, offering his hand. Andrews met with the Secretary of State just twice – in June 2010 and May 2013 – during his time as minister. Given the malleability of education's perimeters, it seemed odd that government ministers should meet so infrequently. The latter of their two meetings, described by the Welsh Government as being "frank but cordial", followed a more provocative letter, written by Andrews and his Northern Irish counterpart O'Dowd.

Writing in August 2012, the ministers said they were concerned about a lack of prior notice from the Westminster Government on qualification policy announcements. They said better communication between all parties would reduce the potential for "mixed messages and confusion" for learners, teachers and other stakeholders going forward. The letter came on the back of a number of unilateral announcements from Gove about his future plans for qualifications in England. Changes to GCSEs and A-levels across the border would, of course, impact on provision in Wales and Northern Ireland and it was no surprise that the ministers had highlighted the importance of prior notice on policy announcements in England as being of "critical concern" to all three administrations. They said being "aware of each other's intentions" was paramount, and added:

> "Whilst we understand your wish to ensure that there are high quality qualifications in England, your announcements on proposed changes to what are jointly-owned qualifications highlight the interdependencies between our respective jurisdictions and the importance of continuous communication. Earlier involvement with us, or our officials, in the policy development process would reduce the risk of misunderstanding. It would also reduce the potential for mixed messages and confusion for learners, teachers and other stakeholders. We believe it would serve our learners and other stakeholders far better if we were to be aware of and sufficiently prepared for announcements which may impact on learners across the three administrations."[7] (Leighton Andrews/John O'Dowd, 2012)

Despite the pressing need to put political differences aside in the best interests of learners, communication was at a premium. While Andrews and O'Dowd were open to discussion, requests for joint talks with Gove fell largely on deaf ears. During the meeting of the Select Committee, Labour MP Ian Mearns put it to Andrews that the UK Education Secretary was acting like a "High Commissioner for education" by making unilateral announcements without consultation. Gove, of course, was perfectly entitled to plot his own course for GCSEs and A-levels in England. But while traditional qualifications remained jointly-owned, Wales and Northern Ireland had a vested interest in any proposed changes. Concluding, Andrews stressed that the events of 2012 had been "unhappy" for everyone. Not even the Welsh Government, which could be commended for re-grading tainted papers, came out of the GCSE fiasco with top marks.

# Forging Wales' future

When all was said and done, Westminster's decision to re-sharpen the axe on GCSEs was another win for Cardiff Bay. Gove was digging his own grave on exam reform and Andrews need not do anything. The Tory MP had made life easy for his counterparts in Wales and Northern Ireland. Conscious that "it will not be sufficiently transparent for what will become markedly different qualifications to use the same title", it was he who had blinked first. But it was not all plain sailing. Assuming the Westminster Government pushed through its new proposals, Gove would be keen to promote English exams as the best available. He had already accused Andrews of "undermining confidence" in the value of Welsh qualifications following his decision to re-grade tainted English language papers – and attempts to smear Wales-made GCSEs could prove damaging. Whatever happened, the Welsh Government would need to be on its guard and the promise of a major "UK-wide communications strategy" to promote its exams system to the masses would be of paramount importance.

Ensuring portability of qualifications was essential and the groundswell of support for traditional exams in Wales meant nothing if policymakers failed to translate that confidence cross-border. And then there was the small matter of A-levels which, to all intents and purposes, carry significantly more weight than GCSEs. While Gove seemed happy to concede ground on the naming of exams at 16, England was apparently hell-bent on keeping the renowned A-level brand. Planned changes to A-levels across the border would see the existing modular structure scrapped in favour of a more traditional "linear" system, with pupils sitting all their exams at the end of their two-year course. But the linear approach was not to everyone's liking and making sure the alternative standard was on a par with that being delivered elsewhere would be Wales' biggest challenge moving forward.

While the majority of 16-year-olds continue their education in Wales, students are far more likely to spread their wings and venture further afield after A-levels. Cross-border flow is at its strongest along Offa's Dyke and with so many youngsters moving away to study, Welsh A-levels would need to command the respect of universities in England. But it can be done and while the advent of free tuition keeps most students in the north closer to home, Scotland has shown the way. Moving forward and as Wales continues to forge its own educational identity, attention will quickly turn to implementation. It remains to be seen how smooth the transition to Wales-specific qualifications works in practice. The Welsh Government is not known for its ability to get things done and this is one area of policy it can ill afford to get wrong.

The planed introduction of new English, Welsh and maths papers – together with a modified Welsh Baccalaureate – represented a more piecemeal approach to exam reform. For all the talk of divergence and the potential for Welsh GCSEs to be considered below par, it is A-level reform that remains the most pressing issue. Early in 2013, the Assembly's Children and Young People Committee heard from two of Wales' leading exam boards who warned – with good reason – against substantial deviation at 18. WJEC and OCR Cymru told AMs that retaining an A-level system that is comparable to England's would be crucial, as other variations could be seen as inferior. Nevertheless, the Welsh Government's decision to retain GCSEs and A-levels was given a significant seal of approval in December 2013, with the visit of Professor Sir Leszek Borysiewicz to Cardiff. Vice-chancellor of the UK's top-ranked University of Cambridge, Borysiewicz said plans to strengthen traditional qualifications in Wales were both "fit for purpose" and "competitive at the highest level". He told delegates at the Swalec Stadium that recommendations made by Evans and his team were "rooted in evidence" and welcomed the fact they had been developed through dialogue. But neither was Borysiewicz ignorant to his home country's plight. He said:

> "Historically, Wales has had and continues to have brilliant teachers and excellent schools, and has sent many thousands of outstanding students to universities including the University of Cambridge. These things continue. But in recent times, some slippage in educational performance occurred in Wales and it is greatly to the credit of the Welsh Government that it has recognised that there is a problem with standards and has taken and continues to take strong action to tackle it."[8] (Leszek Borysiewicz, 2013)

Borysiewicz welcomed plans to retain AS-levels in Wales, given their ability to provide young people with the opportunity to "gauge their progress, build confidence and calibrate their aspiration" halfway through their full A-level studies. He said Cambridge was averse to setting its own entrance exams and preferred to make admissions decisions based on the most recent evidence of academic ability. AS qualifications, which would be scrapped in England under Gove's reforms, were an important predictor of academic achievement at undergraduate level, he said. Concluding, Borysiewicz said Wales' goal, to equip all young people with the education, knowledge and skills to enable them to fulfil their potential, was the right one. But he warned, with good reason, that the challenge of delivering that vision in classrooms should not be underestimated.

# Notes

1. Welsh Government. (2012). GCSE English Language 2012; An investigation into the outcomes for candidates in Wales Qualifications and Learning Division. September 10. p 25.
2. Andrews, Leighton. (2012). Western Mail. December 21.
3. Andrews, Leighton. (2012). Western Mail. December 21.
4. Andrews, Leighton. (2012). National Assembly for Wales. Children and Young People Committee; Transcript. November 8.
5. Andrews, Leighton. (2014). Ministering to Education. p 224-226.
6. Taylor, Cassy. (2012). Western Mail. November 9.
7. Andrews, Leighton and O'Dowd, John. (2012). Western Mail. August 1.
8. Borysiewicz, Leszek. (2013). Swalec Stadium, Cardiff. December 11.

# 7

# A University Challenge

## The changing shape of Welsh higher education

*More than a sideshow. An introduction to Wales' long-term vision for higher education. Institutional mergers begin in the capital and set the tone for increased collaboration between universities*

It is a popular misconception that Andrews was responsible for developing the Welsh Government's higher education strategy. Many believe the belligerent minister pursued a controversial collaboration agenda for personal gain; to build his own empire and show to the world he was capable of stretching the most immovable of institutions. Others felt "political ego" and a steely determination to come out on top – to win Wales' University Challenge – clouded his judgement. Allied to that, there are those who believe the drive for mergers was a smokescreen for the underfunding of higher education in Wales, relative to elsewhere in the UK. But while there may be truth in all elements, we can be sure that reconfiguration of the nation's university sector was not a vision crafted by Andrews. The origins ran much deeper and it is neither fair nor accurate to portray the minister as an architect.

The idea that universities in Wales had to pool resources and work closer together far pre-dated Andrews' appointment and was in fact conceived prior to devolution itself. That is not to say higher education took a back seat under the Rhondda AM and the execution of higher education policy was as prevalent under Andrews as it was any other Education Minister. There was a mandate for change and such was the level of public investment in Wales' university sector, he was obligated to ensure value for money.

Debate on the structure of the higher education sector in Wales dates back to 1406, when Owain Glyndŵr sought support from the King of France for the rebellion against the English and for a plan to create two universities in Wales. Since then, all four of the home nations have considered the size and shape of their university sectors, but only in Wales has it been a recurring theme. Recent developments can be traced to 1993, when the Welsh Office advised that there were "too many HEIs which are too small"[1].

Six years later in September 1999, the Higher Education Funding Council for Wales (HEFCW) provided the National Assembly with a report on The Scope for Institutional Mergers at the Higher Educational Level. It concluded that there was a need "for larger, more vibrant and versatile institutions equipped to occupy major positions in the hierarchy of HEIs in the UK and beyond"[2]. Following devolution, it became clear that the nation's university sector had to move with the times and in an increasingly globalised economy, broaden their horizons beyond which they had ever done before. Emerging institutions elsewhere in the UK increased the haste at which Wales had to respond and a disproportionately large number of small universities – relative to other countries – was considered a hindrance. The Welsh Government has actively encouraged HEIs to collaborate ever since.

The first significant development post-devolution saw a 15-month review of higher education policy commissioned by the Assembly's cross-party Education and Lifelong Learning Committee. Chaired by Plaid Cymru's Mid and West Wales AM Cynog Dafis, the committee recommended a geographical "cluster model" by which universities would be grouped according to region. It doubted that the higher education sector in Wales in its current form was sustainable and said "achieving critical mass in an institution relates to achievement both in teaching and research"[3]. The findings formed the basis for the government's first long-term higher education strategy, Reaching Higher. Published in January 2002, the documented ran alongside The Learning Country and charted a course for the nation's university sector to 2010. Writing in Reaching Higher, Davidson made clear that "the status quo in terms of structure was not an option" and the sector could not achieve what the Assembly Government expected of it without "a radically new approach to the development of collaboration". She suggested universities were not performing to their optimum and "reconfiguration is about making the best use of what we have."

Davidson maintained that "effective collaboration is essential to ensure a sustainable future for the sector" although "it is not for me to be prescriptive about the form that clusters will take". A promise to "focus on reconfiguration and collaboration in the first instance" was thwarted by a mixed response from the sector and the pressure on universities to merge would intensify with the passing of time. A reluctance to intervene would not, of course, weigh heavy on every Education Minister. Davidson explained her reasoning for change during the unveiling of Reaching Higher:

"Reconfiguration is central to promoting the excellence that we seek. Small institutions currently carry disproportionate overhead costs – by collaborating on management systems vital funds could be re-invested in core functions and focused on improvements. Similarly, if institutions are to compete for research funds, contracts and students, then they concentrate effort and focus on excellence."[4] (Jane Davidson, 2002)

Size mattered in the eyes of the Welsh Assembly, at least, and there is little doubt that devolution provided devolved administrations with an opportunity to shape their own higher education sectors according to their own wants and needs. In Wales, the first significant merger took place in the capital and involved Cardiff University, the nation's flagship institution.

# A merger for Cardiff

Not without its problems, Cardiff University had overcome the threat of bankruptcy in the late 1980s (Cardiff was in danger of closing on the eve of the 1987 General Election, before being bailed out by the Welsh Office) but a diligent rebuilding process paved the way for the next step in its evolution. Prior to its merger with the University of Wales College of Medicine, Cardiff was notable in being one of the few Russell Group institutions to not have a medical school. The anomaly left a significant hole in its research capacity and gave competitors an upper hand. The University of Wales College of Medicine, meanwhile, was one of only two medical colleges not connected to a major research university and was suffering in its attempts to attract research contracts and academics of international status. The proposed partnership of institutions in such close proximity was, therefore, considered mutually beneficial and talks were initiated in 2002. Together, the institutions would be much more than the sum of their parts, be able to facilitate enhanced interdisciplinary research and enable capital investment on the scale that would not otherwise have been possible. Cardiff's resurgence during the 1990s provided a strong base from which the University of Wales College of Medicine, which was financially relatively weak by comparison, could evolve.

The merger of Cardiff University with the University of Wales College of Medicine was an unquestionable success and achieved the majority of the specific and strategic objectives set by the Assembly Government, HEFCW and the institutions themselves. A paving stone for subsequent projects, it would set an important precedent for structural collaboration. The relationship between Dr David Grant, Cardiff's newly-appointed vice-chancellor, and Professor Stephen Tomlinson, vice-chancellor of Wales' medical college, was integral to a smooth transition. In fact, even before either had been formally appointed to their posts, the vice-chancellors had met and agreed that working together would be beneficial to all parties. There was, from the outset, a willingness to engage. The merger took place as planned on August 1, 2004, when the University of Wales College of Medicine separated from the collegiate University of Wales.

By virtue of its association with the Welsh capital, Cardiff University's image and performance on the UK and international stage is considered crucial. A path finder for other institutions, it is imperative that Cardiff University features prominently in key performance indicators. As vice-chancellor of the nation's leading institution – Cardiff being consistently ranked the best university in Wales – Grant's legacy was invariably merger with the University of Wales College of Medicine. But so too, it can be argued, were there missed opportunities. Immediately following merger, Cardiff rode a reputational wave and entered in 2007 at its highest Quacquarelli Symonds (QS) World University ranking. But from a high of 99th in the world, Cardiff slipped to 143rd in just five years.

It remains something of a regret to some within Cardiff University that tentative merger discussions with Wales' National Conservatoire, the Royal Welsh College of Music and Drama, did not materialise into anything concrete. Cardiff announced plans to "explore a closer working relationship" with the Royal Welsh College of Music and Drama in November 2004, shortly after the formalities of its merger with the University of Wales College of Medicine had been completed. In a joint statement, Grant and Royal Welsh College of Music and Drama principal Edmond Fivet said location – the college is based on the fringes of the university's Cathays Park Campus – and common values gave cause for further assessment of available options. But the talks came to nothing and the expanding University of Glamorgan stepped in to seal the deal in January 2007. Fresh from its merger with Merthyr Tydfil College – ratified in May 2006 – and shortly before the launch of a new campus in Cardiff, Glamorgan had signalled its intent by welcoming into the Glamorgan Group a niche institution steeped in grandeur. It would open new doors to a city centre audience, harness the Royal Welsh College of Music and Drama's enviable reputation in the arts and music, and add another notch to Glamorgan's expanding empire. Some time later in 2011, governors at the college would discuss separating from Glamorgan with a view to reviving talks with Cardiff, but the conversation fizzled out and was never made public.

The retirement of Grant in August 2012 provided Cardiff University with an opportunity to reassess its position and place on the world stage. Professor Colin Riordan was the man chosen to drive Cardiff to the next level. After five years as vice-chancellor at the University of Essex, Riordan would assume responsibility for nearly 30,000 students, 6,000 staff and an annual turnover of £430m. Considered a rising star of the higher education scene, Riordan was head of the International and European Policy Network of the overarching Universities UK and ranked Westminster's Universities Minister David Willetts among his impressive list of contacts. Not surprisingly, therefore, Riordan was far more inclined to broaden Cardiff's horizons internationally than his predecessor. He would invest heavily in new capital developments and while no-one can doubt that Grant kept a well-oiled ship, Riordan was keen to expand the university's offer.

Invariably, mergers take time to bed in, least not on the scale of that undertaken in Cardiff in 2004, but there was a widely-held view that Cardiff University stagnated in the latter part of the decade – a theory compounded by its slide down the rankings. In fact, one of Riordan's first objectives upon taking over at Cardiff was to re-establish the university in the world's top-100 institutions and he gave it a mere five years to do so. Riordan determined that Cardiff required structural change and even before his arrival from the University of Essex, had e-mailed staff warning of his planned reorganisation. Shuffling the university's pack of 27 academic schools into three overarching colleges was designed to increase accountability and the ease in which the vice-chancellor and his senior leadership team could delegate down the hierarchical chain. A University Executive Board, including pro vice-chancellors for each of the three newly-established colleges, would monitor the operational and financial performance of the university and meet once a week to update on progress.

A known strategist, Riordan launched The Way Forward – the university's vision until 2020 – within his first year in post and aside from his root and branch restructuring, set new expectations for a university in need of invigoration. In February 2013, he offered a "golden goodbye", to all staff with two years' service, in the form of a generous severance package, primarily designed to control costs. Cardiff's Voluntary Severance Scheme allowed eligible workers a year's salary up to £30,000, before national insurance and tax deductions. The cost of staff as a proportion of the university's total income was high in comparison to others' and Riordan was keen to bring Cardiff back into line with the rest of the UK. There was a sea-change afoot and outlining its severance scheme, the university warned: "The changes in overall performance expectations and in the way we will work are significant and may potentially be at a level which some members of staff are not comfortable with."[5]

Cardiff said it wanted to create a "sustainable staffing profile" appropriate to the university's plans and needs for the future. It was anticipated that between 200 and 400 workers would leave their posts, but the scheme was extended two months beyond its initial deadline and downsizing took longer than expected. Although staff were given the power to make their own decisions, all applications were reviewed by senior management and the vice-chancellor had the final say over who stayed and who went. Riordan confirmed in September 2013 that the voluntary severance scheme had come to an end and that the process had cost in the region of £8m. "What you have to do is look at it as an investment," he said. "Our wage bill as a proportion of overall income was around 60% and many of our competitors are around 55%. It means you don't have money to spend on other things, such as investment in equipment, better innovation systems and student resources."[6] Figures released under the Freedom of Information Act showed 285 staff applied for voluntary severance, of which 213 were allowed to leave. For all the upheaval, Cardiff rose to its highest QS ranking – of 123rd in the world – in four years in September 2014.

## Restructuring South-East Wales

The saturation of HEIs in South-East Wales had long been an issue for policymakers. Although the nation's most densely-populated region, the conurbation of four universities – just 20 miles apart – was not considered appropriate. Something had to give and ministers had tried desperately to get neighbouring institutions around the negotiating table. On the rare occasion they did, any fruitful discussion would prove futile and underlying differences prevented meaningful development. There was an undulating back story and while the proposed merger of institutions would come to a spectacular crescendo in the summer of 2012, there had been a considerable amount of time and energy spent posturing for position.

The great irony, of course, is that the headache of South-East Wales could have been addressed – voluntarily – as far back as 2003. The University of Glamorgan and University of Wales Institute, Cardiff (UWIC) established a joint working committee in December 2001 to explore the potential for a more strategic alliance between the institutions. The boards of governors at both institutions agreed in March 2003 that there was a strong case for full merger and a consultation process was drawn. It resolved that "merger will enable University of Glamorgan and UWIC to address the Welsh Assembly Government's goals for higher education far more effectively than either institution can do individually". It was a significant statement which suggested, unequivocally, that the universities alone would not be as strong as the sum of its parts. The document continued:

"The level of investment required to develop flexible and innovative learning opportunities, to support leading-edge learning and teaching technologies, and to provide first-class research facilities, highlight the benefits of University of Glamorgan and UWIC pooling their resources, skills and experiences. The scope for either university evolving in these areas and maintaining a competitive edge both in and beyond the UK would be much greater for the new university, than for the two universities separately. Merger presents both universities with an opportunity to make a major change in their development. Competitive and commercial pressures demand that it is critical for both universities to take that step."[7] (University of Glamorgan and UWIC, 2003)

The document concluded that "Wales lacks and needs a university of the size, power and reputation of the leading new universities in England" and merging the University of Glamorgan with UWIC would be one way of addressing that deficiency. There was no grey area and both sets of governors were complicit in the need for radical structural change. Many of their conclusions are as relevant today as they were a decade ago, and while nothing would become of the plan, it provides valuable insight into the projected mutual benefits of merger for both institutions. Ironically, the resulting institution would have been called "Cardiff Metropolitan University" – a name that would give cause for considerable conjecture some years later – but it was as close as the institutions would come to merging of their own will and after negotiations began to unravel, UWIC's governing body resolved to terminate merger discussions in December 2003.

A review of the aborted merger plan, published after the dust had settled in September 2004, provides little-known perspective on the events conspiring against successful collaboration. Commissioned by HEFCW and conducted by its internal auditor ELWa Audit Service, the report charts the first cracks in an increasingly tempestuous relationship between institutions. But the early signs were good and an initial appraisal of the benefits of merger carried out jointly by UWIC and Glamorgan identified "a prima facie case and no barriers to merger". The presumed benefits to Wales and to individual learners included: a much broader and more flexible undergraduate course portfolio; expansion of post-graduate opportunities; improvements in learning resources; expanded progression routes for further education learners; efficiency gains, creating the capacity for new initiatives; opportunities for continued growth and access to new income streams; and significant opportunities in terms of widening access and participation. ELWa said the case for merger was "demonstrably strong", adding:

"None of the parties interviewed during the course of this review argued that the initial case for merger as set out in the appraisal document was flawed or that the benefits to Wales and to individual learners identified at the commencement of the process were unrealistic. There is general agreement that the termination of the proposed merger is a lost opportunity."[8] (ELWa Audit Service, 2004)

According to the report, preliminary discussions between governors of both institutions were first held at the Hilton Hotel, Cardiff, in November 2002. While there was no formal record of the "Hilton Meeting", the key purpose had been to identify at the earliest opportunity any potential "deal breakers". A range of issues were discussed, most significantly: membership of the newly-merged university of the federal University of Wales; the vice-chancellorship of the new institution; and the fact that the merger should be one of "equals". It was a covert operation not unlike that seen in an Ian Fleming novel.

Interestingly, the notes of the informal Hilton Meeting suggest a high-end job share between the vice-chancellors of the new university's component parts. UWIC representatives proposed that the current vice-chancellor of the University of Glamorgan, Sir Adrian Webb, would become vice-chancellor of the new institution for a year, after which the vice-chancellor of UWIC, Professor Antony Chapman, would assume charge for a period of two or three years. From there, a process of open competition would determine who got the job full-time. But the plan never materialised and a subsequent meeting in March 2003 was silent on the matter. According to ELWa, the two institutions had reached an impasse on the issue of resolving the new university's senior staffing structure.

But while leadership proposals were cut short, the governing bodies of both institutions did agree to an identical set of resolutions and a target date for merger of August 1, 2004, was set. So watertight was the agreement, a statement was issued to the press – but it was not long before good intentions started to descend into ill feeling. ELWa said the importance of the proposed merger being a merger of equals was pivotal, adding: "Progressively, from June 2003, actions by both institutions contribute to a divergence from the apparent united position that had been reached in March 2003." It listed a number of actions that were considered contributing to a breakdown in trust and confidence. They included: disagreement over the membership of the University of Wales and the appointment of a new vice-chancellor through open competition; the publication of an internal booklet on the proposed merger by Glamorgan, which bore UWIC's logo; and a merger message composed by Glamorgan's vice-chancellor that had been published on the joint merger website. The matters were not considered to be significant enough on their own to have stunted progress but, according to ELWa, they illustrated "a lack of a shared vision by the two institutions on a number of basic issues". In fact, stakeholders considered that changes in position on issues "agreed" during the Hilton Meeting "represented a key factor in the termination of merger discussions". The audit service concluded:

"The opportunity to create a large post-1992 institution in Wales was viewed by all parties to be a major step forward in order to remain competitive in the UK and international higher education arena. It is disappointing to note that the termination of the merger discussions did not occur because the principles which led to the initiation of discussions were proved to be unsound, but because the institutions found themselves unable to agree on deal breakers and on point of detail, and because at strategic level, there was a mutual breakdown in trust and confidence between the two institutions."[9] (ELWa Audit Service, 2004)

In May 2005, two years after talks broke down, the first of two major reports into higher education in South-East Wales would strengthen the case for merger, this time involving the University of Glamorgan, UWIC and another of their touted partners, the University of Wales, Newport.

# Notes

1.  HEFCW. (2011). Future Structure of Universities in Wales. Annex A.
2.  HEFCW. (1999). The Scope for Institutional Mergers at the Higher Educational Level.
3.  National Assembly for Wales, Education and Lifelong Learning Committee. (2002). Policy Review of Higher Education.
4.  Davidson, Jane. (2002). Cabinet Statement, Strategy for Higher Education in Wales. March 7.
5.  Cardiff University. (2013). Voluntary Severance Scheme. p 1.
6.  Riordan, Colin. (2013). Western Mail. September 12.
7.  University of Glamorgan, UWIC. (2003). Public consultation on the proposal to create a new university through the merger of the University of Glamorgan and UWIC.
8.  ELWa Audit Service. (2004). Review of the terminated merger discussions between the University of Wales Institute, Cardiff and the University of Glamorgan. p 3.
9.  ELWa Audit Service. (2004). Review of the terminated merger discussions between the University of Wales Institute, Cardiff and the University of Glamorgan. p 12.

# 8

## Re-Make/Re-Model

## Forming an evidence-base for change

*Government calls upon experienced vice-chancellors to plot a course for merger in South-East Wales. Progress is slow until Andrews ups the ante and invites the funding council to reconfigure Welsh higher education. But will universities agree?*

Commissioned by HEFCW following unsuccessful merger talks between Glamorgan and UWIC, the Review of 'Post-92' Higher Education in South-East Wales was conducted by professors John Bull and Sir Ron Cooke, both of whom had experience of vice-chancellorship at Plymouth and York universities respectively. From the outset, the report's authors were at pains to stress the wealth of support for the Assembly Government's reconfiguration agenda, despite Davidson's assertion, in June 2004, that the requirements of Reaching Higher had not yet been met. They said:

> "Our impression is that not only is the Government determined to pursue this policy but also, as far as we can judge, all the main political parties in Wales, HEFCW and the relevant trade unions recognise the need for change. Within institutions we have found a similar recognition, although there is some resentment of external pressure, and there are certainly different views on how and within what timescale change can be successfully achieved."[1] (Bull and Cooke, 2005)

The document itself was overwhelmingly supportive of merger and cited a perceived "spiral of decline" facing many HEIs in Wales as justification for change. In their institutional profiling, the report's authors noted that "financial pressures are growing in all institutions" and "there is little or no margin currently to allow significant investment in infrastructure or new developments". In fact, Bull and Cooke stated that, based on confidential estates condition data and the benefit of their own personal visits, the extent of the universities' "poor" estates impacted on student recruitment.

The perception, as with the earlier merger of Cardiff University and the University of Wales College of Medicine, was that capital investment would flow more readily from a conjoined institution of a firmer base. In reality, however, all three earmarked universities would, in time, significantly expand their stock by investing heavily in new capital projects. The University of Glamorgan's expansion into Cardiff, Newport's impressive City Campus and UWIC's multi-million-pound art and design re-development were all testament to both their ambition and recognition that only the best facilities are attractive to students. But the issue of territoriality would become increasingly prevalent and Bull and Cooke acknowledged that each of the three universities had "ambitious plans to create new campuses and, in one case, to locate an activity in the immediate vicinity of a competitor".

It was Glamorgan's plans for a new Atrium building close to Cardiff city centre that caused most provocation and was considered by UWIC a direct attack on its supply of students, funding and investment opportunities. By extending its reach beyond its more traditional Valley borders, Glamorgan now posed a very real threat. The advantages of reconfiguration and collaboration according to Bull and Cooke are summarised in the following statement, albeit they did not accept the argument for "largeness" without qualification:

"There is a widespread view that Wales has too many small institutions and that it needs to create at least one post-92 university of the size and critical mass necessary to succeed. This is not merely a matter of survival: in fact, institutions rarely collapse, they merely decline. Nor is it a matter of buying time in the hope of a future renaissance. The unequivocal aim, to which we shall return, is to create an internationally competitive, well-founded, world-class and durable arrangement."[2] (Bull and Cooke, 2005)

Bull and Cooke concluded that the consultation paper borne out of the merger discussions between Glamorgan and UWIC in 2003, was still "both compelling and valid". They maintained that there was an "exciting opportunity" to re-engage and develop post-1992 higher education provision in South-East Wales, although a shared vision and determination to succeed was lacking. But there was no suggestion that universities should be pushed into a corner and they warned that enforced mergers were unlikely to succeed, however sensible they may seem.

In relation to aborted talks, Bull and Cooke spoke of "merger fatigue" as having an impact and making staff "extremely reluctant" to engage in any discussions about collaboration unless there was a high probability of success. It is understandable that with no end product and nothing to show for weeks, if not months of high-level negotiation, relations between potential partners could fray as they suggested. Among the "residual, but deep" consequences of previous discussions, they considered that:

"There is a marked antagonism and deep mistrust of the persons perceived as primarily responsible for the failure. Whether this perception is right or wrong does not matter. It is intense, and it makes any revival of that merger difficult if not impossible in the short-term."[3] (Bull and Cooke, 2005)

Bull and Cooke said that general staff may see the need for structural change differently from university leadership, and in some cases their views were more radical. In fact, the University and College Union (UCU), representing staff across the institutions, would remain a vociferous supporter of three-way merger. Concluding, with nuanced reference to overhanging disagreement between affiliated parties, Bull and Cooke wrote:

"In our view, it is both probable and highly desirable that a single, new institution would emerge within the next five years from these proposals and the consequential experience of staff working together. Its realisation will depend upon institutions transcending their historical differences, and working together constructively and purposefully to turn vision into reality. It will also require an overt political commitment, and a willingness to provide appropriate new revenue and capital funds to assist and cement change. We believe that the institutions and most of their staff share much of this vision, but, because of the immediate past, they are both sceptical and nervous of engaging or re-engaging in dialogue."[4] (Bull and Cooke, 2005)

The report was far-reaching and controversial, although its publication did not prevent the University of Wales, Newport and UWIC building on their own tentative merger talks, initiated in December 2004. Vice-chancellors Chapman and Professor James Lusty, who had overseen Newport's progression to full university status earlier that year, were open to the idea of working more formally together. But early promise dissipated and discussions were shelved in July 2005. HEFCW's insistence on Glamorgan's involvement was considered one of the main sticking points, though it was not the last time a possible merger between Newport and UWIC would be entertained. Sadly, Lusty would play no further part in negotiations and after illness prompted his early retirement in 2006, Newport's inaugural vice-chancellor died in 2008.

## The Hopkin report

While Bull and Cooke were supportive of merger, a subsequent report commissioned by Hutt and penned in 2008 by Llanelli-born Sir Deian Hopkin concluded that full-scale mergers in South-East Wales were "unrealistic". Hopkin, vice-chancellor of London South Bank University, denounced that a decade of discussions had been "destabilising and demoralising" and "there was no urgency to seek further major institutional changes". He said two of the three governing bodies did not recognise the touted "spiral of decline" and extensive merger discussions had constituted "a major drain" on senior management resources. Nevertheless, Hopkin said the preceding Bull and Cooke report presented a "compelling argument" for the reconfiguration of three of the four universities in South-East Wales. It was not so much the merger itself, as the proposed timescale that the Welshman was not convinced about.

The Hopkin report was significant in that it brought together formally for the first time the vice-chancellors of all three universities earmarked for merger. Unlike with Bull and Cooke, a Strategic Collaboration Board was convened and, chaired by Hopkin with representation from DCELLS, met on three occasions between February and April 2008. It became apparent during those meetings that one university was pressing for merger more than any other. It is within the Hopkin report that the image of Glamorgan as the linchpin emerges.

> "The board examined the experience of institutional mergers and federations in Wales and the UK more generally. While two members believed there was no compelling business case or broad advantage at present for such reconfiguration among the three institutions represented on the board, one member (University of Glamorgan) believes there remains such a case between at least two institutions."[5] (Strategic Collaboration Board for South-East Wales, 2008)

In a record of the points made by each vice-chancellor with regards their own institutional position on collaboration and reconfiguration, UWIC showed its hand. Chapman, who by now was the longest-serving of all the participating vice-chancellors, is recorded as saying Glamorgan's "competitive approach" had been seen by UWIC as "a barrier to collaboration". It was among the first documented signs of animosity between the two institutions, whose relationship would only sour as time passed. Nevertheless, the report would note the "good relationship between the three vice-chancellors who shared their views openly, honestly and constructively" as one of several "positive features" during the engagement process. For all their differences, those participating in the discussions had done so wilfully and with an open mind. Whether the good-natured talks were matched by genuine apathy is not clear.

Hopkin concluded that "substantial opportunity costs" had distracted staff away from their core business and many felt that the energy and resources devoted to merger discussions could have been channelled more productively. He added that each of the universities represented on the board felt that "continuing doubt" had impacted on the recruitment and retention of staff and students. The analysis chimed with the residual merger "fatigue" cited three years earlier by Cooke and Bull. Clearly, aborted merger talks were not without consequence and every time embers were re-ignited, a considerable amount of time and energy was burned. Consider too that many of those party to merger talks remained in situ and wiping clear the slate was not straightforward. It is ironic that the "continuing doubt" to which Hopkin alluded in 2008 would transcend much longer and the higher education sector itself would become caught up in the lingering uncertainty over mergers in South-East Wales. Seemingly endless speculation around collaboration in the region would ripple throughout the sector and vice-chancellors across the country, albeit removed from the sharp end of negotiations, would share in that frustration. The retention of higher education's reputation became an increasingly pertinent issue.

The wide-ranging Bull and Cooke and Hopkin reports of the mid to late 2000s provide valuable context for the roller coaster Wales' higher education system was set to experience a little while later. The collaboration agenda cooled after Hopkin and while For Our Future, the Welsh Assembly's new higher education strategy published in 2009 asserted that "higher education in Wales needs to change, and change fast", it was not until the appointment of Andrews as Education Minister that things picked up again.

## Andrews signals his intent

Andrews signalled his intentions with a speech to Cardiff University's Regeneration Institute in May 2010. Dubbed "Leadership in Higher Education – In Difficult Times", the speech was considered a wake-up call to a sector that had been left largely to its own devices. The sector's governance was given a particularly rude awakening and Andrews' prescriptive demands of a university system seen to be under-performing put down a marker. The tone was typically direct and his delivery left nothing to the imagination. Above all else, Andrews believed there were too many universities in Wales that were too small to achieve the critical mass necessary to secure excellence in either teaching or research. The speech represented the first drawing of the battle lines and included an undressed broadside at university managers. He said:

"I will be blunt and I will be candid. In the first six months I have been in this post, I have begun to wonder whether the higher education sector in Wales actually wants the Assembly Government to have a higher education strategy, or whether it even believes that there is such a thing as a Welsh higher education sector. I am not alone in this view."[6] (Leighton Andrews, 2010)

Andrews used the speech to reinforce the Assembly Government's strategic approach. He warned that financial pressures in Westminster – and their knock-on effect in Wales – would make life for the nation's universities increasingly difficult. The Assembly Government's education budget, he said, could "no longer be a Christmas tree with presents for everyone" and money would follow ministerial objectives. Financial incentives were, of course, an important lever by which he could manoeuvre vice-chancellors into following his lead.

Subliminally, Andrews was addressing vice-chancellors like they were unruly undergraduates; he was in charge and wanted the entire higher education sector to be in no doubt as to what were his expectations. There had to be recognition, he said, that the development of higher education in any society was influenced by public priorities and universities were accountable to the people they served. The status quo was not an option and, once again, structural change came to the fore. Andrews said that, for too many in Wales, "higher education remains a distant, and irrelevant activity clouded in mystery."[7] He recognised the autonomy of universities and the way in which they attracted inward investment, set their own curricula and appointed staff – but given government was the single highest funder of higher education, said ministers had a responsibility to ensure value for money:

"I believe the legal and administrative set-up we have gives us a halfway house. We have institutions that are on paper organisationally free but in reality would collapse without public funding support; that in theory are geared to be responsive and pro-active, but in reality appear cautious and conservative. A cautious and conservative sector is not what Wales needs right now."[8] (Leighton Andrews, 2010)

Andrews said the Assembly Government was justified in calling for a "better return" on the £450m it invested annually. Ministers would be seeking "to get more out of the same or more out of less" and university managers, he said, would need to look very carefully at the deployment of resources in their own organisations. Nevertheless, Andrews was entering uncharted waters; the efficiency of HEIs, the stately homes of our knowledge economy, had scarcely been called into question before. He cited effective governance – at institutional and national level – as being central to driving forward the required step-change in Welsh higher education. But there was no room for sentiment and vice-chancellors no longer held all the aces. Andrews said:

> "We do not want governing bodies that act simply as a bunch of cheerleaders for university management. I was interested to learn recently that some members of university governing bodies have been appointed on the basis of a phone call. Who you know, not what you know. It appears that higher education governance in post-devolution Wales has become the last resting place of the crachach."[9] (Leighton Andrews, 2010)

With autonomy, said Andrews, came responsibility and it was important vice-chancellors were held accountable for the direction, change and management of their institutions. On the other hand, he said it was "perhaps paradoxical that the academic community gets the notion of collaboration" and had grasped the nettle. It became clear that governing bodies, apparently afforded too much wriggle room in the past, would no longer be allowed to shirk government policy. There was a widely-held belief, apparently shared by Andrews, that Welsh higher education was both narrow-minded and territorial; a backwater operating in the shadows of public accountability. Recognising the opportunity for policymakers to wrestle back control, the minister warned universities to "adapt or die".

Speaking at Carmarthen's University of Wales, Trinity Saint David, Andrews reinforced a familiar message and said Wales had been held back by too many institutions that were "too small to cut a mark internationally, too small to operate effectively and efficiently, and too small to respond to the growing pressure of international competition"[10]. He cited an earlier PricewaterhouseCoopers Review, published in 2010, for highlighting what he called "inefficiencies" within the system that prevented money getting to the frontline. He said the "inequality in resource allocation" needed to be rectified and was at pains to stress that reconfiguration – "based on greater institutional integration and mergers" – was by no means a novelty. Andrews was adamant that the state could not renege on its responsibility to build community cohesion within Wales' university system and said:

"Of course, it is better to use core funding to drive change in a time of rising budgets. But the higher education sector in Wales has had a decade of rising budgets and I am afraid that overall, with some worthy exceptions, higher education managements have failed to respond adequately to our agenda. So, failing to respond is costing the sector money. We carry on with a planned approach to higher education, but we now look to the sector to address the inefficiencies in higher education on lower budgets. As the King James bible says: 'Whatsoever a man soweth, that shall he also reap.'"[11] (Leighton Andrews, 2010)

Expectations were higher than ever and in the same way students would demand more for their investment in higher education, so too would ministers. The economic recession and a subsequent squeeze on public finances would make life harder for vice-chancellors, but Andrews was in no way sympathetic to their predicament. He said there would be fewer HEIs and fewer vice-chancellors in Wales by 2013, albeit that did not mean fewer students or campuses.

Responding, HEW, the body representing Welsh universities, said the government's policy on reconfiguration and collaboration was "well understood" and a number of institutions had implemented or were discussing structural change. Nevertheless, Andrews warned that vice-chancellors would not be guaranteed to charge £9,000 for their courses and there would be no "automatic progression to the new fees regime". It would fall to HEFCW to decide who was allowed to charge what, on the basis of stringent university fee plans. A commitment to widening access to students from non-traditional backgrounds would be among several stipulations set by the funding council. An arm's-length body responsible for managing government policy, HEFCW would play a significant role in facilitating the Assembly Government's controversial reconfiguration agenda.

## A report on future structures

HEFCW hit the headlines in December 2010 when it unveiled a two-year plan to scale back the number of universities in Wales. It said no more than two universities would have an income below the UK median and there would be no more than two institutions per region. In practice, HEFCW envisaged a sector consisting of no more than six institutions, down from the existing 11. The plan set in train firm expectations and demanded rapid change, although vice-chancellors could not say they had not seen it coming.

At first glance, the institutional reshuffle appeared painful, with jobs, courses and university managers primed for the chop. But against a backdrop of swingeing cuts, the clamour for university mergers was actually considered a way of securing their long-term survival. After so many years' procrastination, mergers now appeared inevitable and with funding levers available, HEFCW looked certain to get its way. UWIC, Swansea Metropolitan University and the University of Wales, Trinity Saint David agreed to pool resources within months of HEFCW's ultimatum. Buoyed by an assurance that fewer institutions would not mean fewer students or campuses, plans to create a so-called "super university" were hatched in February 2011. UWIC's involvement in the three-way merger plan raised eyebrows given the considerable geographic divide and it was no real surprise when negotiations broke down five months after they had been initiated. UWIC cited "a lack of good governance, due process and administration" for pulling out and promised to consult staff, students and stakeholders about its options. It may have developed a reputation for opposing reconfiguration, but UWIC had at least dipped its toes in the collaboration pond. Nevertheless, pressure was building and the collapse of talks re-ignited speculation around a possible "super university" in South-East Wales, involving Newport and Glamorgan. At that time, Newport was publicly considering its options and the University of Glamorgan maintained its door was open to potential partners.

Wales' university leaders agreed, in July 2011, to a new "strategic approach" they believed would bring about fewer, stronger HEIs. A firm commitment by vice-chancellors to work collaboratively marked a watershed in the sector's long history and never before had the prospect of university mergers been so readily accepted by the sector itself. In a statement released under the guise of HEW, university leaders confirmed a new approach was "essential" and that they would drive forward plans to scale back the number of Welsh universities. They said:

> "Though universities are legally autonomous and mergers are a matter for university governing bodies to decide, in this changed environment we are working with the approach of HEFCW and the Welsh Government on the size and shape of the university sector. We are clear that this new strategic approach will require further reconfiguration of the university sector and will be of all-round benefit. The gains for Wales of fewer but stronger and more successful universities working collaboratively with the Welsh Government will be substantial."[12] (HEW, 2011)

Faced with an "unprecedented" level of challenge, they said the university sector had to move fast to deliver transformational change for Wales. Professor Sir Steve Smith, president of the overarching Universities UK, welcomed what he called a "significant statement of intent" from Wales' university leaders, but whether or not all signatories were such willing bedfellows was unclear. It was not long before HEFCW published its preference for future structure.

The merger of Newport, Glamorgan and UWIC to form a new "metropolitan" university in South-East Wales was among a host of recommendations put forward in July 2011 by HEFCW, which had been asked by the minister to form a blueprint for reconfiguration. The council also proposed that Aberystwyth and Bangor widen their strategic partnership with a view to merging some time in the future. Wrexham-based Glyndŵr University, which had discussed the possibility of merger with Bangor some years earlier, was advised to work with further education colleges under a group structure led by Aberystwyth and Bangor. Andrews welcomed the report as offering a "clear rationale" for the council's preferred structure of Welsh universities. He said HEFCW had made a "persuasive case for change" and he accepted the "broad thrust" of its recommendations.

While proposals for North-East Wales would prove unpopular, it was the suggested model for South-East Wales that became the major talking point, given past histories. The prospect of renewed merger talks in the region was always going to set the cat among the pigeons but at this stage in the game, there appeared little common ground between respective vice-chancellors and much of the next year would be spent posturing for position. Some time later, HEFCW's chief executive Professor Philip Gummett would concede the council's vision for a new institution in South-East Wales was its "most far-reaching recommendation" and that "anyone designing a higher education system for Wales today would be unlikely to propose the present structure".[13]

In its report, HEFCW said that Wales was not achieving its full potential for the investment made in higher education and the sector was not as strong as it could be. But despite mounting uncertainty over the health of some universities in England, it said no Welsh institutions were at imminent risk of collapse and its findings were not derived out of financial concerns. Crucially, it maintained that its advice was evidence-based but "necessarily moves into the exercise of judgement", based on the extensive experience of its members. Hanging such radical reform on the virtue of "judgement", albeit well-informed, would become a sticking point for UWIC, in particular.

Stakeholders were given a little under three months to submit their observations. Submissions to the Welsh Government's consultation on the future structure of higher education, as set out by HEFCW, tell their own story and highlight the undertones running parallel to the reconfiguration process. Consider first representation from UWIC's chairwoman of governors, Barbara Wilding, which proved beyond all reasonable doubt that relations between institutions were far from civil. The level of animosity between management at UWIC and Glamorgan, in particular, would become a huge obstacle to constructive merger discussions and it was clear that aforementioned merger "fatigue" was still very much a factor. In her submission, Wilding attacked Glamorgan's "predatory attitude" to mergers and accused its management of being "unwilling to work collaboratively" until a date for merger was set. She questioned how the universities could come together with so little in common and appeared to confirm that Glamorgan's expanding presence in the capital had put a strain on relations. She said:

> "Over a 20-year period, UWIC has been subject continually to approaches to merge with the University of Glamorgan which have been characterised by unwillingness on the part of the University of Glamorgan to commit to the creation of a truly 'new' metropolitan university in South-East Wales – a university that would be created by assimilation not takeover... Indeed, the resulting innuendo has been detrimental to UWIC and to Wales. Nor has the University of Glamorgan been willing to work collaboratively with UWIC until/unless a date for merger was first set. As a direct consequence, the development of the Skillset Media Academy and the University of Glamorgan's Atrium campus in Cardiff have occurred without UWIC involvement."[14] (Barbara Wilding, 2011)

By virtue of its location, Wilding said UWIC had "a strong civic tradition in Cardiff" and given its origins as a school of mines in the early twentieth century, "the impact of the University of Glamorgan should continue to be intrinsically linked with the Welsh Valleys". Wilding said the merger proposed by HEFCW and involving Newport as well as Glamorgan, was "highly complex" and would run a "significant risk of being unsustainable and failing". The outcome, she said, would be an "unwieldy institution" of more than 43,000 students and combining three universities with very different cultures, values and strategic objectives would bring about "a loss of institutional distinctiveness". Furthermore, she said HEFCW's report was silent on who would be liable for any possible failings. Glamorgan meanwhile, maintained the view that a merger would be beneficial and Professor John Andrews, Glamorgan's chairman of governors, responded:

> "We see the long-term potential for South-East Wales of a single, modern university of a size and scale to compete with the bigger competitors over the border. Our positive response is that there must be a swift, clear decision to merge or not. Each of the universities has different areas of strength, and comes with a different history, culture and financial position. We will need to see that the new institution will be more than the sum of the parts that went into it."[15] (John Andrews, 2011)

So there was a deadlock; of the three universities earmarked for merger, one was strongly in favour, one was strongly opposed and the other, the University of Wales, Newport, was largely on the fence. By virtue of its size, financial position and relative infancy, however, Newport was not considered a deal breaker. Minutes from an extraordinary meeting of Newport governors held on June 29, 2012, would indeed note that a decision not to proceed in merger negotiations could have "implications for the legal and financial probity of the institution". Newport's long-term future was the most uncertain and UWIC was the main thorn in HEFCW's side. But Chapman, who had been party to all previous merger negotiations and was the only remaining vice-chancellor from talks in 2002, would take some persuading.

UWIC became increasingly isolated following the submission by HEW to the Welsh Government consultation on the future structure of the higher education system. The position of the umbrella body during the reconfiguration agenda is an interesting one. Up until 2011, HEW, the Welsh arm of Universities UK, had taken a largely back seat and steered clear from any public pronouncements with regards merger. Aside from unveiling its new "strategic direction", HEW had been conspicuous by its absence and the organisation's promotion of Wales' offer was nothing if not lacklustre. Representative of all the nation's vice-chancellors, one may have expected a similarly subdued stance to collaboration. The reality was very different. HEW's distinctly pro-merger submission would infuriate UWIC, which along with every other university in Wales, was a paying member. HEW said in its submission:

> "The view of HEW is that the funding council's report and the minister's accompanying statement together provide a compelling context for change. The pivotal role of higher education in supporting and transforming the economy and promoting social justice make it a priority that the longer-term competitiveness of the sector should be addressed. HEW supports the overall argument for change and is confident that further reconfiguration will be of all-round benefit to the sector."[16] (HEW, 2011)

The document left nothing to the imagination and determined it was "vital that the sector reorganises itself effectively to interact with business and the community more effectively" and that HEW looked forward to working with the funding council and Welsh Government "for the ultimate benefit of students and the wider economy and society". HEW was adamant that "reconfiguration should not be seen as an end in itself but a means to a stronger, more vibrant and competitive sector". It added:

"We must start preparations forthwith to ensure that the final shape of the future higher education sector embraces the different missions and strengths of each institution and delivers the transformational change we all wish to see on a pan-Wales basis."[17] (HEW, 2011)

There was a definite sense of urgency and the nation's vice-chancellors were said to be frustrated by overhanging uncertainty. They yearned closure and were concerned that the good name of Welsh higher education was being tarnished by institutional infighting. The pace of change was imperative and with the shackles of speculation broken, it was felt the sector could at last branch out and blossom. Indeed, HEW would maintain that "there is a vital need from both a Wales and broader UK perspective that the sector removes uncertainty as soon as possible about future arrangements and their implications for our many stakeholders in Wales and the international community"[18]. But, of course, HEW's collective approval jarred with UWIC's own position, which was to oppose HEFCW's suggested merger. There was no ambiguity – HEW's support for HEFCW's blueprint was explicit.

By its own admission, HEW was "the voice of higher education in Wales" and negotiated on behalf of the university sector. But on this occasion, HEW's position was clearly not shared by every constituent member. The submissions of both UWIC and HEW proved beyond any reasonable doubt that UWIC and the rest of the sector were singing from different hymn sheets. In fact, HEW's assertion that "members are expected to be mindful... that there is a greater chance of successful merger where the participants are willing" was as clear a broadside as you are likely to see. What followed would threaten the very essence of institutional autonomy and was unlike anything ever seen before in UK higher education.

# Notes

1.  Bull, John and Cooke, Ron. (2005). Review of 'Post-92' Higher Education in South-East Wales. p 4.
2.  Bull, John and Cooke, Ron. (2005). Review of 'Post-92' Higher Education in South-East Wales. p 8-9.
3.  Bull, John and Cooke, Ron. (2005). Review of 'Post-92' Higher Education in South-East Wales. p 11.
4.  Bull, John and Cooke, Ron. (2005). Review of 'Post-92' Higher Education in South-East Wales. p 15.
5.  Hopkin, Deian. (2008). Report of the Strategic Collaboration Board for South-East Wales. p 4.
6.  Andrews, Leighton. (2010). Leadership in Higher Education – In Difficult Times. May 25.
7.  Andrews, Leighton. (2010). Leadership in Higher Education – In Difficult Times. May 25.

8.   Andrews, Leighton. (2010). Leadership in Higher Education – In Difficult Times. May 25.
9.   Andrews, Leighton. (2010). Leadership in Higher Education – In Difficult Times. May 25.
10.  Andrews, Leighton. (2010). Opportunities for a Confederal University for South-West Wales. December 3.
11.  Andrews, Leighton. (2010). Opportunities for a Confederal University for South-West Wales. December 3.
12.  HEW. (2011). Statement on the Future of Higher Education. July 2.
13.  Gummett, Philip. (2012). Western Mail. March 22.
14.  Wilding, Barbara. (2011). Future Structure of Universities in Wales, Consultation Response Form.
15.  Andrews, John. (2011). Western Mail. October 13.
16.  HEW. (2011). Future Structure of Universities in Wales, Consultation Response Form.
17.  HEW. (2011). Future Structure of Universities in Wales, Consultation Response Form.
18.  HEW. (2011). Future Structure of Universities in Wales, Consultation Response Form.

# 9

# A Battle To Survive

## Merger threat a Sword of Damocles

*Andrews locks horns with a university under fire. His all-out assault is unlike anything ever seen before in UK higher education. But academics would not go down without a fight and the minister would not have it all his own way.*

Andrews' battle with UWIC became a feature of his tenure as minister. But as he ratcheted up the pressure on the under fire institution, he may not have anticipated UWIC would put up quite so much fight. UWIC began the sector's winter of discontent relatively inconspicuously, by rushing through a change of name. From November 1, 2011, UWIC became known as Cardiff Metropolitan University, having chosen to distance itself from the University of Wales following claims made on television. A BBC Wales programme aired in October 2011 showed an undercover reporter paying £1,500 in cash for a bogus qualification from one of several colleges linked to the University of Wales. A federal institution which once comprised the majority of Wales' universities, the University of Wales was also a major awarding body for education institutions overseas. And it was that activity that proved decisive and the University of Wales would never fully recover from the BBC's allegations.

The University of Wales later agreed to merge with campus-based Swansea Metropolitan and Trinity Saint David universities, though it was unfortunate that the once formidable institution would embark on the next stage of its evolution under a cloud. While overseas activities could be terminated, restoring the good name of Welsh higher education represented a far harder proposition. The fall of the University of Wales as it was known caused significant damage to the sector's reputation; not least because the institution was so synonymous with the country of its name. Brand Wales was suffering and students across the globe took note. Bad news travelled fast and the rebuilding process would take time.

Aside from severing ties with the University of Wales, UWIC's change to Cardiff Met was significant as it further damaged relations between itself and the University of Glamorgan. The name had been earmarked for a newly-merged institution and UWIC's decision to steal in was considered antagonistic by Glamorgan's hierarchy. Later in November 2011, Andrews upped the ante and by accepting "the overall thrust" of HEFCW's future structures report, gave his blessing to plans for a new three-way "super university" in South-East Wales. Newport's vice-chancellor Dr Peter Noyes was the first to respond, backing the creation of a brand new institution he said would allow the sector to emerge from the "historical hangover" of previous merger talks. But having come down hard on Cardiff Met, Andrews decided not to accept HEFCW's advice to pool Glyndŵr into an umbrella group run by Aberystwyth and Bangor.

In an apparent reprieve for the emerging institution, Andrews chose instead to examine further the options available in one of Wales' most industrial regions. It had not escaped the minister's attention that senior Labour politicians had gone public in speaking out against the plans. Responding to the Welsh Government's consultation, a group including Wrexham MP Ian Lucas and Clwyd South AM Ken Skates, seen as a rising star within Welsh Labour ranks, said the proposals displayed a "woeful ignorance" to the needs of North-East Wales. They warned that, if implemented, the plans would damage the region's economy and competitiveness. It is likely that the university's unwavering support from local members was the determining factor in its retention of autonomy.

In hindsight, it was perhaps just as well that proposals affecting Glyndŵr were put on the back burner as Andrews would have his work cut out trying to shape higher education in South-East Wales. Despite growing opposition in the capital, Andrews maintained he expected formal collaboration to take place and was willing to force change if necessary. He had stressed his preference for voluntary mergers, but resolved there was no point in an Assembly aspiring to have powers if it was not prepared to use them. Andrews had the ability, under the Education Reform Act 1988, to force the dissolution of post-1992 institutions. Sure enough, he threatened to use those powers if universities were not sufficiently forthcoming, but first sought participation by diplomatic means.

Early in 2012, Andrews brought in long-serving University of Exeter vice-chancellor Steve Smith as mediator. Like Andrews, Smith met with each vice-chancellor in turn, and while he never got all three around the table together at the same time, formed the conclusion that a three-way merger was necessary. His influence gave the reconfiguration agenda fresh impetus and it was no great surprise that senior management at Glamorgan and Newport announced in July 2012 that they were in talks to create a "beacon institution" that would be similar in size to Cardiff University. They said the new university would build on the strengths and resources of its component parts and operate under a new name. In a statement, Glamorgan and Newport said their "shared vision" would provide greater depth of support to the students, communities and economy of the region. They said the integration process was based on a "bilateral agreement" between the universities, but there was scope for further expansion in the future. Cardiff Met was not involved in the discussions.

Smith, commissioned by the Welsh Government to consider available options, reported back to the minister shortly afterwards. In his report, he warned that two of the three universities earmarked for merger were "dangerously small" and would not survive in the medium-term. He said maintaining the status quo was no longer a possibility and that the "genie cannot be put back in the bottle". He said a three-way merger – involving eight campuses and more than 40,000 students – "remains the way forward" for higher education in South-East Wales and, having held more than 50 meetings and phone conversations with stakeholders, welcomed moves by Glamorgan and Newport to engage in talks. He urged governors at Cardiff Met to "think again" following their decision – by 13 votes to one – to remain independent. Smith said that while Cardiff Met was strong, well-led and financially sound, staying as it was may not be a viable option. He added:

> "In my view, Wales needs one successful Russell Group university and one successful post-1992 university in South-East Wales. The needs of the country and the city region mean that the current structure of institutions is sub-optimal... I accept that so far Cardiff Metropolitan University has done well in comparative terms, and the staff and leadership of the institution deserve credit for what they have achieved. But looking ahead, unless the Government back-tracks on its stated commitments and priorities, and unless HEFCW alters its funding model, I fear that Cardiff Metropolitan University faces fiscal attrition on a year-by-year basis."[1] (Steve Smith, 2012)

Smith said the leadership and strategic vision of Glamorgan and Newport was "a game-changer" and their decision to formally enter into talks was significant. "In my view the right solution is, as most independent reports have concluded, a three-way merger," he said. Smith's feedback would provide Andrews with the leverage needed to force Cardiff Met's hand.

# The dissolution order

Things came to a head in July 2012 when Andrews stepped up his bid to unite reluctant university partners by announcing a statutory consultation on the dissolution of Cardiff Met, as well as Newport. Andrews said he expected Cardiff Met to join Glamorgan and Newport in forming a new "super" institution by 2015 and, despite vociferous opposition, said merger plans hatched by HEFCW remained "sound". Although subject to consultation, the minister claimed dissolution was the "likely course" that would unfold in South-East Wales.

Defiant to the last, Cardiff Met said it was "disappointed" with the announcement and Andrews' "failure to provide a single piece of evidence" to support the merger. University hierarchy threatened legal action and it later emerged that Cardiff Met had considered privatisation as an alternative, "before being swiftly rejected as inappropriate". Cardiff Met had set up a task and finish group to explore the availability of new funding streams and "other legal models of institutional design". A draft business case for Cardiff Met's "continuing existence as an autonomous university" was tabled at a meeting of the university's board of governors on February 7, 2012. But in a joint statement issued to staff in October that year, Antony Chapman and Barbara Wilding said breaking free from the public sector would be "too much of a risk and too much of a change in the core business". Given its significant business links and blossoming connections abroad, it was no surprise that the possibility of Cardiff Met fighting for independence through privatisation had crossed the desk of governors. But cutting the university's flow of public money, some £25m in 2011-12, would not have been done lightly. Things were getting serious and I was invited to interview Chapman and Wilding at the Vale Resort, in Hensol, Vale of Glamorgan, on October 11, 2012. It was the first time they had agreed to meet me together.

The interview was held a week after Andrews agreed to extend the statutory consultation with key stakeholders into 2013, following a request by Cardiff Met for "substantial additional information". Interested parties were given a further 12 weeks to consider the future of higher education in South-East Wales from when the information requested by the university was provided. Wilding said that, having requested on a number of occasions that the Welsh Government presents its costed business case, she had come to the conclusion it may not exist. "It is becoming apparent that the minister doesn't know how much it will cost; how much the taxpayer is going to have to put towards it; and what the risks are," she said. "Our alternative is low cost, low risk and can deliver very quickly – and what's more, staff in each of the institutions want it."[2]

In its "Vision for Post-1992 Higher Education in South-East Wales",

Ann Keane, Chief Inspector of Education and Training in Wales, during a visit to Cardiff High School in September 2010. A former teacher, Keane joined the Welsh inspectorate in 1984. (copyright: Estyn)

Jane Davidson recalls her time as Education Minister during an interview at the University of Wales, Trinity Saint David's Carmarthen Campus in January 2012. (copyright: Media Wales)

Cardiff Metropolitan University's vice-chancellor Professor Antony Chapman
and chairwoman of governors Barbara Wilding discuss their fight for
independence at the Vale Resort, Hensol, in October 2012.
(copyright: Media Wales)

Leighton Andrews, pictured at the National
Assembly in May 2011, was a belligerent minister
who divided opinion. (copyright: Media Wales)

Leighton Andrews and Robert Hill, right, address the media at the launch, in June 2013, of a major report on the future delivery of education services in Wales. (copyright: Media Wales)

Wales has looked across the globe for inspiration and Andreas Schleicher, director of education and skills at the OECD, was one of several renowned educationalists invited to address sector leaders. He headlined a conference at Cardiff City Hall in June 2014. (copyright: Media Wales)

Huw Lewis endured a baptism of fire following his appointment as Education Minister in June 2013. Here he discusses A-level results at Gower College Swansea in August 2014. (copyright: Media Wales)

Wales' education system has been the focus of considerable attention in the media. This headline was one of many circulating following the publication of PISA results in December 2013. (copyright: Media Wales)

Cardiff Met proposed increased collaboration between institutions as an alternative to full-scale merger. It championed the creation of "subject-based academies", which would be tailored to local needs and Welsh Government priorities, and cited a number of "flaws in HEFCW's thinking", namely that the composite institutions had "significant differences in identity, mission and culture". Glamorgan's "anti-collaboration attitude" towards Cardiff Met was a recurring theme, though reference to a "consequent stranglehold on higher education developments in South-East Wales" appeared needlessly provocative. Wilding suggested Andrews had been put in a "very difficult position" by his advisers and the timing of the minister's dissolution announcement did not help as it was made just prior to the university clearing process. The threat of dissolution is not, after all, a prospect easily saleable to potential suitors.

Chapman, who broke his long silence on institutional merger, said the university had recruited well albeit a lot of his work had been "preoccupied with merger arrangements". He maintained the university was not anti-merger but it was "not clear why Wales needs the largest campus-based university in the UK". Chapman said the university had no plans to break from the public sector and insisted any hint of privatisation had been "cast aside". He described suggestions that the university was opposed to merger as "a myth" and said there was a "sword of Damocles" hanging over Cardiff Met which meant other institutions had been "shy of working with us".[3] It is important to note, however, that the views of management were not necessarily shared by staff and Cardiff Met's branch of the UCU maintained a three-way merger of post-1992 institutions in South-East Wales was "in the best interests of its members, students and other stakeholders".

# The minister backs down

Less than a month after my interview with Chapman and Wilding, the minister backed down. In a surprise development, on November 6, Andrews effectively prolonged Cardiff Met's independence by cancelling with "immediate effect" a consultation on its planned dissolution. Andrews said the universities of Glamorgan and Newport, which feared their desire to merge voluntarily may be hampered by the consultation process, had prompted his decision. He said the planned merger of Glamorgan and Newport was "moving at speed" and those particular discussions "have got to be our focus at the current time". Andrews said he was mindful that Cardiff Met's requests for more detailed information from the Welsh Government could have delayed their coming together. Consider too that the proposed dissolution of Cardiff Met against its will was never going to be easy and was sure to have been subject to a legal challenge by the institution had it been pursued. The willingness of Glamorgan and Newport to come together after a decade of posturing was an opportunity too good to miss. Timing is everything and fearing the Welsh Government's intense negotiations could result in nothing at all, the three-way plan was dropped. Andrews would later confess that he did not believe enforced dissolution was possible without the support of another political party. Plaid Cymru was the minister's preferred option, but members would not be moved.

Reflecting, Wilding said the statutory consultation process had been legally and financially flawed from the start. "The proposals put forward for the reconfiguration of the higher education sector in South-East Wales did not contain enough evidence to enable the governors to take such a decision about any reconfiguration option," she said. "It is our intention to engage enthusiastically with the new university and also to do all we can to explore new ways of working with all education partners in the region." It was a watershed moment and one that ended, for Andrews' tenure at least, the arduous merger saga.

Uncertainty surrounding any merger process is liable to inflame speculation, and, in an increasingly competitive student market, Glamorgan and Newport were right to demand a swift resolution. But it was nevertheless a bad result for Andrews, who had been adamant from the outset that a merger involving Cardiff Met *would* happen. Described as "a massive climb-down" and "a major U-turn" by critics, the announcement effectively left Cardiff Met – the missing piece of the Welsh Government's higher education jigsaw – to its own devices. It is ironic that just two weeks prior to his change of heart, Andrews had attacked Cardiff Met's management and a number of "misleading statements" – namely around its position in university rankings – emanating from the institution. He appeared in no mood to back down and the chances of a reprieve looked wafer thin at best. But a reprieve Cardiff Met got, and, whichever way you looked at it, the university had been handed an indefinite stay of execution.

There was one important caveat to Cardiff Met's lifeline, namely Andrews' steely determination to see Welsh Government policy through. Post-dissolution order, his reaffirmed "commitment" to a single post-1992 HEI in South-East Wales did nothing to quell speculation over Cardiff Met's long-term future. The day after his decision to ditch dissolution plans and with the sound of Chapman's champagne corks still ringing in his ears, Andrews suggested in the strongest terms possible the fate lying in wait for Cardiff Met. When quizzed on the merger issue in the Senedd, he told AMs: "Cardiff Metropolitan University is now largely marginal to the Welsh Government's higher education strategy. We will not be wasting time, energy and resources on institutions that are marginal to our higher education strategy."[4] Subsequent rumours that Cardiff Met's rivals were leant upon to strike lock down agreements with local colleges – with a means to cutting off its supply of students – were not, therefore, considered completely unfounded.

Cardiff Met was, without question, a nagging thorn in the minister's side. But against all odds, it had achieved its primary objective and wrestled independence from the jaws of dissolution. In hindsight, the appointment in April 2011 of Wilding – Britain's longest-serving female Chief Constable – as chairwoman of governors was an unlikely masterstroke. Having served on the board for only a year prior to her promotion, Wilding was fast-tracked to lead her fellow governors following the departure after six years of chairman John Wyn Owen. A woman of no notable higher education experience, Wilding's unrivalled career in the public sector – not to mention her plucky personality – was the perfect fit for a university on the brink. The university needed someone with a public profile and the gumption to tackle Andrews head on. Wilding started her three-year term in office in August 2011 and few knew her selection would end up being quite so pivotal to the university's future.

Wilding spent 42 years in the police service prior to her retirement in 2009. The majority of her operational career was spent as a detective in the Metropolitan Police, before leaving as a Deputy Assistant Commissioner in 2003 to assume the position of Chief Constable of South Wales Police. Prior to heading west, she commanded directorates as diverse as Strategic Resourcing, for the 50,000 staff of the Metropolitan Police, and Security and Protection, which included the protection of the Royal Family. Wilding was involved in the identification of victims from the sinking of the Marchioness on the River Thames in 1989 and also led the UK policing response to Suicide Terrorism from 9/11 to 2005. This was no ordinary adversary and if Andrews did not already know with whom he was dealing, he need not have looked further than Wilding's impressive CV. The staunch and ultimately successful defence of her adopted institution would be another notch on an already impressive list.

Withdrawn from the media glare, Cardiff Met's vice-chancellor was a far less combative personality. A trained psychologist, Chapman was more understated and not the type to engage in an open war of words, which made Wilding the perfect foil. She was far better versed in dealing with the sort of challenge posed by a vociferous politician and in an increasingly embittered and personal battle, gave as good as Cardiff Met got. Her important role in fronting up to a minister on the warpath cannot be underestimated. The former Chief Constable would become the face – and voice – of Cardiff Met's impassioned bid for survival as an autonomous institution.

I met Wilding and Chapman for the second time at the university's Llandaff headquarters on February 20, 2013. There are not many institutions to have stared dissolution in the face and in their first major interview[5] since crisis was averted, the pair explained the steps they would take to ensure survival in the shadows of Cardiff University and the new institution developing nearby. Despite its new lease of life, critics painted a picture of uncertainty, bordering on the inevitable – that Cardiff Met was too small to survive in an era of increased competition and financial prudence. And yet, a decade after reconfiguration was first touted, it remained free-standing and running to profit.

Chapman said: "We had been continually advised that what was proposed would be very difficult to achieve in the particular time-frame proposed, and that we should continue to press for the business case and the rationale for that sort of move... Our students simply didn't swallow the idea that big was better."[6] Nevertheless, there was a feeling that Cardiff Met's self-induced exile could come back to bite if merger talks were revived later down the line. Glamorgan and Newport's decision to merge regardless, with a combined institution of 33,000 students and five campuses, put them in a position of considerable strength. Entering into three-way merger talks would have guaranteed a level playing field and, following its reluctance to engage, dissenting voices predicted Cardiff Met would "wither on the vine" in the shadow of a new university evolving nearby. Cardiff Met had won the battle – but would it win the war?

Far from severing ties, Chapman said Cardiff Met would be keen to work with the fledgling University of South Wales – the result of Glamorgan's merger with Newport – following its planned launch in April 2013. Wilding, who had been head of Cardiff Met's governing body for just 18 months, said past experiences had been invaluable and conceded that ensuring Cardiff Met retained its independence in the face of intense pressure to merge had been "hugely satisfying". When asked how the achievement ranked alongside her 40 years in the police force, she said: "Does it equate to saving a life? No – but nearly. It is actually always about having done the right thing, not allowing yourself to be distracted, and to come out the other end with a sense of purpose and focus."

Chapman hailed Wilding's "forensic" understanding of the issues facing Cardiff Met and looking back on what was a turbulent time for him as vice-chancellor, said: "It was certainly a challenging year but I enjoy challenges and different aspects of the work. I would prefer though, to be focusing on the core mission. I am paid to lead the university and a good proportion of my time in the last 18 months has been spent in meetings talking about reconfiguration." Of that, there was little doubt albeit the reality was that much of the previous decade had been spent poring over collaboration and the university's response to government policy. As the university's figurehead, Chapman himself became synonymous with Cardiff Met's cautious approach to merger and survived a potentially career-ending vote of no confidence from members of the National Association of Teachers in Further and Higher Education (NATFHE) in the summer of 2005.

Elsewhere, the new University of South Wales was to operate across Cardiff, Pontypridd and Newport – as well as maintaining a strong presence in the Heads of the Valleys. It was, to all intents and purposes, a powerhouse of education and while challenging established brands is easier said than done, Wales had given birth to a genuine "super university" of the size and scale to rival any in the UK. All parties, with the possible exception of Andrews and the Welsh Government, had got what they wanted.

# The University of South Wales

The University of Glamorgan and University of Wales, Newport were by no means failing institutions. But while they each excelled in certain areas, they could not on their own offer the range of opportunities required to take them to the next level. There was a strongly-held belief that, together, they would be better-equipped to win favour from a shrinking pool of debt-conscious teenagers. And therein lay the challenge as, without income from student fees, ambitious expansion plans were ultimately rendered pointless. Fusing campuses 20 miles apart (Newport's Caerleon Campus was the farthest from the new university's headquarters in Treforest, just outside Pontypridd) would be no mean feat. But the woman charged with blooding the University of South Wales was supremely confident.

I interviewed Professor Julie Lydon, who was appointed vice-chancellor of the new institution after Newport's transfer of property, rights and liabilities into Glamorgan, on the eve of its launch in April 2013. Wales' first ever female vice-chancellor, Lydon took over at Glamorgan in 2010 after the retirement of Professor David Halton, whom she had worked under as assistant vice-chancellor at the University of the West of England. Lydon had followed Halton to South Wales a year after his appointment as vice-chancellor of Glamorgan in 2005 (she was made deputy vice-chancellor) and as leader of the bigger of the two merger partners, was considered the ideal candidate to oversee the university's latest transition. Lydon gave the university of South Wales a "two-year horizon" to get its new house in order and fully-integrate provision across all sites. The Welsh Government, via the university funding council, made available an additional £24.8m over three years to help smooth the changeover.

The university had undergone a whirlwind transition after the decision by Glamorgan and Newport to merge was officially announced in July 2012. In the intervening nine months, ruling governing bodies settled any lingering differences and worked quickly to establish a new leadership team. Newport's acting vice-chancellor Professor Stephen Hagen, who had since replaced Noyes, played a strong hand and was appointed one of five deputies at the University of South Wales (three had roots in Glamorgan and the other two were from Newport), although he would not stay for long. Hagen left under a cloud shortly after the university's launch and started work as vice-president for change management and internationalisation at the University of Information Technologies, Mechanics and Optics, in St Petersburg, Russia, in 2014.

Figures showed nearly 700 staff considered leaving their posts prior to Wales' biggest university merger. Data compiled using the Freedom of Information Act showed 369 staff at Glamorgan applied or "showed an interest" in taking voluntary severance prior to its joining with Newport. Overall, 308 Newport staff considered the same package, which was introduced to cut costs ahead of the launch of the University of South Wales. According to The Insight, the merged university's student newspaper, 136 former Glamorgan staff who applied between January and September 2013 were allowed to leave. The figure included 49 frontline teaching staff, while at Newport, 114 were granted voluntary severance – of which 25 were academics. Permanent staff with two years' service were offered a "golden goodbye" similar to that unveiled by Cardiff University a year earlier. The scheme entitled eligible workers from both institutions a pay-off worth a year's salary – the first £30,000 of which would be tax-free. The universities said all terms had been agreed by trade unions and senior management had the final say over who stayed and who would be allowed to leave.

For Lydon, the pace of change was crucial. "I think to have achieved a legal integration in that time is going at some pace – but that's quite deliberate," she said. "We realise that we're operating in a pretty volatile time and we therefore wanted to secure the new university as quickly as possible to prevent any uncertainty, least not for staff. Within five minutes of our first meeting, the intent and direction of travel was very clear and we wanted to find a way forward and a way of making it (merger) happen. We were both determined to make it work." Lydon acknowledged that collaboration had been "part of Glamorgan's thinking" for some time and university managers had made no secret of their desire to merge with neighbouring institutions. When asked if she regretted Cardiff Met's self-induced omission from the merger plan, Lydon said:

"Not at all. It's up to Cardiff Met to determine its own future and the market will out in terms of what happens. Why waste any more time and energy? They're not a competitor and we don't see them as part of our future. The door's not closed but if they were to ask [about merger], it would have to be on the basis of a full integration."[7] (Julie Lydon, 2013)

Not surprisingly, her thinly-veiled rebuke would not have warmed the hearts of colleagues in Llandaff. Lydon added that Andrews had been "absolutely right" to press for increased collaboration between universities, which in the current climate, "need to be niche or big" to remain competitive. She added: "I don't think we've had any negatives at all and reaction to the University of South Wales has all been very positive. In no other sector would you have 20 years with no change and business leaders are surprised we didn't do it (merge) sooner. It's the right time and we are all very committed to it."

For all the animosity between the institutions, it was ironic that University of South Wales courses were marketed for the first time, five days after its launch on April 11, 2013, at a UCAS convention held at Cardiff Met's Cyncoed Campus. Fortunately, respective stands were not in close proximity. Moving forward, it is hard to imagine Cardiff Met and the University of South Wales ever coming together meaningfully under the same leadership. Relations between vice-chancellors, in particular, are frayed to the point where they will not willingly be seen in the same room. Experience shows how important personalities are in the merger process and the failed tripartite of 2012 was no exception. It came as no great surprise when the University of South Wales announced in September 2014 the closure of its smaller Caerleon Campus. Attempts to market the site's conference potential appeared futile with the formidable Celtic Manor Resort operating on the other side of the River Usk and the writing was on the wall when a spokeswoman confirmed in June of that year that although no long-term decisions had been taken, management was "carefully assessing, from the evidence, what the future shape of that estate should be"[8].

The Welsh Government's response to news of Caerleon's closure was predictable. Despite announcing in its 2011 Assembly manifesto that it did "not intend to see the closure of any of Wales higher education campuses", the administration sought to distance itself from potential controversy by declaring that overall management of the university's estate "is a matter for them".[9] Politically, there was nothing to gain by the Welsh Government speculating on the future of university campuses, post-merger. It needed a means by which to deflect possible criticism if what many considered to be inevitable, actually happened. In that respect, shifting responsibility back on to the universities themselves was always in the offing. I recall a Freudian slip by the then Deputy Minister for Skills Jeff Cuthbert in June 2012, during which he said he was "loath to give assurance" that no campuses would close as a result of university reorganisation.[10] The Welsh Government was forced to hastily clarify its original position, albeit Cuthbert was almost certainly right to have his reservations.

If Cuthbert's faux pas was unfortunate, there is a lesser-known side story to the merger saga that, given the sensitivities of merger and the obvious animosity between university leaders, could be considered wholly inappropriate. At a meeting of Glamorgan's board of governors on November 19, 2012, members received a report from the vice-chancellor noting that she had been asked by the Welsh Government to sit on the selection panel for the appointment of the new Director General for Education and Skills[11]. Emyr Roberts had announced his resignation and Owen Evans, well-known in the higher education sector following his two-year term as Director for Skills, Higher Education and Lifelong Learning, was one of four candidates shortlisted. There is little doubt that Lydon, who accepted the Welsh Government's invitation to sit alongside Civil Service Commissioner Kathryn Bishop and three other senior officials, ticked all the boxes and would have fulfilled ably what was requested of her. But when you consider that Andrews did not cancel plans to dissolve Cardiff Met until November 6, 2012, and the institution was walking on egg shells well into the new year, the Welsh Government would surely have been better served approaching someone else. There is no suggestion of anything untoward on Lydon's part, but the Welsh Government's judgement is open to debate. If higher education representation was essential, a vice-chancellor not directly linked to merger negotiations would surely have been more appropriate. It is hard to imagine Chapman being approached under the same circumstances.

Andrews brought the curtain down on a long-running drive to restructure the nation's university sector in June 2013. The Welsh Government's new higher education strategy, building on For Our Future, plotted a new course for government and universities in Wales to work in partnership until 2020. It looked at how Welsh institutions could "achieve excellence at every level" and effectively confined the controversial drive for reconfiguration to history. Unveiling the new higher education strategy, Andrews said "substantial progress" had been made in delivering on the Welsh Government's objective of creating fewer, stronger universities. The strategy received cross-party support within the Senedd and highlighted the role institutions played in providing high-quality education and their contribution to industry, research and innovation. Collaboration in South-East Wales was, at long last, off the agenda.

# Funding higher education

Many believe the Welsh Government's drive for collaboration was a smokescreen for its under funding of the nation's higher education sector. Contracting the number of universities in Wales, critics argued, served only to mask the inadequacies of the devolved administration. Although evidence suggests mergers are actually more expensive in the short-term, over a longer period, pooling resources can see courses dropped, campuses closed and students scaled back. Conversely, merging backroom services can free up funds to improve teaching and learning. Invariably, with fewer universities holding out their hands, HEFCW could afford to spread more generously public funds.

The Learned Society of Wales, established in 2010 to foster home-grown knowledge and culture, is one of the more vociferous defenders of Welsh higher education. A group of the nation's most eminent academics, it has described the financial state of the sector as "perilous" and attacked the Welsh Government for confining Welsh universities to the "slow lane" with a decade of under funding. It pointed to a cumulative funding gap of more than £360m between universities in Wales and England from 2000-09. A report published by HEFCW in 2011 showed funding per student in Wales was about £900 less than across the border[12]. The Learned Society warned that such under funding undermined the sustainability of Wales' dominant knowledge base. It said:

> "We recognise that this is a time of inevitable cuts in public expenditure, but emphasise that the Welsh universities have taken cuts in advance in times of plenty elsewhere in Wales. Continued weakening of the Welsh universities on top of a decade of poor support from the Welsh Assembly Government will reduce their attraction to students and hence loss of income. It will also reduce their attraction to staff and hence loss of excellence. All will result in further erosion of our key national knowledge base and so on in a downward spiral which holds out little support for the belief that Wales is to be a small but clever nation."[13]
> (Learned Society of Wales, 2011)

The Learned Society of Wales said it was not surprised that on most indicators Welsh universities were not always performing well, despite some examples of excellence. It blamed a 9% reduction in the university budget and "serious funding uncertainties" created by the Welsh Government's tuition fee policy for an "ominous" outlook.

A report published in 2013 by Auditor General for Wales Huw Vaughan Thomas found there were "limitations" in the Welsh Government's appraisal of its tuition fee options and the cost of its multi-million-pound subsidy was expected to be 24% more than first thought. Thomas warned the controversial tuition fee policy would cost £156m more than planned and said the Welsh Government could have done more to appraise its options before agreeing to existing arrangements. According to Thomas, the estimated cost of the policy had risen from £653m to £809m. He said there had been various changes in the assumptions underpinning the Welsh Government's forecasts and institutions were charging higher fees than had been expected.

Rightly or wrongly, the Welsh Government had made supporting homegrown students, wherever in the UK they studied, one of its defining policies. The idea that access to higher education should be on the basis of an individual's potential to benefit and not on the basis of what they could afford to pay, had been its mantra. It was, of course, a very noble aim and one which even the most ardent critic would find difficult to oppose. But in such austere times, the issue was always going to be one of cost. Could Wales afford to subsidise all of its students wherever in the UK they chose to study? The jury, it seems, is still out. Interestingly, Andrews would later refute claims the Welsh Government had underestimated the policy and said it had actually come in under budget. But while educationalists dispute the best way forward, those in other sectors – most notably health – will forever argue they are more deserving of public investment.

The Learned Society boasted 58 founding fellows who were all prominent figures within their respective academic disciplines. Its opinions, therefore, were not to be taken lightly. The funding argument took on extra weight when one of Wales' longest serving vice-chancellors put his head above the parapet and went public with his concerns. Professor Richard B Davies warned in 2011 that Welsh universities were working on a "shoestring" and the comparative under funding of higher education was unsustainable. Swansea University's leader said there was no doubt universities in Wales had been under funded "for some years" and failure to boost the sector's budget would eventually impinge on performance. In fact, Davies said it was "much more difficult to maintain Welsh universities than English universities, where money has been abundant". He added:

> "Undoubtedly, we (Welsh universities) have been significantly under funded for some years and there is a danger that, if this continues, it will damage performance. There is no reason why it should have damaged performance so far and we can manage things for the short-term. But it does mean you invest less money in the university estate and don't have the flexibility to spend money on new initiatives because money is so tight. We mustn't present too bleak a picture here, as we've managed very well, but continued under funding is unsustainable and you can't work forever on a shoestring."[14] (Richard B Davies, 2011)

Davies had taken a calculated risk. While the majority of university leaders would doubtless echo his concerns, tackling the minister and his government head on was akin to biting the hand that feeds. It is for that reason universities rarely speak out publicly against the administration.

It goes without saying that the balance of power lies firmly in Cardiff Bay and a report published in 2012 suggested funding for Welsh universities may have been scaled back because of their reluctance to engage in collaboration policy. A study by the Higher Education Policy Institute (HEPI) said there had been "continuing political dissatisfaction" with Wales' university sector and its relationship with the Welsh Government. At the same time, it said institutions in England and Scotland had been funded at a "consistently higher level" – and the funding gap was a "major issue" for Welsh universities. The report's author, Dr Tony Bruce, suggested Scotland had enjoyed a better working relationship with its devolved administration.

> "In Wales, the sector has had a much more chequered relationship with government partly because of the continuing stalemate over the reconfiguration issue and concerns about its performance... This may be one of the main reasons why the government has not been prepared to close the funding gap with England that has emerged over the past decade."[15] (Tony Bruce, 2012)

Despite a disparity in funding, the report highlighted a number of similarities between higher education in Wales and Scotland. Although there were at the time 14 universities in Scotland to Wales' 10, the average size of institutions in student terms was almost identical (11,626 in Wales and 11,627 in Scotland). Data showed there were 3.33 HEIs per 1,000 people in Wales, compared to 3.66 universities per 1,000 head of population in Scotland.

Following the economic downturn, universities were forced to refocus their spending in the same way as business. True, vice-chancellors were becoming increasingly adept at weathering financial storms, but often their hands were tied and the longer economic conditions conspired against them, the more likely institutions were to teeter on the brink. A senior manager working at a Welsh university warned in 2013 that universities in Wales could be at risk of collapse if student recruitment worsened over time. They said the situation was "serious" and failure to recruit students well in the future could have far reaching implications for HEIs. Nevertheless, bankruptcy was a last resort and the possible reputational damage was such that universities and their overarching governments would do everything in their power to avoid letting troubled institutions go to the wall.

Consider the University of Wales, Lampeter. When the nation's oldest university hit the rocks, HEFCW could ill afford to sit idly and watch its downward spiral from afar. In 2008, a year after the Quality Assurance Agency (QAA) had warned of "limited confidence" in the university's management and ability to ensure academic standards, HEFCW commissioned external consultants to review Lampeter's managerial capability and whether it had the "viability and ability to deliver a sustainable institution". In its report, HEFCW said the financial position of Lampeter was "weakening sharply" as a result of falling student numbers and increasing costs. It bemoaned weak marketing and recruitment processes and resolved that many of its deficiencies came from "incapacity".[16] HEFCW called for interim management to be put in place and raised the possibility of a merger to save the institution. Negotiations duly began and Lampeter and nearby Trinity University College, based in Carmarthen, announced in April 2009 their intention to come together formally. The launch of the University of Wales, Trinity Saint David would mark a new beginning for Lampeter, whose demise was a lesson for all university leaders and set a benchmark for what could happen when financial issues spiralled out of control.

The Welsh Government's new strategic plan for higher education, published in June 2013, was not as prescriptive as some had anticipated and, to a certain extent, universities were given the space Andrews had initially been less inclined to allow. But the trials and tribulations of the previous three and a half years had changed nothing as far as HEFCW was concerned. In its corporate strategy for the three academic years from 2013-16, the council outlined its position on the issue of reconfiguration and collaboration. It said:

> "Overall, we remain of the view that too many of our universities are too small by UK standards, and that we still have too many institutions, raising concerns over their competitiveness, sustainability, regional coherence and range of provision. Our statement on the future shape of the higher education sector in Wales noted our aim to see six HEIs, with a community focused and a research intensive university in each region. That continues to be the council's position."[17] (HEFCW, 2013)

At the time of writing, there are eight universities in Wales. By HEFCW's reckoning, that means there are two universities too many. So, coupled with subtle funding threats, one suspects there is still life in the merger agenda and the final act may be yet to play. Of those left standing, there is every chance Cardiff Met and Glyndŵr will be the universities looking anxiously over their shoulder.

# Notes

1.    Smith, Steve. (2012). Report to the Welsh Government on South-East Wales Higher Education Provision.
2.    Wilding, Barbara. (2012). Western Mail. October 11.
3.    Chapman, Antony. (2012). Western Mail. October 11.
4.    Andrews, Leighton. (2012). Western Mail. November 10.

5.  Chapman, Antony and Wilding, Barbara. (2013). Western Mail. February 21.
6.  Chapman, Antony. (2013). Western Mail. February 28.
7.  Lydon, Julie. (2013). Western Mail. April 11.
8.  University of South Wales. (2014). South Wales Argus. June 9.
9.  University of South Wales. (2014). Western Mail. September 13.
10. Cuthbert, Jeff. (2012). Western Mail. June 5.
11. University of Glamorgan. (2012). Minutes of the Meeting of the Board of Governors. November 19.
12. HEFCW. (2010). The Funding Gap: 2007-08. p 4.
13. Learned Society of Wales. (2011). Western Mail. March 2.
14. Davies, Richard B. (2011). Western Mail. October 24.
15. Bruce, Tony. (2012). Universities and Constitutional Change in the UK, The Impact of Devolution on the Higher Education Sector. Higher Education Policy Institute. p 97.
16. HEFCW. (2008). Review of University of Wales, Lampeter. p 5.
17. HEFCW. (2013). Corporate Strategy 2013-14. p 24.

# 10

# A Toxic Legacy?

## Jane Davidson: The interview

*Wales' longest-serving Education Minister and the architect of so many flagship policies recounts her time in office. Were there regrets and was she satisfied she got everything right? An exclusive interview provides the answers*

As the architect of so many of Wales' educational initiatives, it is not surprising that Davidson attracts both adoration and criticism in almost equal measure. Rather like her most vociferous successor, she continues to divide opinion and while laying claim to some of the nation's finest policy creations, Davidson also presided over a frustrating period of decline in terms of Wales position relative to others. It is a sad fact that Wales went from performing above average at GCSE and A-level to performing considerably below the UK average. An inquest was launched following Wales' desperately poor PISA results in December 2010 and it was perhaps inevitable that the spotlight would fall squarely on the shoulders of the nation's longest-serving Education Minister. After all, Andrews had been in post only a year when PISA was published and the associated tests had been sat prior to his arrival in 2009. Hutt's brief hold of the education portfolio was negligible so by virtue of her extended run in the role, the finger of blame was pointed at Davidson and critics made their feelings known. The vultures circled and Philip Dixon deduced that Wales had paid the price of Davidson's "toxic legacy". The "national humiliation" of Wales' worsening PISA results, he said, were proof that problems were deep-rooted and not formed overnight. He said of Davidson:

"The leaking roofs, faulty windows and Victorian loos of many Welsh schools are a lasting monument to her seven-year reign as Education

Minister. While New Labour were spending millions on the English school system, transforming buildings in the process, the Welsh education system was being starved of cash. The target of making every school fit for purpose by 2010 was quickly and quietly dropped when it became apparent that it would be missed by a mile."[1] (Philip Dixon, 2012)

Others, like ASCL's Brian Lightman, were far more forgiving. He said Davidson had every right to "hold her head high" and Wales would ignore her achievements "at its peril". A former secondary headteacher in the Vale of Glamorgan, Lightman retained strong ties with Davidson, with whom he had worked before landing ASCL's top job in 2010. It was clear that loyalty had not since dissipated and Lightman said the former minister would be remembered as a "pioneer of an inspiring vision"[2] who worked tirelessly to engage with the profession. Professor Gareth Elwyn Jones, former head of education at Aberystwyth University and a respected voice on the system's origins, was another gushing in his praise. Jones hailed the impact of the Foundation Phase, Flying Start and the Welsh Baccalaureate and concluded that: "Since devolution there has been lots of sun. Jane Davidson has more claim than most to bask in it."[3]

Davidson was an ambitious and self-made politician who worked her way up the Welsh Labour pyramid to very near the summit. In fact, there was only one job left to be scaled at the time of her retirement and there is little doubt that she toyed with the idea of one day becoming Wales' First Minister. Davidson took a populist approach to her time as Education Minister and was always keen to build consensus. She considered herself a "listening minister" and won many admirers by opening her door to sector stakeholders. But so too was Davidson willing to get out into the field. Her stock rose with the more people she met and her goal to visit every school in Wales served as a valuable PR exercise. As it was, Davidson need not have travelled the length and breadth of the country to win favour and her courteous relationship with unions provided a solid platform. She met with them individually – as well as them altogether – twice a year and they appreciated her willingness to consult extensively before cementing policy. Davidson was also popular on her own turf and in 2003, four years after her election to the Assembly, she won a majority more than four times her previous margin. The irony was that Davidson was not from a traditional Valleys' background and unlike the vast majority of her constituents, completed her education at an independent boarding school, Worcestershire's Malvern College.

Nevertheless, Davidson's reign remains the topic of considerable debate and comments made by Helen Mary Jones, formerly Plaid Cymru's education spokeswoman, provide contrast to those summarised earlier. In 2003, Jones said of her Welsh Labour counterpart: "She is like a queen bee, taking credit for everything her government does, but not the discredit for what they don't do. She is a bit of a one person operation, talking about I, I, I, and not enough about we, we, we. And that's not just me saying that. I've heard her colleagues in the Labour party say that too."[4] Davidson was considered by many to be a First Minister-in-waiting and, as a close ally of Rhodri Morgan, would have been one of his more natural successors. There is no telling exactly when she gave up the ghost but if indeed her eyes were on the top prize, a bid to win power would surely have been buoyed by the teachers' vote.

Davidson was a confident speaker both in public and behind closed doors, where she was not afraid of putting misfiring officials in their place. She was very conscious of her own image and some time after her resignation from the Cabinet, admitted taking critical comments from her Wikipedia entry and replacing them with positive material. Among negative references removed from the online encyclopedia were the names of school closures that she did not halt while Education Minister. The accolades and plaudits she was given while Minister for Environment, Sustainability and Housing were among references added to her biography. When asked about her motives, Davidson said she had sought only to update her Wikipedia entry having "ceased to be an AM" and that "someone had been deliberately posting selective information"[5] she had subsequently removed. In an interview with the *Guardian* in 2001, Davidson declared that she had "a working education system in Wales".[6] Right or wrong, the same could not be said of Wales' education system a decade later and by virtue of her extended rule, Davidson must carry a certain amount of responsibility.

I entered Wales' education system in a professional capacity too late to have seen first-hand Davidson's ministerial approach and style. But the ghost of education's past loomed large and it was with that in mind that I sought the first comprehensive review of Davidson's tenure, in her own words. I was intrigued by her seven-year rule and curious about the events leading up to the policy decisions that defined her well-documented educational journey. Davidson agreed, albeit reluctantly, to meet with me in January 2012. Our interview took place in her office at the University of Wales, Trinity Saint David, less than a year after her retirement from politics and almost five years after stepping down as Education Minister. It ran over two parts in the *Western Mail* and remains the only first-person account of Davidson's rule of schools, colleges and universities in the time since her resignation as AM for Pontypridd.

Prior to our meeting, Davidson made clear that she would not answer questions relating to decisions taken outside of her watch. To comment on a successor's course of action was to break an unwritten rule and Andrews himself would attract criticism for displaying the same reluctance to speak more candidly about the legacy he inherited. There was a mutual loyalty between ministers, in public at least. Davidson, a confident and assured subject, retained an air of authority and was not shy in coming forward. Our conversation lasted almost two hours and is recorded here in full for the first time. The interview serves as an important testimony of Davidson's time in office and, regardless of what side of the fence you fall, provides a fascinating insight into one of Wales' best-known politicians.

## University of Wales, Trinity Saint David
## Carmarthen Campus
## January 19, 2012

Life in the Pembrokeshire countryside is a world away from the hustle and bustle of Cardiff Bay. But Jane Davidson has gone home. A former teacher, she lives downstream from Cardigan where her passion for education began more than 30 years ago. We meet in her modest office at the University of Wales, Trinity Saint David where she balks at the idea that a woman of her stature is deserving of something more luxurious. Davidson has a formidable CV and as one of the founding members of the Welsh Assembly, was a close ally to inaugural First Minister Rhodri Morgan. More than a decade later, she is retired from politics and is director of the Institute of Sustainable Practice, Innovation and Resource Effectiveness (INSPIRE) – Wales' first dedicated institute for sustainable practice. As retirements go, Davidson's was particularly lucrative but for all her work in the areas of sustainability and the environment, Davidson was best-known for being Wales' longest-serving Education Minister.

Assuming the portfolio in 2000, the former Pontypridd AM spent seven years nurturing the devolved administration's education vision – The Learning Country. A document based on one of the cornerstones of society, it referred to the National Assembly's formation as a "turning point" for education and lifelong learning in Wales. Success, it argued, depended upon a rapid acceleration in lifting Wales' knowledge and skills-base. The words ring true a decade on – yet the uplifting sense of optimism has long since evaporated. By virtue of her extended run in the role, Davidson's record of achievement is the subject of much debate in education circles.

"I think it's very easy for people to always look back and blame an individual – but go back and look at all the reports I had at the time and ask yourself: 'Would anybody have taken a different action?' I think that's the critical issue," she said. "I was forensic in my use of Estyn reports, I was forensic in my use of academic evidence and all the policy agendas went through the Assembly as well as the Government, because we were either in minority government or in coalition. There had never been an individual party agenda that couldn't otherwise be completely overturned by the Assembly – and I am content the policy initiatives that I took were the right policy initiatives for Wales."

Davidson said that she was always keen to build a solid evidence-base when introducing major new initiatives. She met regularly with Wales' education unions, worked closely with Estyn's Chief Inspector and was open to the views of stakeholders. By the same token, Davidson did not wield the axe lightly and decisions – like that to abolish SATs – were taken only with supporting evidence.

"I've never believed that either the minister – even if they had an educational background, as I did – or their civil servants is sufficient for a big decision," she said. "I always used to ensure that either we had consultations of sufficient time, preferably allied to meetings with groups of people who would be affected by the decisions, and in particular cases around very big decisions – such as the SATs decision – a review group that was chaired by the foremost curriculum academic in the UK at that time. I also thought it was really important that when we were introducing a major new initiative, we actually had baseline information and appropriate monitoring and evaluation."

Davidson considers the flagship Welsh Baccalaureate qualification and early years' Foundation Phase programme two of her major achievements. Sector-leading and universally recognised, the initiatives cater for opposite ends of the educational spectrum, but are both widely tipped to help raise the bar in Wales. She said: "There are certain things you look at in politics where you think if I hadn't been there, would something have happened – and I can with confidence say that neither the Foundation Phase or Baccalaureate would have happened if I hadn't been passionate about taking them forward. I actually attempted an agenda and I always tried, as far as possible, to get all-party support for big decisions, because the legacy of any minister is whether or not the policy carries on. So my legacy in education is the fact that Flying Start is still there and is strongly supported; the Foundation Phase has been supported by all parties; Learning Pathways 14-19 is there; transition arrangements I put in place between primary and secondary school have worked; and the Baccalaureate has widened and deepened opportunity. As a minister, the testament in policy terms, has to be whether or not any of your initiatives stand the test of time, and I hope that the reason that all these initiatives have stood the test of time is because of using a strong evidence-base; of engaging with as many people as possible and having consultation that is real in the context of being prepared to change policy on the back of it."

Davidson was keen to stress the importance of lifelong learning – that is, learning for all age groups. By definition, The Learning Country sought to involve everyone in Wales and the minister was a keen advocate of widening access and opportunity. She said: "I think it's important to say that my full title was Minister for Education, Lifelong Learning and Skills. Lifelong learning has always been a fundamental issue I think, particularly in Wales, because we had a lot of people who left school very young to go down the pit or somewhere who, when they came back into education, did remarkably well. So returning to education is a really important theme, I think, in a country that wants to become a 'Learning Country'."

Davidson said she was confident that the Foundation Phase – which is based on the Scandinavian-style of learning through play – will be borne out with results. She referred to the "cyclical" nature of education and the fact that major new initiatives take time to bed in.

"I absolutely stand behind all the evidence that says it's the early years interventions that have the best outcomes in education – but the children who will be picked up by PISA from the Foundation Phase won't be picked up until 2020," she said. "What I was aiming to do on the Foundation Phase is now being delivered across Wales and is strongly supported by teachers and parents. I think the difficulty, if you're trying to turn around an education system, is that it takes a huge amount of time. There's a long time lag and I took us into PISA because we needed an external assessment of how Wales was doing."

Prior to her intervention, Wales was not a fully-fledged member of PISA and the nation only broke free from the UK's blanket entry in 2006. She said: "I remember the officials telling me at the time that this may not be a good idea because Wales will not fare well against the other countries. And I said: 'In which case it's absolutely the right time to do it,' because I'm a great believer in having solid, external, statistically-valid information. One of the things that PISA has shown us is that we're not as good as we thought we were and that's why I took us in. I think that in a small country, you can often feel very cosy in your system and it becomes quite hard to look outside."

She added: "Although I tried a number of initiatives to try and encourage leadership, to try and encourage best practice and for best practice to be replicable and taken forward in different kinds of schools, it nearly always depended on the individual good will of independent schools and staff. The schools that were good would always do more of it, and the very schools that you wanted to raise their game didn't necessarily see the potential. So it's always a challenge. PISA was a wake-up call in 2006 because people realised they were not as good and we were not as good as a country as we thought we were."

Few doubt that international benchmarks are an important tool in the quest to improve Welsh education. But, as the catalyst for a new 20-point improvement plan, its validity was always open to debate and experts have called for a more balanced view of Wales' schools. Davidson said: "I think although I took us into PISA, I think there is a danger if PISA is treated in the same way that SATs were treated. It is one part of a picture and I think the danger is that the focus on PISA could get in the way of making sure that the education system offered in Wales works with young people, who access school through the Foundation Phase at the age of three and come out post-18, to develop skills that are useful for their future employability." Looking back, Davidson said the Assembly Government had been hampered by a lack of Wales-specific data.

"I suppose, looking at what I came into in the year 2000, there was a very demoralised teaching profession which was a lot to do with the SATs agenda; real issues around poverty in Wales and the opportunity of a new legislature," she said. "But in the period of time up until the year 2000, very little had been done in Wales that wasn't just to direct delivery from Westminster – so we found ourselves very short of Wales-specific information. This was something which affected the whole of the Assembly when it started. You couldn't get access to information, so I worked really closely with the Chief Inspector of Estyn as they were obviously going in and inspecting schools, for example. It's very easy for people to look back and just blame an individual – but if you back and look at all of Estyn's reports at the time, would anybody have taken a different action? I think that's the critical issue."

Davidson said GCSE and A-level results rose steadily under her watch, and there was no suggestion that Wales had slipped behind England when she stood down as Education Minister in 2007. She was reminded that while summer exam results had gone up overall, the comparative performance of Welsh school pupils had deteriorated over time. She said: "I don't think there was any significant gap in any statistically significant way in 2007. We thought that the Baccalaureate would improve GCSE and A-level results – and the evidence suggests that it has."

Funding is a contentious issue. Those on the ground argue the case for more money as the foremost solution to poor performance. Extra resources, they protest, would better equip school staff for a renewed assault on attainment. Others, meanwhile, see funding as a smokescreen. Countries such as New Zealand spend considerably less than Wales on education yet perform better, while, closer to home, authorities such as Blaenau Gwent splash out the most for what appears to be very little return. Nevertheless, the correlation between funding and performance is regularly touted by critics who point to a growing spend shortfall between pupils in Wales and England. The supporting figures do nothing to appease their concerns. Pupils across the border now receive £604 more a year – up from £31 in 2000.

Davidson said the funding debate was prevalent during her time as minister, but maintained there was no evidence to suggest that spending on education went down. "My focus in terms of funding was outcomes and the Foundation Phase required additional funding – so I think you'll find that in early years' education, Wales funds better," she said. "The NUT (National Union of Teachers) commissioned a funding report when I was minister and I think what their research identified was the fact that we funded better in primary education and worse in secondary education. The report came before the Foundation Phase so when we launched the Foundation Phase, we put more investment into primary education." Davidson said it was difficult to draw comparisons when different councils were employing different funding formulas. "The funding issue while I was minister was generally about the fact that the counties in Wales that funded most funded more than their counterparts across the border – but the councils in Wales that funded least, funded less," she said. "The funding debate was always a moving target because it depended which sector you were dealing with. Interestingly enough, there were never representations from the further education sector about funding in comparison to England – but there were representations from secondary schools and from higher education."

When asked if the fledgling Assembly Government "put all its eggs in one basket" when it came to funding, Davidson said: "We certainly wanted to make sure that we funded early years effectively. The big issue while I was minister was not actually the levels of funding so much as whether or not the local authorities passed that money on to the schools; so I did quite a lot of work with the unions and with the local authorities to try and get them to pass more money on." Davidson said she made some inroads but pointed out that the drive to push more funding to the frontline was still "live".

Davidson said: "There are some real advantages to having education as a local authority service but people will always make comparisons. A funding formula has to take certain things into account and the level to which the different elements are funded will often depend on local circumstances, so you will always get an element of variation. I think the difficulty is that most of the debates about funding were way after me." Five years have passed since Davidson stood down from education to assume charge of what she described as the "biggest portfolio in the Cabinet" at the time. As a key figure in Morgan's Labour Government, Davidson was given responsibility for the environment, sustainability and housing in 2007. The holder of only two jobs in 11 years, Davidson's ministerial longevity is testament to the perceived strides made under her leadership. The average life of a minister in England, by contrast, is 18 months. Put simply, Cabinet "reshuffles" are commonplace and, as in any walk of life, those seen to be under-performing can be quickly moved aside.

"I think, probably, I was asked to carry on because of the Foundation Phase," said Davidson. "But once the policy agenda was set, I know that

Rhodri moved me into environment and sustainability so that I could pick up a big new policy agenda there. It's very unusual for people to be kept in a role – normally people always move on."

As the dust settles on her political career, Davidson is certain that many of her interventions will live long into the future. She said: "The vision for The Learning Country was the idea that any political administration should take decisions for the longer term so that you don't end up with the education system being pushed from pillar to post every four years. And in that sense, a legacy that has now consolidated the Foundation Phase and the Baccalaureate, for example, into the Welsh psyche gives those policies the best possible chance of success for the future. But it all needs working at as well and you can never take your eye off anything in education."

It is fair to say that Davidson had a long-term plan for the nation's university sector, with collaboration a central pillar in the Welsh Government's higher education strategy. In fact, plans to create fewer, stronger institutions would far outlive the minister and last for well over a decade. Restructuring higher education proved a difficult nut to crack and the sometimes arduous process was by no means ideal. But nevertheless, as was so often the case after devolution, Davidson had laid the foundations for Messers Hutt and Andrews to follow. In many ways Reaching Higher, published in January 2002, was the catalyst for as much churn as it was stability.

"We were first to recognise the need for collaboration in higher education," said Davidson. "Reaching Higher was about the fact that because Manchester had just gone through its major reconfiguration, we were acutely aware that not far across the border was a university bigger than all the institutions in Wales put together. It was really important to have critical mass in our institutions in Wales. I am a great believer in collaboration but we also looked at having an evidence-base for it. I've always made sure I discussed the approaches with as wide a number of people as possible."

Davidson looks back fondly on her time in charge of the nation's schools, colleges and universities. She said: "If I had remained as minister post-2007, my next big area would have been the eight to 14 age group, because in a sense, we had done the three to seven in the first administration and we did 14-19 in the second. You can't do a whole education system at once and the crying need at the time was for the early years – the other crying need was coming from the employers, who were saying they didn't have enough young people with the appropriate skills. The 14-19 agenda was about creating different types of skills and opportunities and the collaboration agenda was always about making sure that more people were working together to deliver better outputs in terms of students."

For all the success stories, Davidson's seven-year education journey was not without criticism. But as Wales' longest-serving Education Minister, she is an easy target and refutes suggestions current incumbent, Andrews, has undertaken to paper over old cracks. She was asked whether she had left a "toxic legacy", as suggested by union leader Philip Dixon.

"Obviously, I don't think it's a toxic legacy, do I," she said. "The critical thing is that everybody gets behind trying to make the education system in Wales the best possible – and I absolutely had that support when I was in post. My only major point of discussion with the unions was about funding. You also have to remember that in small countries, the number of support officials that you have is very small compared to education departments elsewhere.

"It (criticism) doesn't bother me because the only thing you can do as a minister is your absolute best in the job," she said. "What I wanted to do in my time as minister was to create a vision for a learning country and for that vision to be longer than my time as minister – it has been. I would never say that I achieved everything that I wanted to achieve as Education Minister. But I would continue to put that question: 'if anybody else had been in that place with that set of data, would they have taken a different decision?' What I did was put forward two major policy initiatives at each end of compulsory education. The area which is now rightly being focussed upon is the area in the middle; making sure that the transition from the Foundation Phase into the curriculum works and the opportunities that are offered for the Baccalaureate at Level 2 are being led into by the education system. It's absolutely right that that is where the emphasis should be."

Davidson said she was proud to have "been at the forefront of a new kind of delivery" and developed policies that attracted interest from across the world. She has few regrets but when asked what she would have done differently, the former minister said: "I would have done more work on the eight to 14 area because although we went for wholesale change, I think the majority of children spend the majority of their life in school during that period of time. I think I would have made sure that we started work around the eight to 14 agenda some time around 2004, when we had the agreement on SATs, when in fact what we were focusing on at the time was getting the Baccalaureate in place. I did a lot of work on special needs and I would have wanted to do more work in that area. I still feel guilty now at the idea that there are 19-year-olds who have been in special schools with high-level support on the day before their 19th birthday, but then end up in a community centre the day after without that support. I know that's being addressed now but I would like to have done more work on that – we didn't have the relevant powers at the time. I would also like to have been able to do more work around the experience of deprivation and ensuring that it was properly accounted for in school funding formulas – and I wouldn't have minded more than 24 hours in the day."

As a "bullish and outspoken" minister – her words, not mine – Davidson's style is not a million miles from that of Andrews. Rumour is they don't get on, yet both are reluctant to talk about each other's records of achievement. In fact, Davidson declines to talk about anything outside her tenure but stresses she still gets a "huge amount of support" from parents, the teaching profession and academics for her policy agenda in education.

Concluding, she said: "I think we have to remember that the first 10 years of a new legislature are going to have teething problems and the critical thing is that everybody gets behind trying to make the education system in Wales the best possible. As far as I'm concerned, all the time I have spent in government I have spent doing my absolute best that I could for Wales. I have been really privileged to do the two jobs that I would have liked to have done. I care passionately about education and I care passionately about the environment – and I am confident that both are in good hands with the current ministers."[7]

# Notes

1.  Dixon, Philip. (2012). Western Mail. February 16.
2.  Lightman, Brian. (2012) Western Mail. February 6.
3.  Jones, Gareth Elwyn. (2012). Western Mail. February 1.
4.  Jones, Helen Mary (2003). Times Educational Supplement. May 16.
5.  Davidson, Jane. (2013). Western Mail. February 22.
6.  Davidson, Jane. (2001). The Guardian. October 2.
7.  Davidson, Jane. (2012). Western Mail. February 1-2.

# 11

## Furthering Education

### The fairytale of Wales' Cinderella sector

*A rare success story; colleges in Wales prove their worth by committing to government objectives. But Wales' new skills strategy gets off to a bad start and good intentions begin to unravel*

It attracts fewer headlines and its achievements often go unnoticed. But the fact Wales' college sector managed to stay out of ministers' glare when so many other facets of the nation's education system fell foul of their wrath is testament to its success. Further education's passing reference within these pages to date is testament to its good work and the high esteem in which it is held. But, as sector leader David Jones explained, the role of further education has never been more important. Seen by many as the poor relation of schools and universities, colleges are increasingly emerging from the shadows to drive forward their own agenda. Further education has responded to rapidly changing policy and worked hard to establish its own unique brand of tertiary learning. Colleges are rooted in their communities and with the advent of spiralling university tuition fees, are well-placed to provide a more localised and tailor-made alternative to mainstream higher education. In fact, meeting the needs of individual learners and adapting courses to suit particular wants is one of the sector's foremost selling points.

It may come as a surprise to some that around two-thirds of 16 to 19-year-olds in Wales continue their education at further education colleges. Learners study the Welsh Baccalaureate, A-levels, and work-related and work-based qualifications including NVQs, apprenticeships, technical qualifications and diplomas such as BTECs. Jones spoke in 2011 of his role, as chairman of representative body Colegau Cymru, in raising the profile of further education and challenging misplaced perceptions. The problem, he said, started at the top:

"I don't think there are a very high proportion of school teachers, careers advisers and civil servants in the Welsh education department who have a further education or traditional industry background. Until you get more people involved in these formative roles, perceptions will stay the same. We need more vocational learning role models who are in the positions that make a difference to learners. Further education has an important role to play and we must address these issues."[1] (David Jones, 2011)

Jones, then principal of Deeside College, operating in Flintshire, Denbighshire and Wrexham, said he had seen first-hand the benefits of further education for students of all ages and abilities. But amid fallout from Wales' PISA results, he said colleges were not immune from the drive to improve performance. As standards got better, he said it would be incumbent on colleges to adapt and take their learners to a higher level. But there were more pressing issues afoot and further education lecturers spent too much of their time playing catch-up. Wales' well-documented dearth in key skills transcended the school gates and college leaders spent a lot of time refreshing their new charges with basic literacy and numeracy. There was a knock-on effect and failure to properly educate children at primary and secondary levels would ripple throughout the entire system. Deeside was no different and Jones said "corrective work" – to bring students in line with where they should be on college entry – was hugely frustrating. And he warned there would be no quick-fix, with new policies likely to take as many as four or five years to bear fruit. He said in 2013:

"Some students who come to us don't know they have a problem. We test at the point of entry and very often students will have literacy and numeracy levels a tier below what their GCSEs are saying. For some of them the shortfall is so significant that you have to put on specialist programmes, sometimes as individuals and sometimes within small groups. It's not the easiest thing in the world to say to a 16 or 17-year-old: 'Well actually, you've been in school since the age of four, but 12 or 13 years down the line, you're not going to get a job and you're effectively illiterate."[2] (David Jones, 2013)

Jones said the skills shortage was not a new phenomenon and had been apparent for around 15 years. He said the problem had got progressively worse, however, and warned that, as students' skills improved, staff too would have to raise their own performance to meet new expectations. And he was not alone. Dr John Graystone, chief executive of Colegau Cymru, warned in 2012 that the "shockingly high" number of students studying low-level college courses in Wales was proof that a large proportion of school-leavers needed to go "back to basics". He said every education provider in Wales needed to make increasing high-end enrolments a priority. Figures published that year by the Welsh Government showed enrolments at Level 1 – equivalent to GCSE grades D-G – or below had remained static at around 37% for the previous five years. The proportion entering further education at Level 2 – equivalent to grades A\*-C at GCSE – had fallen by 2% in the same period, though numbers remained high at 34% in 2010-11. Graystone welcomed as "good news" a small rise in the proportion of enrolments at Level 3 and 4 – but said more needed to be done.

> "Everyone above 16 years of age is expected to have achieved the Level 2 benchmark – so to have 40% of enrolments at Level 1 is shockingly high. It indicates that a very large proportion of school-leavers, as well as adults who have long since finished compulsory schooling, need to go back to basics. The focus for Wales as a whole must be to help learners to progress up the education levels."[3] (John Graystone, 2012)

From 2006-07 to 2010-11, the proportion of enrolments at A-level equivalent (Level 3) had risen from 18% to 20% in Wales, while those at degree standard (Level 4) had also gone up marginally. But Jim Bennett, principal of Coleg Gwent, pointed out that even the brightest students had to start at the low end of the scale for certain courses. He said that when a youngster left school at 16, they were not necessarily going on to study academic subjects at college. Nevertheless, Bennett agreed there were "issues" with some students progressing from school into post-16 education, and literacy and numeracy levels were "generally below where they should be". The fact that Wales' further education sector spent so much time worrying about up-skilling its students with basic literacy and numeracy, was yet another indictment of the nation's schools standards. It proved beyond all reasonable doubt that Wales' problems were both chronic and deep-seated.

# College reconfiguration

When it comes to reconfiguration, colleges have been extremely proactive. A feeling that improvements in provision were not consistent across Wales was well understood and a belief that more could be achieved if models were "shared, replicated and modified to meet local circumstances" was the basis for radical structural change. The need to eliminate duplication was paramount and colleges were encouraged to consider formal collaborative measures, including mergers or formal federations, with other further and higher education institutions.

"Notwithstanding the improvements to provider delivery, there is substantial evidence to show that there are too many small sixth-forms and, in a few, areas, too many secondary schools. In addition, there is a large number of further education and work-based training providers in Wales and rationalisation would help strengthen strategic management, improve efficiency and better meet current and future demand for relevant high-quality education and training delivery."[4] (Welsh Assembly Government, 2008)

Andrews, of course, had made no secret of his desire to see colleges, universities and local authorities working together to ensure sustainability and enhance learning. But further education was no stranger to collaboration and a steady flow of high-profile mergers were testament to its ability to think outside the box. In a sense, Andrews was preaching to the converted and college leaders recognised the benefits of pooling expertise. Senior management looked at collaboration as a way of ensuring the future vitality of their colleges. Protecting and improving frontline provision was a focal point for governors who, as unpaid volunteers, many with business acumen, were more open to the idea of merger as a way of strengthening their position. By the end of 2013, there were 16 further education entities (including institutions in the third sector) in Wales, down from 25 in 2006. Together, they delivered around 80% of post-16 qualifications in Wales outside higher education and maintained close relationships with local industry. Few could have predicted the merger of Aberdare and Pontypridd colleges (to become Coleg Morgannwg) in 2003 would set the trend for such a startling overhaul of further education.

A glowing assessment of the sector, published in 2011, included proposals to increase collaboration between providers. The Vivian Thomas review into the structure of education services in Wales recognised mergers that had already taken place but recommended between eight and 12 colleges would best serve the needs of the nation. It called on schools and colleges to work more closely together so learners aged 14-19 were offered greater choice. A separate report, chaired by Open University in Wales director Rob Humphreys, proposed a new system of governance involving an elected board and membership body. Its findings were no great surprise given governance had changed little since colleges became incorporated institutions in 1993. To its credit, the sector responded positively to both reports, with college numbers slashed and several of the nation's institutions piloting Humphreys-style bodies. Resulting boards were both challenging and supportive and were chosen on the basis of the skills, qualities and experience that were deemed most useful to their parent college. The evolution of further education governance brought colleges closer to their communities and ensured learner interests were at the forefront of all strategic decision-making.

Jones, who finalised his third college merger in four years in 2013, warned that Wales' further-education sector could take five years to "settle down" and be held accountable following the ambitious transformation agenda. He said new institutions would take time to find their feet and make the streamlined structure work. Mergers "don't just happen", he said, and they take up a significant amount of time and energy that can go unnoticed. But he was confident the nation's new-look further education system would be stronger than its predecessor and the Welsh Government's collaboration drive was the right one.

"From a college's point of view, we seem to be getting messages from the Welsh Government that once this series of mergers is completed ... then that's it in terms of any plans for merger in the longer term and I think that's right. But what people need to do now is say: 'OK, we've now created, with a voluntary approach, this model of further education and we need some time to make it work for Wales. It's not going to work perfectly in a year or two years, there's no doubt about that, and that's not getting excuses in up-front."[5] (David Jones, 2013)

Jones said numbers of students and staff had a strong bearing on the "weight of responsibility" that an individual institution had. And, working on the basis that every student in higher education brings in around twice the income of the equivalent in further education, colleges were punching well above their weight. Performance continues to exceed expectation and Estyn has been quick to praise the "comprehensive range of academic and vocational programmes" on offer nationally. Standards of teaching are broadly "good" and learner success rates – the proportion of young people that start a qualification in an institution and achieve it by the end of the required period of study – are improving year on year. Supporting figures published by the Welsh Government show the average success rate for further education in Wales has increased from 60% in 2006-07 to 84% in 2012-13. Partnership working is a particular strength and colleges are increasingly adept at strengthening ties with local authorities, schools, employers and the wider community. But it has not always been thus and in her 2004-05 annual report, Estyn's then Chief Inspector Susan Lewis said there were too many sessions with important shortcomings in the "majority of colleges".[6] She said standards varied too much across the sector and too many learners did not complete their courses and gain qualifications.

The rise of further education is one of Wales' real success stories and devolution has been kind to the so-called "Cinderella" sector that is so often pushed to one side. It is, perhaps, ironic that given its burgeoning reputation and willingness to comply with Welsh Government objectives, Wales' further education sector is, at the time of writing, feeling the brunt of central budget cuts. Colleges receive around 80% of their funding from the Welsh Government and are more reliant on the public purse than their colleagues in higher education, which have, by virtue of the nation's tuition fee policy, emerged far more favourably from cost saving measures.

## Literacy and Numeracy Framework

The Literacy and Numeracy Framework (LNF) was the Welsh Government's answer to the nation's skills deficiency. Designed to help teachers monitor pupils' progress against clear annual expectations for all learners aged five to 14, it would become a statutory part of the curriculum for years two to nine from September 2013 and include bespoke reading and numeracy tests. A comprehensive skills package, it represented the Welsh Government's belated response to literacy and numeracy strategies introduced a decade earlier by Michael Barber under Prime Minister Tony Blair. While there are no silver bullets in education, the LNF was a headline invention and Andrews himself described the LNF as a "critical tool" in driving forward school standards. It was his trump card. The principles behind the LNF, especially given Wales' well-documented skills shortage, could not be dismissed but as with anything introduced by government, implementation would be key to its success. Not least because the LNF's predecessor had failed so miserably to address one of Welsh education's perennial problems.

It seems rather sweeping to suggest that getting literacy and numeracy right holds the key to improving classroom standards, but it is surely a solid place at which to start. All good education systems are based on a sound understanding of key skills and the ability to read, write and handle numbers will be high on any employers' wish list. But Wales had been here before and the failure of the Skills Framework (SF) to fulfil what it set out to achieve was not a precursor for success. Launched in 2008, the SF was designed to underpin the national curriculum and help strengthen pupil competency in transferable skills like reading, writing, speaking and listening. But the inspectorate's verdict was less than glowing and despite "good opportunities" to develop key skills across all subjects, Estyn said in 2012 that very few schools had a "coherent and well-planned" approach to their delivery.[7] The framework carried a significant proportion of blame, with teachers paying more attention to the needs of the national curriculum. On reflection, Andrews said its roll-out on a "non-statutory" basis had been a mistake and he admitted certain elements had fallen short of the mark. Put simply, schools had enough on their plate without the burden of a curriculum plan they were not actually required to follow. There was chance, then, to learn from past mistakes.

Suffice to say, the reincarnation made an inauspicious start and the hangover from a series of introductory seminars clouded early positivity. To the Welsh Government's credit and, no doubt, relief, there were few dissenting voices when the LNF was officially launched in May 2012 – just over a year after Andrews' grandstand speech to the National Museum. But all that changed when the LNF bandwagon set off across Wales. School staff, who took time out of the classroom – at considerable cost and inconvenience – to attend, gave the showcase an overwhelming thumbs down. Whispers of discontent had been reverberating around education circles for some time before the extent of teacher dissatisfaction became apparent some weeks later.

A National Support Programme (NSP) to assist schools in implementing the Welsh Government's LNF was unveiled in January 2013 with the promise of an additional £7m funding. Four events, starting at Venue Cymru in Llandudno and culminating in a conference at Chepstow Racecourse, were staged in March across Wales to update teachers on proposals. But teachers reacted angrily to glaring errors in the Welsh language presentation. A series of interactive questions, presented on-screen allowing delegates to respond electronically, did not correspond with their translated answers. Two questions asked teachers if they had seen primary and secondary materials. In response, Welsh-speaking teachers could only answer "yes they were" or "no they weren't". Despite the compere, S4C weatherman Chris Jones, apologising for mistakes in Llandudno, slides were not corrected and were used again at subsequent meetings. Not surprisingly, UCAC said it expected the Welsh Government to employ the same high standards of literacy that it demanded of teachers in the classroom. "It is certainly unfortunate that very basic mistakes were allowed to appear in the Welsh versions of these slides at a national literacy and numeracy conference," it added.

Criticism was compounded when the results of an interactive poll conducted at the end of LNF seminars in Cardiff, Chepstow, Swansea and Llandudno found as many as 80% of delegates were not satisfied with the quality of presentations. As many as 74% said they would not attend similar events in the future. Figures obtained using the Freedom of Information Act revealed just 5% of those present at Venue Cymru thought that presentations were useful and only 5% were satisfied with the event overall. When asked, 44% of respondents at Chepstow Racecourse said "few school staff" understood the LNF and just 4% said they were "very confident" that all teachers could teach its content. One senior delegate feared the seminars had "significantly damaged" headteachers' confidence in the implementation programme. Of course, an unfortunate slip in Welsh language translations did nothing to allay concerns.

Carol Glover, contracts director at CfBT – the consultancy employed by the Welsh Government to deliver supporting NSP events – said timing was an issue. She explained: "We launched the programme quickly in order to coincide with the introduction of the national reading and numeracy tests, and we have already acknowledged that some delegates' expectations were not met as a result of this pace, for which we apologise." True, Berkshire-based CfBT had been awarded the NSP contract in January so it had only a limited amount of time to prepare. But rush through implementation at your peril. Once again, the Welsh Government – albeit it had out-sourced the NSP to a third-party – had fallen woefully short on delivery. Its insistence on introducing the LNF as quickly as possible had put undue pressure on CfBT, which wanted more time to consider how best to launch. Make no mistake, the Welsh Government had contributed significantly to its own downfall.

No sooner had the LNF been formally introduced, that confidence was beginning to evaporate. In fact, it could be said that the NSP never fully recovered from its discouraging debut and the botched job of showcasing the LNF to the teaching profession was a frustration to Andrews, who had been so meticulous in his own planning. The implications were serious; one of his premier educational policies had suffered a serious blow that brought into question its validity long before it had time to bite. That was not to say the damage inflicted on the fledgling LNF by its introductory seminars was not irreparable. But the early signs did not bode well and winning back the trust of teachers would be a priority.

The fact that one of the nation's leading teachers' unions chose to describe the LNF's introduction as an "omni shambles" was indicative of early ill feeling. The NASUWT expressed concern that the LNF would impact on members' "already excessive workloads". Members at the union's 2013 annual conference in Bournemouth approved unanimously a motion calling for an increase in the time teachers were allowed to plan, prepare and assess the LNF. It welcomed the promise of additional funding to administer new reading and numeracy tests, but warned it could escalate its ongoing campaign of industrial action if schools forced teachers into taking an active role in their delivery. Suzanne Nantcurvis, a teacher from Wrexham and a member of NASUWT's National Executive, said moves to "dramatically refocus teaching" would come at a cost. In proposing the LNF motion, she told delegates: "The named word of the year in the Oxford English Dictionary is 'omni shambles'. It refers to a situation which is shambolic from every possible angle. It suggests a badly managed situation which demonstrates a string of blunders and miscalculations. I could use this word to describe the introduction of the LNF."[8]

Regardless of early teething problems, there remained an underlying concern that the framework would be lost among the many other government initiatives that were currently underway in Welsh schools. But Ann Keane, so often a calming voice in Wales' schools system, maintained practitioners should not be alarmed by the plans afoot. She said embedding the LNF across the curriculum "doesn't involve wholesale changes" and "strong leaders" will have already made adjustments. According to Keane, a well-functioning framework was a matter of alignment. This was not, she argued, about asking geography teachers to teach literacy and numeracy in every lesson; but if teachers were using fractions in a subject other than maths, it made sense to be familiar with the maths syllabus. Whatever the expectation on teachers, the LNF would live or die by its reputation as a respected tool in the battle to raise standards.

Despite flaws in the new-look skills framework, Wales was not without hope and the LNF won favour with one of the architects of New Labour's early education policy. Barber said in March 2013 that Wales' school system was "on the move again" and work to drive up standards was paying dividends. He added that developments over the previous two or three years in Wales had been "really impressive". Barber was one of several educationalists invited by the Welsh Government to address teachers, school leaders and council officers at its Raising School Standards Conference in Cardiff. He stressed the importance of setting targets and said the Welsh Government had in place "very clear and very sharp" goals. Barber, an adviser to education ministries across the world, said taking regular "stock takes" within school systems was helpful in gauging performance, while the importance of implementation was often misunderstood. It was a vote of confidence for a department in desperate need of reassurance. But Barber's affirmation about the importance of implementation in government policy only served to reinforce widely-held concerns. He said:

> "One of the most common mistakes that politicians around the world make is this... they think it's 90% getting the policy right and then implementation takes care of itself. Actually, I think it's pretty much the reverse of that. Getting the policy right is only 10% of the task, 90% is making sure it happens in an effective way."[9] (Michael Barber, 2013)

Wales' schools director Chris Tweedale hosted the event and revealed that Barber was first brought in to meet with the Department for Education immediately following Andrews' appointment as minister in December 2009. He said that, under Andrews' direction, Barber "provided quite a lot of challenge" for officials and had since maintained a keen interest in developments this side of the border.

Barber spoke of the need for every child to succeed at school regardless of their background. He said making sure every pupil was "on the agenda" was a feature of the world's best education systems and said there was no reason to assume that children in Wales should achieve anything less than those elsewhere in the world. Speaking at the Cardiff City Stadium, he said there were lessons to be learned from other nations and "global benchmarking" helped gauge performance:

> "We should know that a child at school in Cardiff or London, when we say they are good at maths, would be good at maths in Singapore or Tokyo or Toronto. There is no reason to assume that children in Wales should achieve any lower standards than anybody else, anywhere else in the world."[10] (Michael Barber, 2013)

The best systems in the world, he said, were intent on up-skilling all of their children. But an education system was only as good as its teachers and Barber said recruiting the right people – with good academic qualifications and the right personal characteristics – into the workforce was fundamental to future success.

# Notes

1.    Jones, David. (2011). Western Mail. July 7.
2.    Jones, David. (2013). Western Mail. May 23.
3.    Graystone, John. (2012). Western Mail. April 9.
4.    Welsh Assembly Government. (2008). Transforming Education and Training Provision in Wales. p 7.
5.    Jones, David. (2013). Western Mail. May 23.
6.    Lewis, Susan. (2004-05). Estyn Annual Report. p 66.
7.    Estyn. (2012). The Skills Framework at Key Stage 3; An Evaluation of the Non-Statutory Skills Framework for Three to 19-year-olds at Key Stage 3. p 3.
8.    Nantcurvis, Suzanne. (2013). Western Mail. April 1.
9.    Barber, Michael. (2013). Western Mail. March 21.
10.    Barber, Michael. (2013). Western Mail. March 21.

# 12

## Running Wild

## The enigma of local government and Wales' inspectorate

*The pressing need for reconfiguration becomes apparent. But is there a mandate for reconfiguration and can local authorities retain responsibility for education? Wales' education watchdog was another under justified scrutiny*

In the world of Welsh education, half-term is normally a period of calm before the storm, given the tendency of ministers to research and prepare major policy announcements during recess. And so it proved in February 2013 when Andrews swept back into the spotlight after a week away from the frontline by relighting the fuse on the ticking time bomb of local government. The grip on town halls was tightening and education delivery in its current form – that was, managed and supported by local authorities – looked set for an overhaul. Andrews had given a panel of experts until the end of March to consider whether education was better off in the hands of local or central government. Andrews said local authorities were failing in their responsibility to administer school services effectively and having given them "time and money to get their house in order", had fallen well short of the mark. He said a series of damning inspection reports – conducted by Estyn since September 2010 – had formed the "evidence-base" for his radical school improvement plan. Opening discussion on the future of education delivery was like stirring a hornet's nest and would not have been done lightly. In fact, Bob Wellington, leader of the WLGA, warned that removing education from council control would "fundamentally damage the principle of local democratic control and accountability, and undermine the ability of local communities to shape the educational future of young people".[1]

News that Merthyr Tydfil and Monmouthshire – councils on either end of the social spectrum – had fallen into "special measures" added fuel to the already raging fire. Wales was in the death throes of council-run school services and, while mooted alternatives may have been hard to stomach, even the most ardent of local government champion would recognise the nation could not continue as it was. The evidence was damning and provided Andrews all the ammunition he required to induce radical structural change. The fact of the matter was, special measures – the highest level of support and monitoring – had become all too familiar in Wales and four other councils – Blaenau Gwent, Anglesey, Torfaen and Pembrokeshire – had been tarred with the same brush. Andrews' bullish reaction was to be expected. He said "Wales can't stay with 22 under-performing local education authorities", and a lack of capacity within Welsh councils was holding the nation back. Strong words – but not without substance.

Andrews laid a significant chunk of the blame for the "dissipating" experience in school services on the fragmentation of local authorities in the mid-1990s. True, there was political motivation behind his reasoning (Conservative MP John Redwood's brief and now infamous tenure as Welsh Secretary did not amount to nothing), but you would have done well to find anyone within the sector who believed the current set-up was working. Andrews was right to assert that some smaller Welsh councils suffered from a lack of capacity and many lacked the understanding needed to oversee wholesale change. This was one situation in which "critical mass" really did make a difference, with smaller education services apparently unable to provide the requisite support to schools. It was not that they did not want to, it was that they did not have the level of expertise to drive strategic improvement.

It was no coincidence that many of Wales' councils looked to England for inspiration, with several directors of education – the majority experienced in working in deprived areas – parachuted in from across the border. While the Welsh Government developed policy, town halls had the final say over which school had what and an upturn in performance hinged largely on their ability to support headteachers on the frontline. But for all the rhetoric, Andrews had little to show for his three-year war on local government. Regional consortia, developed tentatively prior to the minister's arrival in December 2009, were not the answer. Council leaders had been given ample time to separate the wheat from the chaff and desperate times called for desperate measures. That said, establishing a national framework for regional working would have at least ensured consistency across the piece and allowing local authorities the freedom to develop their own bespoke consortia was something the minister would later regret.

# Blaenau Gwent

Blaenau Gwent personified all that was wrong with locally-run education services. The first council in Wales to require special measures, Estyn said in May 2011 that children and young people in Blaenau Gwent did not make good enough progress and standards were "well below" expected levels. Support for school improvement and additional learning needs was considered "unsatisfactory" and the "systemic failure of management" had resulted in the authority providing poor value for money – hardly surprisingly given Blaenau Gwent's relatively high education expenditure. The authority, accused by the inspectorate of not knowing all of its schools well enough, promised an urgent response and accepted a "step-change" was needed to improve standards. But the step-change was not forthcoming. Fast-forward 18 months and the outlook remained shockingly bleak. Returning to the authority in January 2013, inspectors cast doubt on Blaenau Gwent's ability to improve without "continued external support". They said provision remained "unsatisfactory" and recommended the council stayed in special measures.

There are a few points worth noting from Estyn's re-inspection of Blaenau Gwent. Consider first its observation that pupil attainment was still painfully short of what was expected. Blaenau Gwent laid claim to Wales' highest proportion of learners eligible for free school meals, but even when deprivation was taken into account, performance was still well below average. On this occasion, funding was no excuse. The council spent more than most on education, yet too many pupils were leaving school desperately short of basic skills. Huge improvements would not, however, materialise at the click of a teacher's finger and change on the scale of that required in Blaenau Gwent would take time. Eighteen months from May 2011 only really gave those responsible the summer exams of 2012 to make a difference. You could, therefore, forgive the authority for not making significant gains in what was a relatively short period of time. What was harder to forgive, however, was Blaenau Gwent's inadequate direction and "unsatisfactory" leadership. Estyn said council officers, managers and school leaders had not been held to account for their performance. They said leadership of education services was "unstable" and, most damning of all, a "lack of capacity and competence" in key roles at all levels hampered progress.

True, there had been some improvements and elected members were becoming more adept at scrutinising what went on in Blaenau Gwent schools. But, said inspectors, reports from officers often lacked necessary information. Put simply, Blaenau Gwent's education services were rudderless. How could they expect schools to improve when they could not get their own house in order? Local authority support was crucial and, inevitably, problems at the top would filter down. The Welsh Government's chosen remedy was the appointment of "education commissioners". But while inspectors said in 2013 that they had helped facilitate "recent progress", serious issues remained. It is important to note that Estyn's criticism of direction at Blaenau Gwent was not unique and a separate report by the WAO bemoaned "long-standing cultural, performance and leadership problems"[2] at the authority. There had been some improvements since Estyn first visited two years earlier, but a rise in primary school attendance – mirrored across the rest of Wales – was of scant consolation for parents.

## Pembrokeshire

So what next for council-run education services? Blaenau Gwent proved that special measures can only have a limited effect and there are only so many times you can rearrange the deckchairs. And, of course, Blaenau Gwent was not alone. Five other authorities had been deemed "unsatisfactory" by Estyn and since the launch of its new inspection framework in 2010, only five were considered "good" and just Ceredigion was graded "excellent". Blaenau Gwent's re-inspection was more power to the elbow of ministers and proved significant change was necessary. Too many education services in Wales had proven themselves beyond help and poor standards was not the only risk to children. Pembrokeshire council's propensity to put the good reputation of education professionals before its duty to safeguard children was described as "deeply disturbing" by Wales' Children's Commissioner Keith Towler. A report published in August 2011 by Estyn and the Care and Social Services Inspectorate Wales (CSSIW), revealed Pembrokeshire council's shocking failure to manage allegations of child abuse in schools.

The report investigated 25 cases of allegations of child abuse in the county's education services by professionals, ranging from headteachers to youth workers, between April 2007 and March 2011. It reviewed 14 cases more closely and found that almost half referred to more than one child and 35% involved children with additional learning needs. Two of the cases – one in a primary school, the other in a secondary – were treated under "organised or multiple-abuse" procedures, where there may have been more than one abuser or where an individual may have groomed children for abuse. The report found that in three cases a decision was taken not to suspend the accused, despite views of social services and the police to the contrary. In two cases, the authority decided to assign the accused to different duties in another location rather than suspend them, leaving them in a position of authority and trust. In half of the cases, there was no evidence parents had been given full information about an allegation. Furthermore, the report found that of the 642 staff who were identified as working with children in the summer season of 2011, 18 were found not to have an active CRB check and 41 were not found to have required written references. Of the 41, eight had only one reference and the remaining 33 had no reference at all. It meant that 9.2% of staff working with children for the summer either did not have a CRB check or written references in place.

A ministerial board was set up in October 2011 to help the troubled council overcome failings in its child protection procedures. But progress was slow and despite the seriousness of allegations made against the authority, ministers felt it necessary in June 2012 – almost a year after the CSSIW and Estyn had brought Pembrokeshire's shortcomings to light – to write to council leaders expressing their "continuing grave concerns" over safeguarding issues. In a fresh development, they hinted that other safeguarding matters had come to light and the ministerial board had found that at least 18 school rooms were being used to incarcerate children for "time out" purposes. They said the authority's education service had failed to disclose their existence and an allegation about a teacher tying a child's hands behind his back had been made since the report.

As well as being completely unsettling, there was something archaic about revelations in Pembrokeshire. How local government officials could take such a laid-back and apparently apathetic approach to issues of pupil wellbeing and child safety – least not in this, the twenty-first century – was difficult to comprehend. One suspects the subsequent high turnover of staff was essential given the unacceptable levels of service in the region. But if we accept that relative incapacity is an issue in Wales, it is important to note that deficiencies transcended smaller councils and the likes of Cardiff and Swansea were by no means shining lights either. Interestingly, Cardiff's new director of education Nick Batchelar, who joined the authority from Bristol Council in August 2013, suggested some time after the city's inspection in 2011 that Estyn had looked too favourably on its performance. Batchelar said in January 2014 that the inspectorate, which deemed Cardiff's education service "adequate" three years earlier, had "compounded rather than assisted" the tackling of certain problems.[3] It was a remarkable admission, but one not without substance.

Pressure was mounting and you felt certain that something had to change. There could be no more tinkering around the edges and if the current system was failing Welsh children, policymakers had to take stronger action to make it work. Too many education services in Wales had proven themselves beyond help and not even the belated introduction, in April 2014, of a new national framework for regional working could allay school improvement fears. Given local government's obvious inadequacies, it came as a surprise to many that directors of education in Wales were being so well remunerated. Councils were criticised in September 2013 for paying senior education officers large sums of money amid mounting evidence of poor standards. The fact it came as changes introduced by the Westminster Government saw teachers' pay linked to performance in the classroom – with schools themselves setting salaries – only served to compound matters. Since launching its new inspection framework, Estyn had deemed that only seven councils had "good" or better leadership. Philip Dixon said teachers and parents would be "stunned" by some of the salaries being pocketed, adding:

> "There seems to be no rhyme or reason as to the variation in what is being paid. It does not seem to be done on responsibility for the number of schools, nor on the number of pupils. And it clearly bears absolutely no relation to the achievement of the authority as shown in its Estyn grading. The performance of teachers and heads is rigorously examined. The same sort of scrutiny needs to be visited on those who run local education services."[4] (Philip Dixon, 2013)

Data compiled using the Freedom of Information Act highlighted the variation between the salaries of directors of education, ranging from £61,476 in Pembrokeshire to £120,000 in Cardiff. Councils whose leadership was considered "unsatisfactory" paid education leaders as much as £98,581 a year for their services. Leadership of Denbighshire's education services was considered among the best in Wales and was ranked "excellent" after a remarkable turnaround in fortunes. In its 2012 report, Estyn said relationships with schools had improved significantly since Denbighshire's previous inspection in 2007, which found education provision "unsatisfactory". Karen Evans, a former headteacher who started as Denbighshire's new head of school improvement and inclusion in 2010, was paid a relatively meagre £74,771 a year. Evans had responsibility for 57 schools and 15,630 pupils. By comparison, Hilary Anthony, who presided over 62 schools and 22,480 pupils in Bridgend prior to her retirement, received an annual salary of £104,068. But Bridgend's education services and leadership were deemed only "adequate" by inspectors in 2012.

Andrews had ample ammunition to force through radical structural change long before the publication of Robert Hill's review of education delivery in June 2013. A former policy adviser to Prime Minister Tony Blair, Hill's broad experience of public services and understanding of government was appealing to Andrews, who asked officials to research the consultant's credentials and suitability. A meeting between the pair was held on December 11, 2012, and Hill was appointed to conduct the minister's review shortly after. The subsequent report was arguably one of the most significant ever to fall on the desks of Welsh ministers. Andrews said:

"This review is fundamental to the success of our education system. I have said repeatedly I would not have invented 22 local education authorities, and that the fragmentation of education authorities in the mid-1990s was one of the contributing factors for the downturn in performance a decade later, as effective challenge and support was lost in many parts of the system and time, energy and resource was dissipated. This is the opportunity to get things right."[5] (Leighton Andrews, 2013)

Hill's report was radical in the extreme and it had major implications for the future of local government in Wales. But council leaders could not say they did not see it coming. Andrews had been on the warpath for years and with so many council education services in special measures, he had a mandate for change. Headline recommendations included transferring some statutory local authority education functions to Wales' four regional consortia. If approved, the move would effectively cut out the layer of accountability provided by local authority education services and make consortia directly answerable to elected members on matters of school improvement. Hill also suggested reducing the number of local education authorities in Wales by a third by April 2014. But with summer recess on the horizon and so little time after the report's publication, Hill's preferred pace of change was always highly unlikely.

One thing was for certain – Hill's proposals hinged on regional consortia rising to the challenge. The South-East Wales cluster, although in its infancy, appeared the yardstick for others to follow. Hill said the Education Achievement Service (EAS) – consisting of Blaenau Gwent, Caerphilly, Monmouthshire, Newport and Torfaen councils – had a "clear structure" and was "developing well". Hailing the consortium's strong partnership with school leaders, he said: "It's still very much a work in progress but it is doing the right things. Others have got their differing strengths and weaknesses – but we need to get them all to that sort of level." True, talk of restructuring education services was always going to attract the most headlines. But Hill's wide-ranging review put forward 85 options in a comprehensive analysis considering all facets of delivery. Frontline teaching and learning did not go unnoticed and mooted changes at classroom level had potential to go a long way. Lead practitioner departments, stronger emphasis on leadership and the scope for more networking between schools were all welcome developments. A suggestion that Wales could introduce a "Co-operative Trust Model" – giving parents, learners, staff and community organisations a stake in the running of their schools – was one of the only contentious issues, given its similarities with the hugely unpopular "academy" approach being modelled in England. Hill's review opened several doors and time would tell through which the Welsh Government chose to walk.

## Estyn's judgement

As Chief Inspector of Education and Training in Wales, Ann Keane was well-placed to judge exactly where the nation's schools system stood – and indeed, how far it had still to travel. So when Keane admitted in April 2013 to being "frustrated" by the pace of improvement in Welsh classrooms, the sector pricked up its collective ears. This was one opinion that definitely did matter and Keane's frustrations could not be waved away or ignored. Keane said levels of literacy and numeracy remained a "major issue" in Welsh schools and inspectors were not picking up the "systemic improvements" she wanted to see. Keane, who had now been in post for three years, warned that education was "a big ship that will take time to turn around" and parents may have to wait before dramatic changes begin to surface. A full two years after Andrews' call to arms, it was not what the Welsh Government wanted to hear. There was little doubt that the minister himself knew acutely the extent of the task in hand. But for those clinging to the hope that Wales would make a miraculous short-term recovery, it was a crippling reality check. And it was not made lightly. Keane urged caution:

> "The initiatives that are supposed to shift the direction of things in schools are only just emerging. The NSP hasn't started properly and the LNF only becomes statutory in September. It's frustrating for me because I want to see standards improving and I want our inspections to be reflecting that improvement – but when I think about the fact these initiatives will not actually be having an impact until September onward, I can understand that this is a big ship and it's going to take a while to turn it around."[6] (Ann Keane, 2013)

But Keane was not without hope. She said there was at least "more power in the engine room" and new regional consortia "have an energy and a focus" which boded well for the future. So too did she have faith in measures put in place by the Welsh Government. She maintained that Wales had the ability to create a "world-class" education system – but there was significant work to be done and still a long road down which to travel.

Reflecting, Keane pinned some of the blame for Wales' plight onto the nation's local authorities, which had fallen spectacularly short of the mark in Estyn inspections. Keane said there were "issues of capacity and capability" with regards to Welsh councils and, in many cases, elected members did not play a strong enough role in driving school improvement. She said she agreed with the notion that there were "too many" local authorities in Wales and drew comparison with the nation's versatile college sector. She pointed to the many mergers to have taken place because "smaller colleges struggled to cover all functions with an in-depth level of expertise" – but warned that "restructuring will not solve all the problems" facing Welsh education. She said:

"A lot of the ones (councils) that are in category – Merthyr, Monmouthshire, Blaenau Gwent and Anglesey – are small. When we went in them, we were finding the number of officials devoted to educational services was very small – so you have no economies of scale. What you have is one official that has a bigger span of responsibility than another official in a larger authority. When you don't have economies of scale, you get a wider span of responsibility and a more superficial response to the issues they face and none of the depth of expertise that you can have if you are a bigger unit."[7] (Ann Keane, 2013)

Writing in her third annual report, Keane said 48% of primary schools and 54% of secondary schools required a follow-up visit in 2011-12, with inspectors returning later to consider whether sufficient improvements had been made. She said more than half of all primary and secondary schools needed to achieve better standards of literacy and standards of writing were a particular concern, with some pupils not given enough opportunity to write independently in different styles and for different purposes. Overall, there were fewer schools awarded "good" or "excellent" judgements in 2011-12 and nearly half of those inspected required a follow-up visit. Keane outlined the traits linking schools in need of more support in a column for the *Western Mail*:

"Schools that need follow-up by Estyn – and, to a lesser extent by local authorities – tend to have some characteristics in common. Outcomes for some, if not all, groups of pupils will be weak. Teachers will not be providing enough challenge for pupils in lessons and expectations of pupils will be too low and undifferentiated. The progress that pupils should make in literacy and numeracy will be limited. Planning and assessment practices across the school will not be co-ordinated well. The leadership in the school is likely to have some significant shortcomings and governors will rarely challenge performance in depth. Self-evaluation will be sporadic and superficial and will not be used to inform school development plans."[8] (Ann Keane, 2012)

Keane said she was pleased to report that few schools stayed in categories causing concern for very long. Most of them, she said, came out of category within two years. But having warned that schools must do more to address "mediocre teaching performance" and inconsistencies between classes, she maintained it was not for Estyn to tell headteachers what to do.

Keane's surprise attack on school leaders was a welcome aside to the then customary assault on key skills; Wales' long-standing deficiencies in literacy and numeracy had, of course, been extremely well-documented, not least by Keane herself. Laying blame at the classroom door, on the other hand, had long been taboo for educationalists and few had been prepared to stick their heads above the parapet. Nevertheless, the critical eye of an objective inspectorate would be vital to ironing out the inadequacies of the nation's schools system and, to a certain extent, Keane was only peddling what was well known already. But was all as it seemed at first glance, and were there ulterior motives? Conspiracy theorists argue Estyn was not as "arm's-length" from government as it would have us believe. By its own admission, areas identified by Keane as needing attention – namely literacy, numeracy and school leadership – "mirror" government priorities and were "at the forefront of what we're working hard to deliver". Some were of the impression Keane was employed simply to do the minister's dirty work.

The NASUWT made its feelings known at its annual Welsh conference in November 2013, declaring that Estyn had lost credibility and the respect of teachers. Delegates at the conference, held in Llandudno, heard that Estyn was no longer perceived to be an independent body and was "so aligned with the political system that it is failing in its core principles of providing an independent, high-quality inspection and advice service". Rex Phillips, NASUWT Wales organiser, said: "If Estyn is to regain the trust of the teaching profession, the inspectorate must do more to demonstrate that it has not become an arm of government. Special measures may be needed if the inspectorate continues to allow itself to be compromised." Keane was said to spend an awful lot of time in the corridors of the Welsh Government, though you would have worried if she had not. With 30 years' experience, Keane had been immersed in Welsh education longer than most and if the minister wanted a guide, she would have a significant claim. It helped that Keane and Andrews had a good working relationship and a mutual respect for each other as professionals. The same is not always true for ministers and their chief inspectors.

## Estyn toughens its stance

Since its introduction in September 2010, Estyn's new inspection framework had found a significantly higher number of schools requiring extra help. In fact, Keane said the number of schools requiring closer monitoring and follow-up visits during its latest six-year inspection cycle had been higher than expected. It is a poorly-kept secret that the nation's schools inspectorate toughened up on Andrews' watch and there was no doubt Estyn's gloomy outlook gave weight to the minister's mandate for change. Keane herself had admitted there was once a "complacency" about Estyn's work that contributed to a slide in school standards. She said scrutiny of the nation's schools had lacked rigour and the inspectorate was not "above or outside" criticism. Her assertion that – "if you want to blame somebody, then we are in there as well" – was refreshingly honest. Yet for a publicly-funded organisation that had afforded its staff steady salary increases, it did not sit comfortably.

> "We have to be honest and say that Estyn was part of the complacency that affected the education sector. I don't put Estyn above or outside that and if you want to blame somebody, then we are in there as well. There was a complacency about our inspections of local authorities in the past and we were not sharp enough. We are now more robust and rigorous and we focus much more strongly on outcomes for learners and how local authorities get to grips with improving those outcomes. That is the big focus of our inspections now and we're also more rigorous in the schools themselves."[9] (Ann Keane, 2012)

It was perhaps inevitable that Estyn was accused of "rewarding failure" after it emerged more than half of the inspectorate's 113 staff earned more than £50,000. Keane, meanwhile, was remunerated with a salary higher than those whom she replaced. Figures released using the Freedom of Information Act showed Estyn's Chief Inspector received a salary in the bracket "£100,000 to £105,000" in 2010-11. A year earlier in 2009-10, Keane's predecessor was awarded "£95,000 to £100,000". Overall, the inspectorate – which is independent of but funded by the Welsh Government – spent £7.3m on its 113 staff in 2010-11. The figure, which was equivalent to £65,150 per person, was significantly higher than the average spend in 2006-07, when 115 staff cost Estyn just £6.6m. In total, Estyn received £13m from the Welsh Government in 2010-11 and, as of April 2012, there were 58 members of staff earning more than £50,000 a year. The Tax Payers' Alliance said the revelations were "infuriating" and "pay and other rewards should be commensurate with results". Keane's earlier admission – that the nation's inspectorate was complicit in nurturing a culture of complacency – raised a number of questions far more serious than pay and remuneration.

Estyn's new inspection framework placed greater emphasis on key skills and supported more joined-up working across different sectors. Subsequent reports were proof the inspectorate had toughened its stance. But while some believe the timing of Estyn's mutation from sheep to wolf was too much of a coincidence, the makings of a new six-year inspection framework pre-dated Andrews and sector leaders agreed that Estyn was, at long last, on the right track. Having waited so long for an efficient and fully functioning inspectorate, one would have expected the Welsh Government to assume little more than a watching brief. It was a surprise, therefore, when Estyn was asked in 2013 to consider judging schools on their ability to support pupils from deprived backgrounds. The Welsh Government saw fit to add to Estyn's workload as part of its bid to break the link between poverty and low attainment. Later, in March 2014, campaign group Chwarae Teg suggested Estyn begin assessing how well schools challenge gender stereotypes in the classroom. After such a sustained period of inadequacy, anything to jeopardise the inspectorate's newfound stability was perhaps better avoided.

So what does one take from Estyn's scrutiny of education services? On the face of it, it is not the quality of inspections today but the dubious quality of those that went before that are most questionable. Keane's assertion that Estyn is "now more robust and rigorous" is as plain an admission of guilt as you are likely to get. It is inexplicable how many schools and local authorities have gone from performing relatively well with little or no cause for concern – to returning inspection reports so bad they are in need of life support. Playing devil's advocate, there is every reason to doubt the validity of some of Estyn's findings in the mid to late 2000s. That is not to say all education providers inspected in the past decade were looked upon too favourably, but one questions whether standards can slide so dramatically in such a relatively short space of time. When asked, Keane dismissed suggestions earlier Estyn reports were not credible:

> "I think it's fair to say, if you look at the raw statistics, that overall it's harder to get 'good' or 'excellent' judgements now than maybe it was in the last cycle... we've re-calibrated and it is a more rigorous framework. But broadly speaking, if you've got a grade one in the last cycle and you've got the same leadership, you're not going to be 'unsatisfactory' in this cycle. It's very unusual for drastic drops and if you were top of the pile, unless there's been a complete disaster in a school, you're going to be doing OK."[10] (Ann Keane, 2013)

Keane said that while the scale for ranking schools was different, those that had shifted up and down had done so proportionately. She accepted that primary schools given top marks in their previous inspection may not have been so fortunate under the current regime – but said reports had not been re-calibrated to the extent that results were "shockingly different". As an indicator, if a school got an "excellent" in its last inspection cycle, Keane said they were still likely to be at least "good". She added:

> "You don't want to frighten parents into thinking that what Estyn said in 2006 was completely off the wall and is no indicator to what the

school is like now. If the same head's there, the likelihood is it's still going to be a good school."[11] (Ann Keane, 2013)

However significant one considers Estyn's change in tack, inflationary school assessments would have given headteachers across Wales the impression they were performing better than they actually were. Keane spoiled the illusion by pursuing a more rigorous inspection framework, but the damage had already been done and many schools were given the freedom to coast. That is not to say everyone was satisfied with the watchdog under its new Chief Inspector.

In Cardiff, Batchelar's concerns appeared vindicated when the authority was deemed as requiring "significant improvement" following a monitoring visit in February 2014. Estyn said the city council had not made enough progress in the three years since its last major inspection and it would be increasing the level of follow-up activity required in the Welsh capital. Inspectors said standards in Cardiff schools had not progressed sufficiently and there were concerns about primary provision as well as secondary. They said changes in senior leadership had impacted on continuity and pace of change and most outcomes for children and young people had not improved well enough. Estyn's intervention meant Cardiff's education services were dangerously close to requiring special measures, but the city's plight did not come as a surprise to many and education in Cardiff had been a concern for some time. Reflecting on Estyn's report, Batchelar said: "For so long the reality of the situation had not been properly identified and people thought things were better than they were. The system didn't recognise it had a problem because it was told it was adequate and it thought adequate was alright."[12]

Cardiff was the first council in Wales to be looked upon using Estyn's new inspection framework and there was a strong suggestion it may have got off lightly. The fact the authority had failed to improve sufficiently in the three years until its next major report seems to support that argument. It is entirely plausible that Cardiff was given a reprieve because inspectors had not yet calibrated its new marking system. We know that Estyn had toughened up its regime but with nothing to compare against, there is every chance it looked too favourably upon Wales' capital city. But those of a more cynical disposition will say that is precisely why Cardiff escaped without the embarrassment of special measures. The reputational damage Cardiff's plight could inflict on the nation as a whole was an extremely high price to pay for the shortcomings within its education services. The Welsh Government would take no pride in watching the Welsh capital fail. Looking back in 2014, Andrews acknowledged that tackling the areas where failing schools were concentrated – "notably the two biggest local authorities of Cardiff and Rhondda Cynon Taf" – could make a significant difference to GCSE performance.[13]

The volatility in Estyn's inspections is perfectly encapsulated in the following table of local authority judgements. A change in Estyn's marking system makes direct comparisons difficult, but if we assume the strategic management of education services to be of paramount importance – support mechanisms are unlikely to operate without due direction – significant conclusions can be drawn. Under the earlier inspection framework, a local authority's performance in discharging its responsibilities was rated on a four-point scale from "good with outstanding features" to "shortcomings in important areas". Nowadays, inspectors rate on a four-point scale of "excellent", "good", "adequate" or "unsatisfactory". The marked difference in performance from one inspection cycle to the next speaks volumes. Not one local authority was graded the lowest rung on the ladder for strategic management between 2004-10. True, there will be mitigating factors and it is not unprecedented for well-oiled systems to break down over time. But it is hard to imagine so many Welsh councils deteriorating over such a short period and there is every chance they too had been looked upon with rose-tinted spectacles.

**Table 4 Local authority education services: Estyn judgements 2004-2016**

| Local authority | Strategic Management: 2004-10 | Current Provision: 2010-16 |
|---|---|---|
| Anglesey | Good features outweigh shortcomings | Unsatisfactory |
| Blaenau Gwent | Good features outweigh shortcomings | Unsatisfactory |
| Bridgend | Good features and no important shortcomings | Adequate |
| Caerphilly | Good features outweigh shortcomings | Adequate |
| Cardiff | Good features outweigh shortcomings | Adequate |
| Carmarthenshire | Good features and no important shortcomings | Good |
| Ceredigion | Good features and no important shortcomings | Excellent |
| Conwy | Good features and no important shortcomings | Good |

**Table 4** *Continued*

| Local authority | Strategic Management: 2004-10 | Current Provision: 2010-16 |
|---|---|---|
| Denbighshire | Good features outweigh shortcomings | Good |
| Flintshire | Good features outweigh shortcomings | Adequate |
| Gwynedd | Good features outweigh shortcomings | Adequate |
| Merthyr Tydfil | Good features and no important shortcomings | Unsatisfactory |
| Monmouthshire | Good features outweigh shortcomings | Unsatisfactory |
| Neath Port Talbot | Good features and no important shortcomings | Good |
| Newport | Good with outstanding features | Good |
| Pembrokeshire | Good with outstanding features | Unsatisfactory |
| Powys | Good features outweigh shortcomings | Adequate |
| Rhondda Cynon Taf | Good (inspected using new-style report) | Adequate |
| Swansea | Good features and no important shortcomings | Good |
| Torfaen | Good features outweigh shortcomings | Adequate |
| Vale of Glamorgan | Good (inspected using new-style report) | Adequate |
| Wrexham | Good features and no important shortcomings | Adequate |

SOURCE: Estyn

Allied to the idea that some in Wales may have been operating under false pretences, Estyn's generous school notice period is worth considering. Schools and other education and training providers are given four weeks' written notice of an inspection, with the exception of local authorities which receive 12 weeks' notice. There is a strong argument to suggest legislation should be changed so providers cannot predict when their next inspection is due. It seems entirely appropriate that schools are inspected as they appear day-to-day. Visitors need to see a school as it operates in real-life, so as to highlight its limitations and flag requisite support. For schools to dress themselves up as something they are not would be to defy the object. There is nothing to gain, in the longer-term at least, from concealing flaws and thereby contaminating evidence. For example, it is not uncommon in Wales for struggling schools to parachute in staff especially for forthcoming inspections. Superficial window-dressing is like revising the night before an exam – you will get found out in the end and if schools are given licence to paper over cracks, they will only serve to deny their pupils. Conversely, the idea of inspectors calling in unannounced will be enough to keep some teachers awake at night. A decision by England's education watchdog Ofsted to introduce "no-notice" inspections was not, it is fair to say, inspired by a desire to reduce anxieties. There is a balance between observing schools in situ and causing unnecessary panic to be struck. In future, there is every chance Estyn will be able to dictate what notice it gives schools of an impending inspection and, provided their newfound powers are not abused, the discretion should be no bad thing.

News that Keane would not be extending her run as Chief Inspector beyond the expiration of her five-year contract in 2015 was considered a blow to Welsh education. Keane's independent thought and measured approach to challenging situations won her the respect of sector leaders and her vast experience would be difficult to replace.

# Notes

1.  Wellington, Bob. (2012). Western Mail. November 20.
2.  WAO. (2013). Annual Improvement Report: Blaenau Gwent County Borough Council. p 3.
3.  Batchelar, Nick. (2014). South Wales Echo. January 14.
4.  Dixon, Philip. (2013). Western Mail. September 25.
5.  Andrews, Leighton. (2013). Oral statement. January 22.
6.  Keane, Ann. (2013). Western Mail. May 7.
7.  Keane, Ann. (2013). Western Mail. May 7.
8.  Keane, Ann. (2012). Western Mail. April 26.
9.  Keane, Ann. (2012). Western Mail. March 24.
10. Keane, Ann. (2013). Western Mail. May 16.
11. Keane, Ann. (2013). Western Mail. May 16.
12. Batchelar, Nick. (2014). South Wales Echo. March 28.
13. Andrews, Leighton. (2014). Ministering to Education. p 112.

# 13

## Out Of The Blue

## The Cabinet creaks after a row over school places

*A shocking end to an equally shocking reign as Andrews walks out under a cloud. Who would step into his shoes and what would await Wales' newly-appointed Education Minister?*

When Andrews and his Welsh Government colleagues were summoned into Cathays Park on March 14, 2013, the sector held its breath. For months, speculation had been rife that the tough-talking Rhondda AM would be central to a Cabinet reshuffle and the wait was almost over. There were all sorts of jobs rumoured to be lined up – business or finance were front-runners, while tips at the turn of the year had Andrews down as Wales' first "Chancellor". The permutations appeared endless but all the while there remained a nagging spanner in the works. What would become of education? There are few things more important than improving the life chances of young people and given the limited pool from which to choose, empowering the wrong AM could undo all of what the Welsh Government had set out to achieve. Deficiencies in the Welsh education system were well-documented and a boost in standards was essential while the economy and jobs market continued to struggle. Getting the right person into the hot seat would be crucial to Wales' economic prosperity and the Welsh Government's decision to break its new hierarchy online – via social networking site Twitter – only served served to fuel apprehension.

Andrews himself was braced for a change. The ministerial shake-up had been mooted for some time and there appeared every chance he would be moved up the pecking order. But given the challenge still facing education in Wales, there were only a handful of jobs suitably demanding for a man of Andrews' undoubted intellect. Either way, the minister made a conscious effort to clear his desk ready to hand over the reigns. Everything overhanging was set in train and or resolved to the point where someone else coming in would be able to do so seamlessly. When the reshuffle was finally announced, the fall of Health Minister Lesley Griffiths set the cat amongst the pigeons, although her departure was no real surprise given her tumultuous term in office. The fact she was axed so soon after her appointment suggested there may be other casualties and the Wrexham AM had, in fact, been one of those tipped for the education portfolio were Andrews' relieved of his duties. As it was, Edwina Hart's retention of the economic brief all but sealed his fate.

"Bad luck, I'm back," said Andrews to reporters outside Welsh Government headquarters in Cardiff's Civic Centre. It was a provocative turn of phrase and not one to warm the hearts of his critics. The minister's popularity within the teaching profession had soured and the pace of change was proving too fast for many. Then again, Andrews was working to a deadline and the nation's education system had no time to waste if his target – of a place in the world's top 20 by 2015 – was to be realised. Andrews' re-appointment as Education Minister was always going to be divisive, but the sector craved stability and those at a policy-level welcomed his chance to see through what he had started. With so many plates still spinning, there was always the possibility that a change at the top could bring every new initiative crashing back down. The building blocks were in place and, like or loath him, there appeared no pressing need to rock the boat. Andrews himself had unfinished business. The small matter of Wales' qualifications system was perhaps highest on his list of priorities and while the sector was settled on retaining GCSEs and A-levels, there remained several unanswered questions. The future of the WJEC was still shrouded in uncertainty and Qualifications Wales was little more than an ideal. Establishing an organisation to award and regulate a new suite of Wales-specific qualifications remained a formidable body of work and there continued to be serious doubts over the Department for Education's capacity to raise standards.

But the relative calm would not last long and a frantic period of change was set in motion two months later when Chris Tweedale announced his resignation as the Welsh Government's schools director after four years in post. A former secondary school headteacher, Tweedale was a senior civil servant at the Department for Education in England prior to moving west shortly before Andrews' appointment in January 2009. He became Andrews' right-hand man and, as a senior adviser on schools policy, was responsible for delivering much of the minister's 20 point plan. Nevertheless, Tweedale's decision to leave the Welsh Government in May 2013 was not unexpected, given he had been overlooked for the position of Director General of Education twice – both Emyr Roberts and later, Owen Evans, having been selected ahead of him. In a letter to Permanent Secretary Derek Jones confirming his departure, Tweedale hinted that the job he would be leaving was very different to the one he had begun. He said:

> "In that time we have shown that the young people of Wales have needed more support from their teachers and schools. We have also come to terms with the fact that our school system has needed major and far reaching reform."[1] (Chris Tweedale, 2013)

Tweedale said corrective measures were in their "delivery phase" and Wales was already seeing measurable improvements at school level. He said the Welsh Government had put more challenge and support into the system and been able to build a high quality team of civil servants and seconded practitioners who had the confidence of both the minister and education professionals. But his assertion that Wales' schools system had required "major and far reaching reform" proved beyond all doubt the extent of the challenge that had faced practitioners upon his arrival. Tweedale's personal account serves to reinforce the view that Wales' education system was not functioning properly – and had not been for some time.

The resignation of Tweedale meant the department would soon have three new directors in post. Evans, a man of little experience in education policy and with a career spent largely in the private sector, had only been promoted to the role of Director General a short while earlier in December, while Professor Huw Morris, his successor as Director for Skills, Higher Education and Lifelong Learning, had yet to fill the void. The acting deputy vice-chancellor of the University of Salford, Morris had spent his entire career in academia and was not due to take up his new post until September. The high turnover of senior management was a concern to unions, who considered changes in personnel an unwelcome distraction during what was a critical period for education in Wales. With a host of new initiatives in the pipeline, they feared too much "churn" could prove damaging. Philip Dixon said "musical chairs" at the top of the department was unhelpful and schools would be concerned about stability and strategic direction. He went on:

> "The roll-out of the LNF is now at a crucial stage, and reviews of teacher training and the delivery of education services are imminent, so we could do without any new 'cunning plans' being dreamt up by incoming bureaucrats. It is vital that Mr Tweedale's successor has an in-depth knowledge and experience of schools, and also commands the respect of the sector. With the spectre of PISA looming, the department will have to convince other stakeholders that it really does know what it is doing."[2] (Philip Dixon, 2013)

The Welsh Government passed off unions' apprehension as "nonsense", adding that the minister – now a veteran of some three and a half years in post – provided "strong leadership for the department as a whole".[3] It was an unfortunate response to what many in the sector considered to be very genuine fears for a department lacking in experience. However, it would not be long before their concerns would take on a whole new level. The revolving door of Wales' education system would swing wide open just a month later with what was arguably the biggest shock in Welsh politics for a decade.

## Andrews leaves the Welsh Government

The events of June 25, 2013, came as a complete surprise and attracted headlines across the UK. Not one to go quietly, Andrews left the Welsh Government dramatically after First Minister Carwyn Jones told him he had broken the Ministerial Code by campaigning against the closure of a primary school in his Rhondda constituency. The resignation of one of the biggest hitters in his Cabinet was doubtless a major blow to Jones, who won the Welsh Labour leadership on the back of his campaign. It goes without saying that Andrews was a close ally of the First Minister, but relations between the pair had soured over the summer and the wheels came off spectacularly following a highly-charged plenary meeting in the Senedd. News of Andrews' departure followed a turbulent day in which Jones pointedly failed to back the Education Minister as opposition politicians lambasted him over his support for Pentre Primary School. They claimed it was untenable for Andrews to back the campaign when Rhondda Cynon Taf Council's proposal to shut the school was in line with guidance over surplus school places issued by himself as minister. Jones' silence was deafening.

According to Section 4.4 of the Ministerial Code: "Where ministers are uncertain about whether a conflict arises between their ministerial and constituency/regional responsibilities they should consult the First Minister, for decision as to how the business is to be handled."[4] It became apparent that Andrews had not consulted Jones before backing the Pentre Primary School campaign. In a letter to the First Minister, Andrews expressed regret that his commitment to constituents may have led to "an apparent conflict" that made life difficult for the Welsh Government. Responding to his departure, Jones said: "I recognise very well that there is sometimes tension between the role of a government minister and the demands of a constituency AM. The Ministerial Code aims to define the boundaries between the two roles and, on this occasion, I believe those roles were confused. It is for that reason, and that reason alone, that I accept your resignation as Education Minister."[5]

But Jones' letter was little more than a formality and a smokescreen for the tensions that had been underlying for some time. Two weeks earlier, Jones expressed his displeasure at a campaign backed by the Rhondda Labour Party against the potential closure of the consultant-led accident and emergency department at Royal Glamorgan Hospital in Llantrisant. The First Minister ruled that party logos should not appear on campaign material but opposition politicians smelt an opening and accused Andrews of campaigning against hospital reconfiguration plans that grew out of Welsh Government policy. Nevertheless, it was Andrews' backing for the school campaign, and its relationship to his own education portfolio, that proved decisive. It was, without question, the straw that broke the camel's back. Welsh Conservative leader Andrew RT Davies was particularly unforgiving and said that, after Jones had failed to endorse his Education Minister's position during First Minister's Questions, it was "inevitable" that Andrews had to go. Plaid Cymru's Simon Thomas said Andrews had undermined the Welsh Government and having argued against his own policies, his decision to step aside was the correct one.

As the ministerial obituaries began to surface, teachers' unions painted a mixed picture of the minister's rule of schools, colleges and universities. But amid an overwhelming sense of shock, there was a general consensus that Andrews' departure had come at a crucial stage in the development of Wales' education system. With PISA looming and summer exam results pending, the sector called for the quick installation of a new minister capable of commanding the confidence of the profession and parents. Anna Brychan said she was "stunned" by the news and while they may not always have seen eye to eye, maintained that Andrews had made a "powerful contribution to education policy in Wales and beyond during his tenure".[6] However challenging some of their conversations, she said there could be no doubting his personal commitment to the standards agenda and for that he should be congratulated.

The door to the Cabinet, however, was by no means closed and in his letter acknowledging Andrews' resignation, Jones hinted a return was in the offing. He said he had "high regard" for Andrews' skills and abilities and "very much hope that you may be able to serve the Welsh Government again in the future". Assuming Andrews was intent on continuing his political career – there was some speculation that, at the age of 55, he would contemplate standing down in 2016 – it appeared fair to venture he would not be frozen out for long. Historically, the Assembly did not luxuriate in a plethora of Cabinet-capable members and Andrews was far too shrewd an operator to be left languishing on the backbenches. In the meantime, critics mused over the events leading up to his sudden departure from government and why Jones had not sought to support his Education Minister when backed into a corner. In his first interview after resigning, Andrews said the First Minister had reached a decision that some of his campaigning had transgressed the Ministerial Code and notably, that "he asked me to resign"[7]. It was a telling revelation. While it was true Andrews had written to Jones with his resignation, it was not immediately clear that he had been told to do so. Having been in possession of a job he "loved" and with so many irons in the fire, it appeared highly unlikely that Andrews would have offered his hand so willingly.[8] There was little doubt, therefore, that the nation's most belligerent minister had in fact been sacked.

There are bound to be many reasons behind Andrews' sudden departure. Conspiracy theorists will tell you that he manufactured his own exit and with much-vaunted PISA results on the horizon, created the perfect storm by which to jump ship. After all, ministers are ultimately judged by their results and Andrews would surely rise or fall by Wales' PISA scores. There was no suggestion Welsh teenagers were going to perform significantly better in 2013 than they had in 2010 and Andrews knew his reputation was at stake. Given his robust style and high expectations of others, there would have been many leaping for the minister's throat had PISA gone sour. Calls for the minister to fall on his sword were inevitable if Wales' leaning tower lurched further and the pressure on Andrews may well have been too much to bear. The minister was dealt a blow shortly before his resignation when Michael Davidson, who led PISA on behalf of the OECD, warned Wales had to improve in 2013 if it was to achieve its ambitious top 20 target. Davidson said progress would be essential if Wales wanted to compete with the world's best education systems. So in that respect, Pentre Primary School offered a way out. And what better way to do it, than in the name of those who voted for you.

Suffice to say, Andrews' decision to stand down in support of Pentre Primary School did his reputation locally no harm at all. Plaid Cymru leader Leanne Wood's decision to contest the minister's seat at the next Assembly election was an issue and, rightly or wrongly, Andrews took the threat seriously. Wood's challenge, regardless of how realistic her chances of success, called into question Andrews' future as an AM and undoubtedly sharpened his focus in the constituency. He had, after all, witnessed first-hand Plaid's ability to win in what was a traditional Labour stronghold during the inaugural Assembly election in 1999. Wood was not only born and raised in the Rhondda, but she had proven in her shock victory in Plaid's 2012 leadership race more than capable of upsetting the applecart. A regional South Wales Central AM since 2003, Wood started as a rank outsider in the quest to succeed Ieuan Wyn Jones before emerging victorious by almost 1,000 votes. Then again, the minister would be defending a significant majority (Labour won the Rhondda by 6,739 votes in 2011) and you felt sure that if anyone could emerge from the PISA mire, it would be Andrews.

Andrews was a minister who polarised opinion and for many, his resignation would have been long overdue. He was no shrinking violet and his combative approach was unlike anything anyone in devolved Wales had ever experienced before. Large swathes of the education fraternity took umbrage. They felt the weight of a demanding new minister on their shoulders and, to some extent, believed his very public scorn was unjustified. Welsh education was in "crisis", he said, and we were all responsible. There could be no alibis or excuses; the drive for improvement and a renewed focus on standards had begun. But it was for that reason many others within the nation's education system would be sorry to see Andrews leave. His unashamed quest to raise the bar in Wales was to be commended and without his leadership, there were concerns the pace of change would stagnate. It is inevitable that the appointment of a new minister brings with it a period of flux in which the incumbent takes time to get their feet under the table. Andrews' departure would leave a significant void, not least because this particular minister had his finger so firmly on the pulse.

There is little doubt that Andrews had been nearing the end of his tenure before his sacking. Having prepared so diligently for a new brief earlier in the year, he was ready to move on and had he gone in March to become Wales' inaugural Chancellor, there would not have been many asking questions. When the spring-clean did not extend to education, however, it seemed Andrews would be in post at least until PISA. If anything, the fact he lasted just three more months in the role provided the strongest indication that Andrews' departure had not been planned and was the net result of Jones' refusal to bail his once close ally out of a hole. The First Minister's patience had worn thin and it is likely a breakdown in relations triggered a premature end to Andrews' tenure. Jones could have bided himself time by referring the matter to the Permanent Secretary, as indeed he did a year later in June 2014 when Natural Resources and Food Minister Alun Davies stepped out of line. The fact he did not, spoke volumes. If Andrews' faux pas had taken place in Westminster, there is every chance the minister would have survived. Accounts were sanitised in the days and months following Andrews' exit albeit the event is sure to have been a matter of great regret to all parties.

Moving forward, Andrews' would be an extremely hard act to follow and of most pressing concern was that the previous three and a half years would amount to nothing if the nation's new Education Minister failed to build on his foundations.

# Huw Lewis appointed Wales' new Education Minister

Merthyr Tydfil and Rhymney AM Huw Lewis was the man charged with picking up the education baton. A former chemistry teacher, Lewis trained in Scotland and, an Assembly "original", was first elected in May 1999. He was assistant general secretary of the Welsh Labour Party prior to his election and had held a number of Cabinet roles since. Formerly Deputy Minister for the Economy and Transport, Lewis was appointed Deputy Minister for Children in December 2009 – briefly working as understudy to Andrews – after an unsuccessful leadership challenge. Following his re-election to the Assembly in May 2011, Lewis was appointed Minister for Housing, Regeneration and Heritage and in March 2013 was appointed Minister for Communities and Tackling Poverty. But nothing could have prepared him for the high profile and high pressure role of Education Minister.

Speaking of his appointment some months later in December 2013, Lewis admitted to being taken aback by his predecessor's departure from the Cabinet. "I was surprised and I won't disguise that – but that's politics," said Lewis. "I suppose it's a very unusual job in that sense. You can't plan your route through politics and you have to do your best, wherever you're sent." Lewis was on his way to Neath in his former role as Minister for Communities and Tackling Poverty when the call came. He recalled: "I was told that I had to return to Cardiff for unspecified reasons. It was all a bit mysterious. I found out when I got back that the First Minister had offered me the job."[9] Three and a half years after defeating him in the race to become Welsh Labour leader, Jones had entrusted Lewis with one of the government's biggest and most demanding portfolios. Lewis vowed to follow on where his predecessor left off and build on the "fantastic foundations" Andrews had laid with regard to school standards.

Albeit he had masterminded Jones' campaign to lead the people of Wales, there was no animosity and Andrews would be a key asset to Lewis in the days and weeks following his appointment. In fact, one of the first things Andrews did after leaving office was to draw his successor a list of priorities. Far from washing his hands, he retained a keen interest in the nation's education system and was willing to help guide the fledgling minister through stormy waters. Nevertheless, Lewis started with a blank canvas and with so many new faces in post, had chance to mould his own department and create a clarity of vision for all. But driving a wedge into the revolving door of DfES appeared an impossible task and there was no guarantee anyone would be around long enough to see the Welsh Government's school improvement plans through. One of Lewis' first public appearances came within two months of his appointment as minister, when pupils across the country opened their GCSE and A-level envelopes.

For thousands of students across Wales, August marks the culmination of two years' hard work and the start of a bright new career. But for all the ecstasy and celebration, there is also disappointment and heartbreak. Not everyone gets the grades to become a doctor and, while some exceed expectations, many fall agonisingly short of the mark. It is often said that newspapers, film crews and education journalists, in particular, miss the boat on A-levels and GCSEs. Our tendency to compare and contrast is considered in some way disrespectful to the application shown by teachers and pupils. It goes without saying that achieving a D, against all odds, could be equivalent to an A or A* for some students. Pupils often face significant barriers to learning that make their achievement during exam time all the more extraordinary – and that should not be overlooked or in any way down-trodden. But by the same token, we cannot ignore the bigger picture and year-on-year statistics do matter.

In 2013, the percentage of A-level students in Wales being awarded at least an A grade fell for the fourth year in a row – and at the fastest rate since devolution. Official figures showed that while the overall A-level pass rate remained stable at 97.6% in Wales, 22.9% of entries scored an A or A*, down from 23.6% in 2012. Records showed there had been no higher fall since 2000. Allied to that, a breakdown by nation revealed an alarming widening of the attainment gap between Wales and England across two key indicators. England's overall pass rate had increased by 0.1% to 98.1%, while the percentage of pupils obtaining at least an A grade had fallen by 0.2% to 26.3% – a far slower rate than that recorded in Wales. There was a narrowing of the gap in A* grades – but only because England had fallen 0.3% to 7.7%. The proportion of pupils obtaining A*s in Wales remained at 6%. The results were a rude awakening for an Education Minister still wet behind the ears.

When challenged on the figures, Lewis said there would be an analysis as to why Wales' students were continuing to lag behind England's when it came to top grades. He described the nation's A-level results as "good" but conceded the "small but stubborn" gap in overall attainment between Wales and England needed to be addressed. The problem, of course, was that many ministers had tried and failed to bridge the results deficit and Lewis had merely inherited an age-old problem. The following table articulates perfectly how Wales slipped behind the rest of the home nations since publication of The Learning Country.

**Table 5 A-level comparisons – percentage of pupil passes per country**

| 2002 | A | C | E | 2013 | A | C | E |
|---------|------|------|------|---------|------|------|------|
| UK | 20.7 | 65.3 | 94.3 | UK | 26.3 | 77.2 | 98.1 |
| England | 20.3 | 64.5 | 94.1 | England | 26.3 | 77 | 98.1 |
| Wales | 21.5 | 70.4 | 95.8 | Wales | 22.9 | 75.2 | 97.6 |
| NI | 28.1 | 76.8 | 96.4 | NI | 30.7 | 83.5 | 98.2 |

SOURCE: Joint Council for Qualifications (JCQ)

While there were far more Welsh pupils achieving the crucial A, C and E grade benchmarks in 2013 than in 2002, Wales had gone from performing significantly above average to significantly below average. The decade charts an alarming slide and while Wales' pass rates had improved markedly, they had done so at a far slower rate relative to other countries. It is also notable that, during the same period, England's teenagers had moved from well below Wales and Northern Ireland to around the UK average. Whatever your opinion of modern-day qualifications and their validity, the comparison cannot be argued away or excused.

Wales was underachieving compared to the rest of the UK and the gap was widening. There was no escaping that fact. The nation's fledgling Education Minister needed look no further than his own constituency for a steer on the sort of challenge that lay in wait. Merthyr Tydfil was one of Wales' worst performing education authorities and Estyn had criticised senior officers and elected members for not challenging under-performance and poor learner outcomes. In a report published early in 2013, the inspectorate said Merthyr's education service had not responded well enough to recommendations dating back to 2004 and nearly 40% of pupils left primary schools in the region with sub-standard literacy skills. It found "systemic weaknesses" in delivery, high exclusion rates and too many young people not in education, employment or training. The Welsh Government had toyed with the idea of merging Merthyr with nearby Rhondda Cynon Taf, but when the plan went stale (due in part to unforeseen legalities), the advent of special measures saw a ministerial board parachuted in to take charge of the council's schools. And it was not before time.

The percentage of pupils who achieved A-level grades A*-C in Merthyr fell to 66.9% in 2013 from 68.6% a year earlier, while the overall pass rate at grades A*-E also dropped to 96.3%, from 97.3% in 2012. The percentage of pupils securing coveted A*-A grades stumbled from 15.8% in 2012 to 14.4% – some way off the all-Wales average of 22.9%. Notwithstanding the efforts of pupils and teachers, against a national backdrop the results were a damning indictment of Merthyr's ailing education service. But this was not an attack on schools themselves and all of Merthyr's four secondary schools were performing well at the time of their last Estyn inspection and it was not they who were deemed to be "unsatisfactory". According to the inspectorate, the authority's "lack of leadership at all levels had failed to secure continuous improvement across education services and had resulted in standards remaining too low". True, the proportion of learners in Merthyr who were eligible for free school meals was the third highest in Wales. But even when these high levels of deprivation were taken into account, performance was still well below average.

# Notes

1. Tweedale, Chris. (2013). Letter of Resignation. June 20.
2. Dixon, Philip. (2013). Western Mail. May 17.
3. Welsh Government. (2013). Western Mail. May 17.
4. Welsh Government. (2011). Ministerial Code. p 15.
5. Jones, Carwyn. (2013). Letter to Leighton Andrews. June 25.
6. Brychan, Anna. (2013). Western Mail. June 27.
7. Andrews, Leighton. (2013). Western Mail. June 29.
8. Andrews, Leighton. (2014). Western Mail. June 25.
9. Lewis, Huw. (2013). Western Mail. December 26.

# 14

# End Of The Line

## PISA heralds the start of a new chapter

*Lewis sets out his stall. But international rankings are a rude awakening to a minister still finding his feet. Wales looks to England for inspiration as a new school improvement strategy is unveiled*

It was no great surprise when Lewis made breaking the link between poverty and low attainment his number one priority for Wales' schools system. No two ministers are the same and while there would be nuances in approach, Lewis had chosen to prioritise an agenda he knew well. Delivering his first major speech to sector leaders in October 2013, Lewis announced a renewed focus on deprivation and its impact on school standards. He warned that pupils who were eligible for free school meals were far less likely to achieve good GCSE grades and vowed to develop a plan to tackle the issue. Lewis' statement of intent represented a reshuffling of Welsh Government priorities – his predecessor, it is fair to say, had focused more on literacy and numeracy. Andrews had made tackling deprivation the lesser of three evils during his term in office. Addressing stakeholders at the University of South Wales' Atrium in Cardiff, Lewis said "poor pupils do less well in school" – and that was something he was not prepared to tolerate. Poverty aside, the new minister's direction of travel was along the same lines as Andrews' and improving key skills would remain high on the agenda. Otherwise, Lewis' eagerness to engage fully with the teaching fraternity was worthy of note. The sector, he said, would get his "absolute respect" in return for "absolute responsibility".[1] That, of course, was an area Andrews had struggled to negotiate.

In truth, the new minister's tenure started brightly and, after talking unions from the picket lines – teachers in Wales had threatened to strike with colleagues in England in October 2013 – Lewis brokered an unlikely deal with local government. He described a commitment from Welsh councils to drive forward regional school improvement as a "breakthrough" in the quest to raise standards and a warm response from stakeholders gave cause for optimism. But life got decidedly tougher for the fledgling minister later in 2013, when Robert Hill's calls for radical structural change (the former Blair aide having suggested reducing by a third the number of education authorities in Wales) were kicked into the long grass. Lewis was accused of "delaying" school improvement by shelving the plans, which had been widely supported within the sector. Accepting 80 of the former UK Government adviser's 85 options for change, Lewis chose not to act on calls to restructure school services, pending the results of the Commission on Public Service Governance and Delivery being led by former NHS Wales chief executive Sir Paul Williams. Lewis said he had already taken action and if the WLGA failed to deliver on its commitment to ring-fence regional school improvement funding, money would be top-sliced. He maintained that a radical restructuring of education services before the next Assembly election in 2016 was "unlikely".

Andrews, now watching from the backbenches, described Lewis' response as "a game-changer". But one wondered whether councils would have enjoyed the same stay of execution had the former minister still been in post. A promise of a new national model for regional working was long overdue and, in itself, unlikely to bring about the level of improved school support required in Wales. For many, introducing what the minister called a new "lever" amounted to little more than a rearranging of the deck chairs. Without radical structural reform, regional consortia appeared doomed to fail. Schools turned to councils or consortia for advice, training and support and, with officials seemingly incapable of addressing their problems, it was no wonder education in Wales was suffering. Teachers could not shoulder all responsibility and local authorities – in all their different guises – had to be held to account as well. There were not many dissenting voices following Hill's intervention and you would have done well to find anyone within the sector who believed the current set-up was working.

There was a fear that the Welsh Government would do everything possible to avoid taking the toughest of tough decisions. It goes without saying that education takes up a considerable chunk of the local government budget and cutting all responsibility would have far-reaching implications, not least for those in power. The fact that many councils in Wales were Labour-run was not lost on critics, albeit party politics could not be allowed to muddy ministers' views. There may well have been a mutiny within Welsh Labour ranks if a shake-up on the scale of that recommended by Hill was accepted, but improved school standards – and with it, better prospects for young people – was surely a price well worth paying. That is not to say wholesale centralisation of education services was necessarily the best way forward.

The government's dubious record since devolution did not inspire confidence, although there were other options on the table. The creation of a buffer, in the form of regional school boards accountable to ministers, for example, would disconnect Cardiff Bay from the sensitivities of the coal face. Either way, having 22 local education authorities appeared a hindrance in a country as small as Wales.

## PISA results

If response to his seemingly lacklustre plans for the future delivery of education services rocked Lewis onto the back foot, then the barricades came down a few days later on December 3, 2013, when PISA results were published. In total, 3,305 pupils from 137 schools in Wales took part in the 2012 tranche of tests, which involved 65 nations. But the findings were grim and just when you thought it could not get any worse, Wales slipped further down the international scale. Wales' average score in maths dipped for the second time running to a lowly 468 points – a full 30 points below Scotland and 27 behind England. Science, traditionally Wales' strongest PISA suit, also fell to its lowest recorded level and while the nation's average reading score rose from 476 to 480 points, Wales failed to improve its ranking against other participating countries in any of the three measures. Its scores in each domain were significantly lower than more countries in the 2012 cycle than in the 2009 cycle. The nation was heading in the wrong direction and slipped to 43rd for maths, 36th for science and 41st for reading. Rather than rubbing shoulders with Finland and Shanghai, China – the doyennes of the education world – Wales languished alongside European minnows Hungary, Luxembourg and Lithuania. To put Welsh performance into context, Croatia, one of the nation's closest comparators, was at civil war when PISA was being developed in the mid-1990s.

Wales' inaugural PISA results, published in 2007, were a rude awakening to an education system caught napping. The nation had underestimated the level of challenge required and a belated introduction to the world stage made clear Wales' inadequacies. Three years later in 2010, scores showed evidence of further decline and were the catalyst for system-wide reform. But this, the most recent international assessment of Wales' schools, was nothing short of damning. A Lazarus-style revival was never likely, but to make no meaningful stride forward defied belief – and was rightly cause for serious concern. It is not often that the UK's media sits up and takes notice, but Wales' sorry decline was so pronounced it could scarcely be ignored. There is a lot riding on PISA and while each of the home nations is given its own individual breakdown, the cumulative UK position depends entirely on its constituent parts. If reading, maths and science scores dipped in Wales, the eyes of the world would fall on Cardiff Bay for all the wrong reasons – and so it proved.

Wales' PISA results were cause for much consternation in Fleet Street. While the *Huffington Post* declared that "Wales has worst education in the UK", the *Daily Mail* supplemented its coverage with a story called "Wales gets the wooden spoon". The *Telegraph* was the most scathing of all the London-based press. Columnist and free school founder Toby Young wrote on the paper's website that Wales' education system was "a basket case" and the nation itself, "the sick man of Europe". He warned: "If this is the future you want for the rest of the UK after 2015, vote Labour." The article itself was entitled: "I have seen the Labour future and it doesn't work. It's called Wales."[2] It may be the most openly Conservative of Fleet Street broadsheets, but its conclusions were doubtless echoed by millions of like-minded critics across the border. Closer to home, the *Western Mail* led with comments made by Gove in the House of Commons. Whatever the context, "Wales is a nation going backwards" is a provocative headline that leaves nothing to the imagination. Nevertheless, a Westminster smear campaign was, perhaps, inevitable and opened the door to Labour sceptics who required no invitation. Responding to a question from Tory Vale of Glamorgan MP Alun Cairns, who described Wales' PISA scores as "nothing short of a scandal", Gove said: "If you want to know what our (England's) education system would be like if the country were foolishly to vote Labour at the next election, you need only look over the Severn to see a country going backwards." Far from being the educational Garden of Eden, Wales was becoming a warning to other nations of how not to do things. In typically forthright fashion, David Reynolds said Wales was in danger of becoming a "theme park". Only this was an attraction it could have done without.

As Wales' education system clicked back into gear after the Christmas break, there was pressure on everyone to raise their game. The nation's plight was becoming an embarrassment and, having been singled out as the UK's weak link, PISA was causing serious reputational damage both at home and abroad. The advent of the internet means bad news travels fast and the message that Welsh schools were failing to properly educate their children was starting to reverberate. Once was a blip; twice was a problem; but three dismal tests in a row was inexplicable, regardless of the measures being taken to redress the situation. PISA cast a dark shadow that extended beyond the confines of Wales' education system. Veteran broadcaster Jeremy Paxman, who seldom missed an opportunity to twist the knife, was particularly brutal. The *Newsnight* host asked viewers on February 18, 2014: "What's wrong with Wales?" as if it were riddled with some kind of infectious disease. "The fact is," he continued: "Wales is in trouble, particularly in education.

As it's ambitions have grown, it's achievements have tumbled." But we did not need Paxman to tell us of our predicament and so low was the level of expectation, educationalists had seen PISA coming.

**Table 6 Wales' PISA results and rankings (brackets) 2006-12**

| Wales | 2006 | 2009 | 2012 |
|---|---|---|---|
| Reading | 481 (27) | 476 (38) | 480 (41) |
| Maths | 484 (31) | 472 (40) | 468 (43) |
| Science | 505 (20) | 496 (30) | 491 (36) |

Source: OECD

Closer analysis found morale among Welsh teachers significantly below average. In a report published after headline scores were released, it was revealed that the number of headteachers in Wales who believed there was high staff morale was nearly 10% behind that of other countries taking part in the study. When asked whether morale of teachers in their school was high, 83% of school leaders said they agreed or strongly agreed. The average of headteachers in other countries who believed morale was high was 91%. Given the weak relative performance of Wales' education system, and a perception in some quarters that teachers were somehow responsible, the findings were hardly surprising.

Lewis himself described Wales' lowly position in international rankings as "unacceptable" and called on the nation's teachers to "step-up" in the drive to raise standards. He said the PISA results were "disappointing" and there would be "no shirking of responsibility" from the Welsh Government. But he rebuffed suggestions Wales was becoming an embarrassment to the UK and said no minister, including Gove, had cause for self-congratulation. Leading business groups, meanwhile, described Wales' rankings as a "wake-up call" that made clear the importance of good schooling on the nation's economy. Confederation of British Industry (CBI) Wales director Emma Watkins said no issue mattered more to the UK economy over the long-term than the quality of its education system and "it's not acceptable for Wales to have slipped so far behind".[3] Robert Lloyd Griffiths, head of the Institute of Directors in Wales, was no less forgiving and said the PISA figures were cause for "grave concern". Countries with an unrelenting focus on the quality and rigour of their education systems would be the ones that win the race, he warned. Griffiths said the figures put Wales at a "considerable disadvantage" and the UK, whose collective results were nothing to write home about either, appeared to have "its feet shackled at the starting line".[4] Teachers' unions, meanwhile, called for patience after the mini revolution set in train by former Education Minister Andrews in 2011. David Evans, secretary of NUT Cymru, said he was "disappointed" Wales had not improved its PISA standing – but warned that educational change did not happen overnight.

On the face of it, you would have thought the new emphasis on PISA – and with it, the availability of new tests and materials – would have left a mark, however small. Wales had made no real ground and a laser-like focus on standards had failed to translate into anything meaningful or of substance. Wales remained bottom of the UK pile and while its reading score had improved, the nation's maths haul had dipped to chronic levels. A fall in science was a serious blow, not least because critics were relying on Wales' trump card to pull the nation's education system up the rankings in 2015, when the subject would feature more prominently. As it was, one of the Welsh Government's few hopes gave cause for no optimism whatsoever. But standards in Wales were so poor when countries were pitted against each other in 2010, a marked change in fortunes was always highly unlikely in such a short space of time. To recap, Wales was ranked 38th for reading, 40th for maths and 30th for science three years earlier, when Andrews called for collective responsibility. But the "systemic failures" to which he alluded, would take time to weed out. Wales' problems were deep-seated.

The nation's abject PISA standing was a damning indictment of 14 years of devolved government, in which the Labour Party had held the education brief uninterrupted. Recent developments – including the overarching LNF – had been broadly welcomed as the right way forward, but February 2011 – when Andrews unveiled his root and branch response to PISA – was effectively too little, too late. Hampered by a growing number of participating countries, the Welsh Government was bound to be licking its wounds again and the 2013 results came as no great shock to the system. Newfangled policies designed to raise the standards bar had not had opportunity to bear fruit and the advent of more competition meant improvement would take a lot longer than the 18 months between the introduction of Andrews' 20 point plan and November 2012, when PISA was next sat. Indeed the challenge was made considerably harder by the fact that other countries shared in Wales' unwillingness to settle for mediocrity.

Wales' failure to improve at all in 2013 made it highly likely the Welsh Government would fall well short of its top 20 target. Why? Because no country had ever made the level of improvement required to bridge the plunging gap between Wales and the so-called powerhouses of education. And there was little to suggest a precedent would be set. A Research Note put forward by the National Assembly in the wake of PISA said the rate of improvement by 2015 would need to be "considerable". In maths, it said Wales would have to improve by 33 points and 23 places in the rankings to be in the top 20 in 2015. In science, Wales would have to improve by 24 points and 16 places and in reading, Wales would have to surge 28 points and 21 places to reach its target. So all things being equal, what then would the OECD recommend? An analysis of the world's high-performing education systems would suggest that the ingredients of their success are far from random and all possess common underlying principles. According to the OECD:

> "PISA defines countries as high-performing if almost all of their students are in high school at the appropriate age; the top quarter of performers place among the countries whose top quarter are among the best performers in the world, with respect to their mastery of the kinds of complex knowledge and skills needed in advanced economies, as well as their ability to apply that knowledge and those skills to problems with which they are not familiar; student performance is only weakly related to their socio-economic background; and spending per pupil is not at the top of the league tables. Put another way, PISA defines superior performance as high-participation, high-quality, high-equity and high-efficiency."[5] (OECD, 2011)

There was a lot riding on PISA and it was not just reputation and political point-scoring at stake – experts believe a poor showing will inevitably impact on economic prosperity. Business leaders will be less likely to settle on your shores if you are seen by PISA to be ailing. The reaction of Wales' own business leaders – the aforementioned Watkins and Griffiths – were a case in point. In the aftermath of results in 2013, Michael Barber wrote:

> "The arrival of new PISA results every three years focuses minds in education ministries around the world like nothing else. The objective data encourages ministers to take a fair view of their system's performance, and review which education reforms are having the greatest impact... The result is that education ministries and officials around the world now engage in continuous dialogue about education reform. None can afford to ignore the mounting evidence of what works and what doesn't."[6] (Michael Barber, 2013)

PISA tests what all good education systems should be striving to teach – namely quality reading, maths and science skills. The ability to reason and consider real-life scenarios is a crucial by-product and one all employers look for in their new recruits. Sceptics need only look at the growing number of PISA participants – there are more than 70 countries signed up for the 2015 test and, like it or not, the world's biggest education survey is both respected and here to stay. Despite a plea from teachers' unions to avoid knee-jerk reaction, the so-called "PISA panic" kicked off the minute scores were published.

Lewis was already a man under pressure when rankings went south. This was one bullet he could not dodge and when asked whether it would be better for the Welsh Government to apologise and accept it had got things wrong in the wake of December's PISA results, Lewis said: "If it helps, yeah sure. I think there probably was a period in the mid 2000s when, particularly, those basic pupil experiences on literacy and numeracy weren't properly there and the challenge wasn't properly there. I suppose we all need to apologise to young people. Every element of the system – from the minister's office right through to the school governors, local authorities and headteachers – has to step up to this challenge."[7] It was a significant development and the minister's clearest admission of guilt since assuming the education brief. The Welsh Government was at least partially responsibility for the parlous state of education in Wales and Lewis was right to take ownership of the nation's foremost problem.

But if the Welsh Government thought the Christmas break would detract attention and soften the PISA blow, it was very much mistaken. No sooner had Parliament reconvened in January than Conservative Monmouth MP David Davies reopened old wounds and poured scorn on the devolved administration's handling of education. Addressing members in the House of Commons, Davies said: "The PISA results... showed that things in Wales have not only stagnated, but gone backwards and that educational standards in England are still far higher than they are in Wales, where the Welsh Assembly's Labour minister recently had to make a fulsome apology on the front page of the *Western Mail* for his party's abysmal failure."[8] Responding, UK Education Minister Elizabeth Truss said Lewis was right to apologise for letting children in Wales down. "The reality is that the Welsh Government caved in to the unions and abolished national tests and league tables, and their results in maths have plummeted to lower than 40th in the PISA tables," she said. "That shows how vital it is that we increase accountability in this country and keep up the pace of our reforms to make sure that we push ahead like countries such as Germany and Poland, rather than fall behind like Wales."

The finger-pointing had started and with a General Election on the horizon, the Welsh Government could expect a bumpy 2014. Gove was sure to turn up the heat on his Welsh Labour adversary during the countdown to polling and Prime Minister David Cameron did not need a second invitation, either. In a highly-charged speech to the Welsh Conservatives' Spring conference in Llangollen, Cameron accused the Welsh Government of "appalling, inexcusable complacency" in its handling of education. He said: "Wales is falling behind not just the rest of the UK, but the rest of Western Europe. And what is Carwyn Jones' response? He says: 'We took our eye off the ball.' I'm sorry? It's like the guy in the crow's nest of the Titanic saying 'I took my eye off the horizon'. This man and his government are sinking the hopes of a generation." But the Tories were not the only threat and Jones would face pressure from within his own ranks as the opposition in Westminster stepped up its fight to win back power. UK Labour leader Ed Miliband could not let Wales' inexcusable school standards hamper his challenge for a majority. Wales was not a beacon of light worth parading to the masses and regardless of public opinion towards the ruling Conservative-Liberal Democrat coalition, failures in both education and health were not a glowing endorsement of the Labour Party. The chickens had come home to roost and no amount of spin could paper over these cracks.

# A new challenge for schools

There is a strong argument for the introduction of a more formal, government-led drive to tackling one of Welsh education's most perennial problems – namely that of breaking the well-known link between poverty and low attainment. The Universities Heads of the Valleys Institute (UHOVI), launched in 2010, was a step in the right direction and has made considerable strides in the further and higher education sectors in one of Wales' most deprived regions. But a new systemic approach was long overdue and it was no great surprise when Schools Challenge Cymru was launched early in 2014. The Welsh Government's headline response to Wales' poor PISA rankings, it would build on similar "challenge" programmes in London, Greater Manchester and the Black Country and involve bringing in expertise from all over the UK. While the Welsh Government had scoured the world in search of best practice, there were surely lessons to be learned from closer to home and city regions in England had shown school-led improvement could work in the right conditions. Not only would Challenge Cymru focus on those underachieving, it would strive to negate the impact of poverty on attainment and the promise of an additional £20m a year was a shot in the arm for schools which needed support the most.

The London Challenge was hugely successful in raising standards in one of England's most disadvantaged areas and there was every chance its model could be adopted in Wales. Launched by Tony Blair in 2003, the London Challenge was a partnership between all those seeking more for the city's young people. Its strength lay in its unification, with all parties working together to ensure best practice became the norm. Initially reserved for secondary schools, the scheme expanded to incorporate primaries in 2008 and benefited from a significant amount of government investment. The strategy was credited with transforming the targeted London boroughs of Islington, Hackney, Haringey, Southwark and Lambeth by providing support for schools on the frontline of breaking the link between disadvantage and low attainment. It used independent, experienced education experts, known as London Challenge Advisers, to identify need and broker support for under performing schools. The advisers were supported by a small administrative team, based in and funded centrally by the UK Department for Education. The net result saw exam results in London secondary schools improve at a faster rate than those in the rest of England. Primary schools that became partners with London Challenge also improved rapidly. The contextual value-added measures of the participating schools, taken altogether, rose significantly from below average in 2008 to above average in 2010. Writing on its impact, the nation's inspectorate said:

"From the beginning of London Challenge, London schools have received clear, consistent leadership from the team leaders appointed by the Department for Education. Their message has been the pressing need to improve educational standards and the sense of professional duty incumbent on teachers to do this for London children. Over time, that message of commitment and encouragement has been repeated consistently by the London Challenge leadership team. These endeavours have reinforced a clear sense of moral purpose among teachers and school leaders to close attainment gaps between London and the rest of the country... Their sense of pride in being part of a city-wide education service, irrespective of whether they were receiving or providing support, was a fundamental characteristic of London City Challenge."[9] (Ofsted, 2010)

As the inspectorate suggests, the way in which leaders of the London Challenge motivated teachers to think beyond their intrinsic sense of duty to their own pupils was crucial. A commitment to serving youngsters across London was an underlying feature that, in turn, encouraged successful collaboration between school leaders and teachers. It was a perfect example of school-to-school learning and while divisive in some areas of the UK, proved an overwhelming success in London. Participants and providers questioned as part of a review of the strategy were unanimous in their appreciation of the positive impact the approach was having on raising standards in both host and participant schools.

Designed to raise performance in Wales' weakest secondaries, Challenge Cymru would bid to drive up standards and bridge the gap with the rest of the UK using the same collaborative approach. Additional money would see struggling schools – the majority in the South Wales region – given targeted support to help drive up classroom standards and pupil attainment. Selection centred around school banding scores and how well pupils eligible for free school meals had performed in their GCSEs. Participating schools would be monitored on a regular basis as the programme developed and headteachers were under no illusions that they could be stripped of Challenge status if their schools failed to improve quickly enough. The Welsh Government demanded a return on its investment, but so-called failing schools would not be expected to bring about improvement by themselves. Some of Wales' best performing schools would be encouraged to take part in the programme by sharing expertise and supporting teachers in Challenge Cymru schools.

The programme was full of promise and sector leaders welcomed its long-awaited introduction – but having waited 10 years for a Challenge, only in Wales would two come along at once. The Central South Wales Challenge was based on the same premise of school-to-school working and was launched – on a smaller scale – less than two weeks before the Welsh Government unveiled its own version. Driven by the Central South Consortium, it involved schools in Cardiff, Bridgend, Merthyr Tydfil, Rhondda Cynon Taf and the Vale of Glamorgan setting aside past rivalries and working together in the best interests of their pupils. Rumour had it, the consortium stole in ahead of the Welsh Government and not everyone in the Department for Education was impressed by its forward-thinking. Then again, many of those involved in the Central South Wales Challenge were oblivious to the fact there was another Challenge project in the pipeline.

The appointment in an advisory capacity of Professor Mel Ainscow, who led on the Greater Manchester Challenge for the UK Government, was a solid start in Central South Wales. A £50m initiative, the Greater Manchester Challenge launched in 2008 and, mirroring the earlier London Challenge, sought to locate and extend the best practice that already existed within the city region. Results were below the national average and non-attendance was sky high – a joined-up strategy between Government, more than 1,100 schools, 10 local authorities and all those working to raise standards was required. And it has stood the test of time. Designed to crack the cycle of disadvantage and educational underachievement, the Greater Manchester Challenge continued making a difference long after the end of its grant. Primary schools outperformed national averages and, in the public exams taken by all young people at 16, secondary schools in Greater Manchester improved faster than schools nationally in 2011. The percentage of primary and secondary schools performing below the Government's floor targets fell sharply over the initial three years of the Challenge and significant gains were made in schools serving the region's most disadvantaged communities. Ainscow had been there and done it. A self-proclaimed "stimulus to get things moving", his knowledge and expertise would be invaluable as the pan-Wales project developed.

But clarity was essential and getting Challenge programmes to dovetail would be crucial or Wales risked diluting their impact. To muddy matters further, there was a third school-to-school improvement programme already in operation in Wales. The Lead and Emerging Practitioner Schools initiative had been around since May 2013 and sought to match high-performing schools with "emerging" schools to disseminate and implement best practice over an 18 month period. Funding of up to £90,000 was awarded to each partnership and was only released when schools could demonstrate that milestone targets had been met. You would be forgiven for thinking the arrival of two Challenge programmes on the scene would have marked the beginning of the end for Wales' Lead and Emerging Practitioner Schools. But there appeared little sign of it slowing down and stakeholders were duly encouraged to make their applications for a fresh tranche of funding shortly after the launch of supplementary challenges. Ainscow's appointment in April 2014 as Chief Adviser to Challenge Cymru was sensible and would help facilitate a merging of the two Challenge programmes.

Ainscow's desire to blur the boundaries between schools – as well as bordering local authorities – was radical in the extreme. He said he wanted Welsh and English-medium schools to work together with Church in Wales and Roman Catholic schools, but breaking down age-old barriers would be no mean feat and the sector would have to wait and see if headteachers were willing to play ball. They were not, after all, legally obligated to partake in school-to-school collaboration and partnerships were reliant upon goodwill. As a show of the Welsh Government's commitment to the project, Lewis said he planned to visit all 40 participating "Pathways to Success" schools. Given the minister had made few forays into the field, that in itself was a positive sign and while some would be sceptical of yet another initiative, no school was in a position to turn its nose up at a share of £20m. There was genuine hope that Challenge Cymru could pay dividends and although the prospect of more PISA humiliation was another three years in the making, a health-check carried out by its creators at the OECD came far too early and was never likely to make for pretty reading. A review of the "quality and equity" of education in Wales was commissioned by Andrews in December 2012 and published in April 2014. It focused on children aged three to 16 and considered alternative policy areas that could add value to the Welsh Government's existing reform programme. Albeit the report was the latest in a long line into Welsh education, seldom were they so dismissive of central government and the inadequacies of policy implementation by civil servants.

In a startling offensive, the OECD said teachers had been "overwhelmed" by a continuous flow of changes to Wales' education system and the nation lacked a long-term vision. Officials said the Welsh Government's tendency to introduce multiple initiatives in such a short space of time risked "reform fatigue" and accountability had "not been adequately matched with the provision of additional support to meet the raised expectations". They said there was no consistency in the services being provided by local authorities and regional consortia and, overall, "there is no consolidated approach to support schools in implementing the new policies and responding to low performance". The OECD said Wales had "struggled to strike a balance between accountability and improvement" and a number of "concrete policy options" would help strengthen the nation's education system over the long-term. Experts from the OECD visited Wales in 2013 to take evidence from a cross-section of stakeholders. It said:

"Wales has started a reform journey and the profession and the public share the sense of urgency to take action and the reform directions set out by the Government. However, it appears that the many reform initiatives pursued in the last few years have left the profession with a growing sense of feeling overwhelmed by a continuous flow of changes, and a lack of clear direction beyond 2015."[10] (OECD, 2014)

A document spanning 143 pages recommended raising the status of teaching and developing a culture of "collective responsibility" for improved learning and achievement for all students. But it was hopeful the Welsh Government could build on the current situation, given its "culture of consultation" and "positive relationship" with the profession. There weren't many immersed in Welsh education who would have found the OECD's findings surprising and the Welsh Government was to be commended for commissioning the report in the first place. Allowing the producers of the world-famous PISA study to shine a light on your education system is nothing if not bold and the former minister attracted praise for opening the closet to the department's skeletons. After all, the vast majority of stakeholders would not have known the OECD was available to carry out country-by-country reports. It is by no means a regular phenomenon and only Scotland, way back in 2006, had done similar in the UK.

Continuing on the OECD theme, Andreas Schleicher warned at a major education conference in June 2014 that almost a third of students in Wales were at risk of failing to meet the expectations of modern society. He said 30% of Welsh teenagers "are not demonstrating the outcomes that you need to be successful in today's world and today's economy". Addressing delegates at Cardiff City Hall, Schleicher said there were a "very significant share of low-performing students" in Wales and improving learner outcomes was the biggest challenge facing the nation's education system. Introduced by Owen

Evans as the "David Beckham of the educational world", Schleicher said Wales was "not currently living up to its potential" and raising expectations among teachers, pupils and parents was key. He said the "high degree of equity" between schools was a strength of the nation's education system, but noted that schools in leafy, affluent areas were not performing a great deal better than those in more challenging environments.[11] His assertion that the child of a room cleaner in Shanghai outperforms the child of a doctor or lawyer in Wales, was certainly food for thought. So too was his perception of school class sizes, which he said were not as big an issue as some countries – like Wales – had made out. Schleicher's assessment, made using a host of detailed graphs and tables, was as convincing as it was sobering. The conference served as a stark reminder that Welsh education remained a long way off world-leaders, some three years after Andrews stirred the pot.

Moving forward, there was all to play for and politicians would be doing everything in their power to ensure ballot boxes returned favourably in May 2015. But you felt sure that the heat on Lewis to stand firm in defence of "the Welsh way" would intensify and unless results improved, he would find it increasingly difficult to stave off those calling for an English-style approach. The marketisation of education, with academies and greater autonomy for schools, was not an avenue down which the Welsh Government wanted to walk. But failure to raise the bar would make it more of a possibility.

The Welsh Government was running out of chances to get education right. Heckling from the Commons was getting louder and rumours that Lewis was finding life as Education Minister tough were growing. It was not long before sector sources started harking back to the previous regime, albeit criticism of the former chemistry teacher was harsh given the circumstances in which he had found himself. The PISA results of 2013, for example, had nothing to do with him and he had inherited what was, in reality, a problem many years in the making. But all was not well and the fact that a minister as divisive as Andrews was being talked about so favourably less than a year after his resignation spoke volumes. Could Wales' most vociferous politician really be allowed back into the fold? Whatever happened, you felt sure Andrews had unfinished business.

# Notes

1.   Lewis, Huw. (2013). Reform, Rigour and Respect. October 16.
2.   Young, Toby. (2013). The Telegraph Online. December 6.
3.   Watkins, Emma. (2013). Western Mail. December 4.
4.   Griffiths, Robert Lloyd. (2013). Western Mail. December 4.
5.   OECD. (2011). Strong Performers and Successful Reformers in Education p 228.
6.   Barber, Michael. (2013). The Pearson Blog, Sir Michael Barber. December 3.

7.    Lewis, Huw. (2013). Western Mail. December 26.
8.    Davies, David. (2014). Education Questions, House of Commons. January 6.
9.    Ofsted. (2010). London Challenge. p 4.
10.   OECD. (2014). Improving Schools in Wales: An OECD Perspective. p 118.
11.   Schleicher, Andreas. (2014). Western Mail. June 12.

# 15

# A Time To Reflect

## Leighton Andrews: The interview

*Looking back on his three and a half years as Education Minister,
Andrews recounts his sudden departure and the policy initiatives
introduced on his watch. But what of the future and would the Rhondda
AM be back?*

I was approached by Andrews in summer 2014 with a means to an interview
marking his first anniversary since stepping down as Education Minister. We
met on June 16 a short distance from the National Assembly at the Wales
Millennium Centre, Cardiff Bay. I was keen to give Andrews the same
opportunity to reflect publicly on his tenure as I did Davidson, some two
and a half years earlier. We spoke for just over an hour and, as well as being
the first comprehensive interview he had given since his departure from the
Welsh Government, it was also the first time I had interviewed the former
minister alone and without an entourage. In terms of what was said, Andrews'
recollection of June 25 the previous year, his thoughts on PISA and a thinly-
veiled broadside at his predecessors, struck a chord. Andrews' reasons for
introducing both the LNF and school banding were particularly revealing.
Above all it was clear that Andrews remained emotionally attached to Welsh
education and his impending book, the first by a former Welsh Government
minister since the creation of the National Assembly, was indicative of his
ongoing association with the brief. A supporting website, in which he would
comment on the policy announcements of his successor, was most unusual
and gave fuel to rumours Andrews was pulling the strings. Musing as to
the reasons why Andrews had arranged to meet, it dawned on me that he
may have wanted the world to know he was ready for a comeback. The full
interview is published for the first time in this book.

# Wales Millennium Centre, Cardiff Bay
# June 16, 2014

He shook up Wales' schools system, locked horns with Westminster and waged a war on vice-chancellors. And that's not the half of it.

Leighton Andrews' reputation precedes him and there was doubtless a collective sigh of relief for many within Welsh education when the former minister stood down in 2013. Andrews' three and a half year term in office came to a dramatic end on June 25, following a row over the planned closure of a school in his Rhondda constituency. Amid accusations he had broken the Ministerial Code by campaigning to keep open Pentre Primary School, Andrews tendered his resignation. Opposition parties claimed it was untenable for Andrews to back the campaign when Rhondda Cynon Taf council's proposal to shut the school was in line with Welsh Government guidance over surplus places.

Recalling the day's events, Andrews said: "I resigned. There was a story running about my support for a group campaign against the closure of a school in the Rhondda, in Pentre. Clearly, I wasn't happy with the proposals that Rhondda Cynon Taf council had made. To some people, that appeared to be a conflict with my role as Education Minister. But your constituents put you in the Assembly and you've got to stand by them when you think they have a just cause. I wouldn't have chosen to have left in that way at that time, but I respect the right of the First Minister to make those decisions."

It was Andrews' clearest indication that his position in the Welsh Government had been taken out of his hands. Other than a profound sense of shock, Andrews said he felt "bruised" and "numb" having relinquished his first senior Cabinet role. He acknowledged that "political life is very changeable" but maintained he "didn't go into work that morning expecting to be ending in the job that evening".

Andrews said: "You serve at the pleasure of the First Minister. I couldn't have told when I was appointed in December 2009 how long I would be in the job. There was no guarantee that we would have had a majority in the election of 2011. Political life is very changeable. The key thing for me was that we had a clear manifesto which set out the course for this Assembly – and there was a lot of detail in there. So in effect, taking that agenda forward was the job of whoever was the Education Minister."

Given his tempestuous relationship with Wales' teaching fraternity, reaction to Andrews' surprise departure was somewhat mixed. But while it is true the belligerent minister made almost as many enemies as he did friends – and his aggressive style was not to everyone's liking – large swathes of the sector appeared sorry to see him leave. The day after his resignation, Andrews wrote on social networking site Twitter that he had always wanted to live long enough to read and his obituaries. So, did he like what he saw?

"I thought people were very kind and very complimentary – and I felt it was sincere," said Andrews, whose headline speech as Education Minister came in February 2011. Two months after Wales flunked its PISA test, Andrews took a book to what he called a "complacent system". It ended up being a defining moment, but was Andrews conscious of how significant his line in the sand was likely to be?

"I did think it was likely to be important and be seen as a turning point," he said. "It was the core of what we put in our manifesto. It felt like part of a seamless change moving forward, but it was also at the end of coalition government so it was partly about Labour staking out its territory as we went into the election." Wales' PISA results were well below expectations and triggered a robust response from Andrews, who unveiled a 20 point improvement plan to revive Welsh fortunes.

"I think people were broadly in agreement with the direction of travel, even if they didn't agree with every single point I made," he said. "I found that, by and large, the profession respected blunt speaking – and they respected that I'd always take questions at events and engage in dialogue." Andrews said PISA was "the wake-up call" and it was important the profession had time to "digest the implications". But his target – to be in the world's top 20 PISA nations when results are next published in 2016 – has long been a subject of ridicule. To succeed, Wales would need to make one of the biggest leaps ever recorded by the overarching OECD, and critics believe Andrews asked too much of an ailing education system. Reaching his goal appears all the more unlikely given Wales' failure to make any ground in December 2013, when the nation slipped further down the PISA rankings. Looking back, does the former minister regret setting the bar quite so high?

"I think that the policies we announced were right; I think the target I announced was not as smart as it could have been," he said. "One of the things we didn't allow for was the fact that the number of countries taking part in PISA changes from assessment to assessment." Reflecting on his response to PISA, Andrews hailed the introduction of Wales' LNF as an important development. "As I look back over it, it seems to me that this was something that the headteachers' unions, particularly, thought was very worthwhile," he said. "I think the LNF was pretty commonsense – it breaks down literacy and numeracy and sets out where you expect pupils to be at each stage of their development. It helps to provide the framework for the reading and numeracy tests, which I think parents have found gives them valuable information – so it's probably the major curriculum reform I instituted."

Given Wales' shortcomings in literacy and numeracy, the LNF was indeed considered a sensible addition by sector leaders. But why did it take Welsh ministers more than a decade to introduce a statutory skills framework?

Andrews said: "England, clearly, in the early New Labour years had done a lot on literacy and on numeracy. In that first New Labour term, from 1997-2001, it made a real impact. It was something we didn't do in the early days of devolution. I think it's important to have high expectations. We needed to raise the bar and make it clear across primary and early secondary that we had high expectations for all. And it's (the LNF) a recognition, I think, that without those core skills of literacy and numeracy, it's very hard to build a platform for further learning for any individual."

If the LNF won plaudits, reaction to another of Andrews' headline initiatives was far less favourable. School banding was launched in December 2011 and every secondary in Wales has since been grouped into one of five bands annually. It is credited with helping to raise attendance levels but stakeholders have grown increasingly frustrated by the volatility of a system which has seen schools leap from Band Five to Band One in a year. Unions question the level of support on offer to those struggling towards the bottom of the pile and critics have likened banding to league tables – a system currently employed in England which ranks schools on their exam results alone.

"It was clear to me that local authorities didn't have any idea of how well their schools were performing," said Andrews of banding's introduction. "We didn't have sufficiently strong measures in place to allow parents to make judgements. We know from inspections in places like Monmouthshire that although they were performing well as an authority as a whole, they should given their demographic be performing a lot better. So it was about introducing more challenge and what we regarded as acceptable." Andrews was asked about deficiencies in the Welsh Department for Education, of which he had been openly critical.

"There was huge progress," he said. "The department became better at using data; better at using relations with stakeholders; better at bringing in external advice; [it was] much more focussed; [there was] much better alignment with core government priorities; and it was much more transparent. For that, a lot of thanks goes to Emyr Roberts and Owen Evans. In my experience, officials appreciate clarity – and I had clear priorities from the beginning. I'm not saying that changes happened overnight – they didn't – but we moved in the right direction."

Among Andrews' other notable achievements was his radical tuition fees policy and decision to subsidise Welsh-domiciled students wherever in the UK they chose to study. In a way that no other Welsh politician has done before or since, he took on Westminster and proved, unequivocally, there was another, Welsh way. Not surprisingly, his long-running battle with Gove was the source of intense media coverage although the former minister saw things slightly differently.

He said: "I'm not sure I saw it as a personality battle between us. He (Gove) is a very ideological politician, with a clear agenda; I'm a politician with a clear agenda – and our agendas are different. There were clearly areas – such as qualifications – which had previously been decided on a three-country basis, which became more and more difficult. But it wasn't up to just me, of course – it was about Northern Ireland and Wales going the same way and England going off in another direction. At a personal level, he was immensely polite, normally, and I think that's the way he always behaved – in a perfectly polite way. It would seem there were other people putting fuel on the fire."

When it came to higher education and his well-documented tussle with university leaders, Andrews said the building blocks had been laid down long before his arrival. He added: "We were very clear on what we needed to do on higher education and moved very fast on that because Jane Hutt had published For Our Future, so in a sense we already had the tramlines for our higher education policy. I gave myself three years to finish the reconfiguration agenda – and we finished the reconfiguration agenda in not much more than three years. The inconclusive nature of it I think effected relations between government and HEIs in Wales, which did not appear to see themselves as part of a national collection. The higher education policy document that we published in June 2013 was a genuine attempt to say: 'We now want to promote the best in Welsh higher education.'"

Responding to accusations he tried too much, too soon, Andrews said: "I think in politics you get accused of one thing or the other; you are either accused of moving too fast or moving too slowly – and it depends on which side of the bed the opposition get out of on a particular day as to which they accuse you of. We need a bit more longevity in educational policy making in Wales, in my opinion."

Regional consortia were undoubtedly one thing Andrews did give sufficient time to develop organically. But despite a strict deadline of September 2012, progress was patchy and not every consortium is properly developed. A new blueprint for driving school improvement at a regional level was launched in April 2014, following local government's pledge to ring-fence voluntarily £19m. Reflecting on his approach to regional working, Andrews said: "We wanted to get them moving fast – but they were consortia of local authorities, so we didn't impose as much of a formal structure as perhaps we should have done at the outset. The leaders had said that education was their top priority and we gave them the chance to get it right. Clearly, they needed more direction. If I had my time again, I would have been more dirigiste at the beginning."

Andrews said he had not wavered from his view that having 22 local education authorities operating in Wales was "too many". He added: "If we get local government reorganisation right, will the regional consortia be necessary in five to 10 years? I don't know."

Leaving the past to one side, Andrews was asked to consider a more recent addition to the Welsh education scene that he had no hand in implementing. Schools Challenge Cymru was unveiled by Andrews' successor to help raise performance in Wales' weakest secondaries. Andrews welcomed what he said was a "very good initiative", adding: "I think officials were starting to think about it when I was leaving, but bear in mind it needed £20m – and they got it through [Barnett] consequentials. We had the Lead and Emerging Practitioner Schools when I was in post, but I didn't have that extra money to put into it."

Expanding on what he thought about the current regime, Andrews said he was "delighted" that Lewis had been appointed Education Minister, having worked closely with him in the past. "Huw has always been absolutely supportive of the standards agenda and I never had any doubts that he would take that forward and develop it in his own way," said Andrews, who had "no input at all" into the choosing of his successor. Freed from the pressures of running such a significant government portfolio, Andrews has, it is fair to say, slipped from the limelight in Wales. But there has, in the absence of education, been more than enough to be getting on with. When it comes to Assembly business, Andrews said he had enjoyed "playing a role" on cross-party health and local government committees. "I wanted to be on a committee where I wasn't going to be continually in the face of my successor – so it's been interesting for me to be working in new policy areas," he added.

In terms of his own personal interests, Andrews remains a keen supporter of Cardiff City Football Club and has spent much of his spare time writing a book based on his in-depth knowledge of Wales' education system. Nevertheless, when you consider the undoubted impact he made while Education Minister, the sight of Andrews on the Senedd's backbenches is still hard to comprehend. Having such a capable and committed politician hidden largely from view in the National Assembly does not seem a particularly good use of resources. Which begs the question: how much longer will the First Minister be able to leave the vociferous Bluebirds fan out in the cold?

"At the moment, I'm focused on the publication of the book and the initiatives we've got going on in the Rhondda," he said. But what if Carwyn Jones were to ring up tomorrow and invite him back into his Cabinet?

"You don't turn the First Minister down, do you," he said. And would he go back to education?

"Well if he asked me, of course I would," said Andrews. "I loved the education portfolio. But I would be very surprised if that were to happen."

One thing was for certain: Wales had not seen the last of Andrews and, having confirmed he would stand again in the 2016 Assembly election, there was every chance the nation's most belligerent politician would be around a fair while longer yet.[1]

# Note

1.    Andrews, Leighton. (2014). Western Mail. June 25.

# 16

# Lessons Learnt?

## A Conclusion

Reflecting on the state of Wales' education system and the events contributing to its unfortunate plight is not straightforward, given the relative infancy of the National Assembly. The cyclical nature of education and the tendency of policy to take time to manifest itself makes drawing definitive conclusions challenging. Such is the weight of initiatives unveiled since devolution, my closing remarks will be necessarily selective and I will seek only to highlight what I consider to be the most significant factors conspiring against Welsh practitioners.

Andrews once described claims he had responded to international criticism of Wales' school standards in a knee-jerk fashion as "complete tosh". He, like his predecessors, believed PISA was an important tool in the quest to improve Wales' education system. Accountability in the nation's schools is key and, with supporting evidence stacked in his favour, Andrews was duty-bound to tighten his grip. Clearly, PISA is one of several performance measures and its findings must be considered in the round. But I defy anyone who believes entry into the world's biggest education survey was a bad move. That said, there are doubtless many within the Department for Education and the Labour Party at large who wish they had talked Davidson et al into staying on the periphery. After all, if it was not for PISA, Wales would rank only against Northern Ireland and old foes, England. Coming bottom of a three-country pile rankles a lot less than it does an international list 70 deep.

Figures obtained using the Freedom of Information Act show the Welsh Government agreed to pay up to £560,741 to take part in PISA over the four years from 2010 to 2014. It shelled out a further $206,000 (circa £163,000) inviting the OECD into Wales to review its educational offer. But you can consider all of that money well spent. While Wales has not yet reached the PISA heights to which everyone aspires, our abject performance serves only to reinforce the nation's continued involvement. Regardless of its apparent pitfalls, the tri-annual test continues to grow and therein lies the real acid test; countries across the globe are signing up voluntarily and in their droves to a study that could cost them as much embarrassment as it could plaudits. Confirmation in August 2014 that the provinces of Beijing, Jiangsu and Guangdong would be joining Shanghai in representing China in the 2015 PISA study would not have warmed the hearts of ministers in Cardiff Bay. Given Shanghai's dominance in previous studies, the presence of three more East Asian regions was likely to hamper further Wales' chances of breaking into the world's higher echelons.

The Welsh Government, as the guardian of education services in Wales, rightly shoulders a significant portion of blame for Wales' PISA scores. All lines of accountability lead to the top and policymakers are as culpable as any for the sorry predicament in which we find ourselves. The role of Estyn in contributing to the illusion that all was well in Wales' schools system cannot be waved away, either. Picture the scene: first, schools are stripped of SATs and league tables, with their replacement teacher assessments not up to standard. Then, with increased onus on the nation's inspectorate to hold schools accountable, it too was found wanting. Inflationary school assessments helped no-one and Estyn's failure to keep an honest and reliable record of performance raises serious questions over its integrity, albeit noticeable improvements have been made since the introduction of its new framework in 2010. The whiff of blame does not stop there, however, and if the Welsh Government and Estyn are part responsible, then so too is everyone else.

Politically, minority parties did not do nearly enough to scrutinise ruling administrations as Welsh pupils started sliding behind their peers during the early to mid 2000s. The Welsh Conservatives, Welsh Liberal Democrats and Plaid Cymru were by no means innocent bystanders and closer scrutiny of policies could have prevented some of the known failures from unravelling. And, assuming funding was a factor, all parties were complicit in starving Wales' education system of cash; the Liberal Democrats and Plaid Cymru had been in government, while the Tories had in the run-up to the 2011 Assembly election pledged to protect health by cutting the education budget by as much as 20%. To a certain extent, those steering the ship were allowed to navigate through troubled waters unopposed. But politicians do not hold all the cards and trade unions, which appear to have more power over Wales' public sector than they do in England, were partners in our decline. The nation's media must also hold up its hands. No-one is immune from criticism and together, journalists in Wales did not sufficiently question the Welsh Government's divergence in education policy. Ruling ministers should not have been given the freedom to do as they wished without justification. That said, the known frailty and gradual contraction of the Welsh media does not bode well for the future.

Following devolution, Wales saw merit in Scotland's distinctive education system as a possible model for its own. But a long history of shared qualifications meant breaking significantly from the norm would be easier said than done. Wales is closer to England than it would care to admit and in GCSEs and A-levels, possesses a link that transcends generations. Severing ties was always going to be a gradual process and while there is further change in the pipeline, Wales should not dismiss out of hand developments being made in Westminster. Andrews once said that one of the benefits of devolution is that it allows England to be a laboratory for experiments. But hugely successful Challenge programmes, involving school-to-school working in some of England's most deprived regions, are proof policy borne out across Offa's Dyke can pay dividends. Schools Challenge Cymru, for example, was an adaptation long overdue and, when it suits, policy can travel.

Finland, considered by many to be the educational doyenne, is often looked upon as a model of how best to innovate. Its schools system is based on the premise that all people have equal access to high-quality education and training and teaching is rightly hailed as one of the nation's most respected professions. In Finland, every teacher must obtain a master's degree – which takes around five years to complete – from one of the nation's eight universities and for every 8,000 applicants, only 700 are accepted. Competition is fierce, but aside from its unwavering commitment to a skilled workforce, Finland's approach is largely atypical. Finnish children do not begin school until the age of seven, they are given more time for recreation and, compared to many other world-leaders, enjoy a shorter working day. There are no high-stakes external tests and teachers are entrusted to craft the best learning conditions for all learners based on a more versatile national curriculum. Crucially, Finland's inclusive education system has not developed overnight and is the product of many years' social and capital investment. A radical overhaul during the 1970s started a process that developed gradually over a 30 year period.

Dr Pasi Sahlberg, a former Director General of Education in Finland and a visiting professor at Harvard University, believes education ministries have become obsessed with "shopping around the world" for the best strategies and warns that policy reforms are "very bad travellers". That said, Wales has caught what Sahlberg calls the "GERM". An "epidemic like Bird Flu", the Global Educational Reform Movement infects countries obsessed with mirroring world leaders and Wales must be careful not to imitate without due care and attention. Finland may well be a beacon of excellence, but no one nation has all the answers.

Closer to home, a nagging thorn in the side of Wales' education system is rampant and inexcusable variation among providers. There are pockets of excellence on Welsh shores, but good practice has not yet manifested itself in every school, across every local authority and pupils invariably suffer from a postcode lottery. The challenge is ensuring all children benefit from the same quality of teaching and are thereby provided the same opportunities to progress in life. Those at the chalk face may think, quite reasonably, that it is what happens in their own classroom that matters most. But if every teacher took the same pride in their pupils' performance, Wales would not be in the position in which its finds itself today. The issue is that headteachers do not have a conveyor-belt of talent from which to draw upon and attracting the cream of the profession into Welsh schools is becoming increasingly difficult. Wales' reputation has been tarnished by a steady flow of negative publicity and its education system has scarcely been less appealing to new starters. It is a vicious circle. We need top teachers to trigger a revival in Welsh fortunes, but there is little incentive to join the profession while performance is under such intense scrutiny. Welsh education has scarcely been so unappealing.

To his credit, Andrews, who like Davidson will be forever synonymous with Welsh education, was the first to properly acknowledge Wales' shortcomings and left no stone unturned in pursuit of system-wide improvement. But his determination to raise performance across the board would also work to his detriment. It was not so much that Andrews had bitten off more than he could chew, than bitten off more than his relatively small army of civil servants could stomach. Andrews' forensic analysis of schools and what needed to be done in compulsory education, coupled with his ferocious assault on Wales' university sector, was unwavering. But there were, in my opinion, too many plates spinning at once. It was a classic case of quantity over quality and if Andrews had focused his attention on one area over several others, he would surely have walked away with more obvious gains. While the nation's well-documented plight gave fuel to his impatience, there is little doubt that Andrews tried too much, too soon. In fact, so preoccupied was the minister with new initiatives that he did not monitor sufficiently those which he had already introduced. It is ironic that Andrews would reflect in 2014 that he thought "there were too many initiatives, strategies, and policies" besetting Welsh education upon his arrival in the department in 2009.[1]

Documents provided by the Welsh Government using the Freedom of Information Act show there were 24 reviews relating to DfES commissioned during Andrews' reign as minister. Given the known inadequacies of the civil service, this was far too many. So determined was he to overhaul every facet of the system, Andrews ended up overloading his officials and putting undue pressure on those whose job it was to develop and implement policy. Take for example, major reviews of the arts in education, ICT and computer science, Welsh history and physical activity. Seldom will a task and finish group or its resulting report recommend a watered-down version of their specialist subject. An independent team of experts in a chosen field will inevitably seek to promote what it is they have been asked to analyse. The fact of the matter is, schools have enough on their plate without widening the net yet further and when you throw in the teaching of drug misuse, physical violence or financial awareness, it is easy to see how teachers can become distracted from their primary purpose. The role of educator has changed dramatically in the last few decades and teachers often double as carers, psychologists, social workers and, to a certain extent, second parents. While these problems are not unique to Wales, schools do not have the capacity to take on more responsibility and should not be expected to rid society of all its problems.

**Table 7 Reviews commissioned by DfES: December 2009-June 2013**

|    | Review | Date commenced |
|----|--------|----------------|
| 1  | Frontline Resources | June, 2010 |
| 2  | Higher Education Governance in Wales | July, 2010 |
| 3  | Future Structure of Universities in Wales | March, 2011 |
| 4  | Digital Classroom Teaching | September, 2011 |
| 5  | Masters in Educational Practice | October, 2011 |
| 6  | Qualifications 14-19 | November, 2011 |
| 7  | GTCW and Development of Education Workforce Council | December, 2011 |
| 8  | Child Development Assessment Profiles | February, 2012 |
| 9  | Consortia and Shared School Improvement Services | March, 2012 |
| 10 | Higher Education Provision in North-East Wales | April, 2012 |
| 11 | Arts in Education | May, 2012 |
| 12 | Schools and Physical Activity | May, 2012 |
| 13 | Literacy Grants | July, 2012 |
| 14 | Initial Teacher Training | September, 2012 |
| 15 | Welsh for Adults | September, 2012 |
| 16 | Impact of Curriculum and Assessment Arrangements within High-Performing Countries | October, 2012 |
| 17 | The Future of ICT and Computer Science | October, 2012 |
| 18 | History, Welsh History and Curriculum Cymreig | October, 2012 |
| 19 | Assessment and the National Curriculum | October, 2012 |

**Table 7** *Continued*

|    | Review | Date commenced |
|----|--------|----------------|
| 20 | Welsh Second Language | October, 2012 |
| 21 | Digital Learning | November, 2012 |
| 22 | Future Delivery of Education Services | November, 2012 |
| 23 | 14-19 Learning Pathways: Learner Travel | November, 2012 |
| 24 | Local Collaborative Provision at Key Stage 4 | February, 2013 |

SOURCE: Welsh Government

In the short-term, rectifying Wales' chronic key skills shortage is of most pressing concern. A solid grounding in literacy and numeracy is essential in an increasingly competitive jobs market and proficiency in the Three Rs is as prevalent now as it was 100 years ago. The teaching of core skills should not be compromised by calls for more physical education in schools. Our economic prosperity does not depend on Wales qualifying for football's World Cup finals. Teachers spend too much time and energy fretting over a convoluted curriculum that is already bursting at the seams. A short while ago in January 2012, there were 10,400 qualifications on the Database of Approved Qualifications in Wales for the 14-19 age group. If the Welsh Government is serious about redressing the nation's skills imbalance, then the LNF must be a focus moving forward; the success of our universities, colleges and indeed secondary schools is largely irrelevant if our youngest pupils are forever playing catch-up. But that is not to say the LNF is a silver bullet and the answer to all our problems. The framework has so far promised a lot and delivered very little. Critics have every right to be sceptical of the Welsh Government's implementation and there is a real danger that the LNF could, in some cases, become counterproductive. The framework must be strengthened as a matter of urgency or many millions of pounds will be wasted.

I was told recently about an English teacher and her junior protégé. When given a book, the pupil – a mere three-year-old – ran her finger across the pages as if to change screen on an iPad, so accustomed was she to new inventions. It is now patently obvious that times have changed and technology in education must be seen as a help not a hindrance. Teachers have to embrace technological developments and in this, the twenty-first century, schools can not afford to turn a blind eye. There is no room for dinosaurs and where finances allow, schools should be encouraged to broaden their horizons. Andrews was a keen advocate and positive strides were made under his leadership, although the minister was at times criticised for his own carefree use of social media. Provocation on such a public forum can paint a certain picture and while greater interaction with constituents can only be a good thing, a line must be drawn. Nevertheless, there is far more scope for technological advancement in Welsh schools and while the advent of new technology should never substitute for good teaching, its benefits are unquestionable.

There is little anyone can say about funding that we do not know already. Money matters in every walk of life and no matter what public service you have a vested interest, there will always be a clamour for more. True, funding is not the answer to all our education woes and a boost to Welsh coffers will not itself bring about the level of improvement needed. But an additional £857 per pupil in Wales – the projected shortfall with pupils in England – would surely help. The trouble for Welsh schools is that they are still bound by the same pay and conditions arrangements as those across the border, where we know there to be more money available. Inevitably, as soon as schools have paid staff salaries – accounting for upward of 80% of their overall budgets – there is significantly less left over for innovation. But some have it easier than others. Consider Wales' only "excellent" local authority education service. Ceredigion spent £5,146 per primary pupil (well above the all-Wales average of £4,550) and £5,823 per secondary pupil (the average was just £5,120) in 2013-14. Overall, Ceredigion was the biggest spender on schools in Wales and the fact did not escape unions, who have long argued for extra resources to support teachers on the frontline. There are exceptions to the rule and Blaenau Gwent is perhaps the best example of an authority that spends very well on education for very little return.

Funding in isolation can be a very different story, however, and I have seen first-hand the struggles that some schools have in balancing their books. Reserves are not a luxury bestowed on every governing body and the fact there are headteachers in Wales regularly covering teacher absence – or worse, taking classes on a permanent basis – is an indictment on the sector's parlous financial state. An inflated Pupil Deprivation Grant to support those least well off is to be welcomed, but rumours of flagrant misuse are of little comfort. In an age of austerity, education must be prioritised. It is no good paying lip service and if we are serious about plugging the attainment gap, we must focus hearts and minds.

Qualifications are another quandary that Wales has yet to fully come to terms with. Governments' tendency to tinker with curriculum and qualifications has been likened to a "disease" and it is easy to see why, given politicians fiddle so often with classroom learning. Take the Westminster administration, for example. Having won power in May 2010, Gove was hell-bent on exam reform amid suggestions GCSEs and A-levels had gone "soft". Years of "dumbing down" under Labour had, according to the Conservatives, given way to a culture of complacency. Pupils in England, they said, were not being suitably challenged and "grade inflation" had conspired against them. A scatter-gun approach to restoring confidence in the nation's exams system saw O-levels, EBaccs and I-levels touted as possible replacements. But despite his posturing, Gove appeared no closer to implementing sweeping changes when he was relieved of his duties in July 2014. Traditional qualifications have always been on the menu in Wales, though one suspects GCSEs and A-levels will end up looking a lot different here.

Barring incident, from September 2015 Wales will have its own bespoke GCSEs in maths, English and Welsh, as well as a revised and overarching Welsh Baccalaureate qualification. Qualifications Wales will be established to facilitate the changes and, over time, be responsible for the regulation and awarding of all qualifications aside from degrees. Together, the change represents a significant body of work and a radical overhaul on the scale of that suggested will require meticulous planning. Regrettably, there is little to suggest DfES is up to the challenge and more uncertainty over GCSE English language in January 2014 – following the Welsh Government's hurried introduction of new-look qualifications – does not augur well. According to figures released under the Freedom of Information Act, the qualifications and curriculum divisions within DfES employed 94 people in July 2013, up from 73 in July 2012. On the face of it, 94 is not nearly enough.

The delivery of education services remains the elephant in the classroom and few with a genuine interest would argue in favour of the current support structure. Local authority education services are, on the whole, too small and incapable of providing the level of support required by schools. Suffice to say, some school leaders will suffer their just deserts when Estyn visits and not everyone will have grounds for appeal. But the plight of a school should not come as a surprise to its local authority. A well-oiled council will be one step ahead of the inspectorate and, barring unforeseen circumstances, be able to prevent any school descending into special measures. As it is, far too many require external intervention and the inadequacies of local government are plain for all to see. Radical thinking is needed and reorganisation is essential. A new style of education delivery is long overdue; the Hill report provided an early blueprint and a basis from which to work, but the Welsh Government must throw open its doors and consult widely with stakeholders as it did so successfully with its reform of qualifications. Party politics must be put aside in the best interests of learners and the sector itself must be allowed its say. The Welsh Government's lukewarm response to the findings of the Williams Commission did not bode well albeit Andrews' appointment to the newly-created role of Minister for Public Services will doubtless provide the agenda with fresh impetus.

It goes without saying that everyone involved in education shares the same goal – to educate and inspire those in their care. But all too often in Wales, providers conspire against each other. There is currently too much animosity between those responsible for administering education. There is no fluidity and a lack of trust is holding the nation's education system back. Schools have little or no faith in local authorities and regional consortia which, in turn, feel at odds with central government. And who can blame them? DfES, in all its various guises, has such a poor record of delivery that stakeholders are rightly sceptical of its ability to implement policy and make good promises of support. Coincidentally, if school-led improvement is given greater precedence and Wales' Challenge programmes do impact on standards, the need for a middle tier will dissipate.

Quality leadership at every level is paramount and teachers must take responsibility for their own improvement journeys. It is predicted that a third of headteachers in Wales will retire over the next decade and it is important to stay ahead of the game by nurturing young talent. Recruiting is easier said than done, however, and it is not uncommon for school governing bodies to advertise posts at least twice, such is the dearth in applications. It could be said that Wales is paying the price for its failure to invest in school leaders at the turn of the last century, when England established the National College for Teaching and Leadership. Dubbed the "schools' Sandhurst", it was England's first prestige academy intended to train the next generation of headteachers and won high praise from sector leaders. Federating is little more than a quick fix and a longer-term solution is needed in Wales. An education system is only as good as the quality of its practitioners and there are none more important than those leading on education's frontlines. That said, it is higher up the food chain that gives cause for most concern.

As I have already alluded, Wales' problems at department-level are extremely well documented and long-standing deficiencies have still to be addressed. Implementation is a perennial problem and Wales is being held back by the obvious inadequacies of its civil service. We have little hope of system-wide change while DfES remains so dysfunctional. Owen Evans, to his credit, has battled manfully to restore order but the added burden of a minister still finding his feet doubtless weighs heavy. Although their professional relationship was relatively short-lived, Evans proved the perfect foil for Andrews and his powers of mediation ensured fruitful discussion. A change in minister and, with it, the shouldering of more responsibility would have been both unforeseen and challenging. Moving forward, Wales needs to attract the best but, like teachers, our sorry position on the world stage makes attracting experienced officers into Cardiff Bay difficult. If, even after 15 years of devolution, the department continues to plateau, a root and branch overhaul may be the only solution. A clear-out will not come cheap, but Wales can no longer settle for mediocrity – or worse, incompetence – at the highest level.

Higher education represented something of a mixed bag for Andrews, as it has the Welsh Government more generally. The pressing need for collaboration, particularly in times of economic hardship, was well understood but getting institutions down the aisle was not as simple as it sounded. Many ministers had tried and failed to solidify relationships and pulling universities around the table rarely resulted in amicable resolutions. If anyone was going to merge long-standing foes it was Andrews, but the defiance of Cardiff Met's vice-chancellor and chairwoman of governors in staving off the threat of dissolution, cannot be understated. Wilding, in particular, played a crucial hand and without her stonewall approach to a minister on the warpath, there is every chance Cardiff Met would have succumbed.

The Welsh Government saw value in merging three universities in South-East Wales, Cardiff Met did not. But regardless of whether or not you agreed with her motives, Wilding fulfilled her brief and failure to deliver a three-way university merger in South-East Wales represented one of Andrews' only headline defeats. It remains a sore subject, softened only by Newport's union with Glamorgan. Nevertheless, both Cardiff Met and Glyndŵr can ill afford to rest easy and one suspects that collaboration is only temporarily off the Welsh Government's higher education agenda. The merger plan is not yet dead in the water and you would not bet against its resurrection some time in the not too distant future. It is worth noting that as the vice-chancellors of some of Wales' smallest universities near retirement age, there could soon be a vacuum in which merger would become a more distinct possibility. It will be interesting to see who picks up the mantle as and when they decide to hang up the cap and gown, and whether or not their successors choose to oppose so vehemently formal collaboration. The financial state of Glyndŵr, in particular, could quicken the process, with financial statements for 2012-13 revealing a group deficit of £4m equivalent to 9% of its total income. Having fallen foul of the Home Office for admitting international students with invalid English language test results, it appears inevitable that Glyndŵr will evolve yet further and Professor Michael Scott's decision in November 2014 to stand down as vice-chancellor could well be definitive.

A lot has been made of Andrews' assault on Wales' higher education system and battles with vice-chancellors, in particular. Like others, I always saw merit in plans to merge Glamorgan, Newport and Cardiff Met into a powerhouse of higher education in the South-East Wales region. Having four universities – each with their own vice-chancellor, registrar and governors – competing to attract the attentions of students, businesses and local authorities is not in and of itself an efficient use of public resources. Regardless of whether or not the Welsh Government had compiled a working business case, Andrews ultimately failed in his attempts to translate to all parties a positive message. Instead, he allowed his frustration at the pace of change to boil over and by issuing a dissolution order, cut short any hope of an amicable resolution. It was a defining moment and the minute Cardiff Met's shutters came down, the three-way merger plan was as good as over. Andrews was determined to flex his ministerial muscles and prove to the nation he could achieve what his predecessors had not. But in doing so, he overstepped the mark and his pursual of Cardiff Met wasted time and energy that could have been better used elsewhere. Nevertheless, the former minister still walked away having achieved more in higher education than his predecessors and on the basis that any new entity should set out to achieve more than could be delivered by its individual parts separately, the merged institution has potential.

It is often said that we in Wales must aspire to be a small, smart country. And, with a population of just three million in such close proximity, there should be no reason why that basic premise cannot be achieved. But being small, I would argue, is as much a hindrance as it is an aid. The incestuous nature of education in Wales means everyone tends to know everyone else. It is an issue that transcends all sectors and cosy consensus can give way to complacency. Impartiality is often called into question and past history is difficult to overlook. Higher education is one of the more obvious breeding grounds, with skills easily transferable between institutions. The danger when so many familiar faces are swilling around the nation's education system, is that it becomes too sterile. True, there has been some outside influence and recent additions to Wales' university sector – the vice-chancellors of Aberystwyth, Bangor and Cardiff have all migrated from elsewhere in Britain – are all very welcome. But there remain too many with a strong influence who have yet to make their mark on standards. The Welsh Government can ill afford to be too insular and a freshening up of its top team is long overdue. Just as in the review of qualifications, there is a fine line between understanding the wants and needs of your own learners – and opening up an external eye on what it is you are trying to achieve.

The National Assembly for Wales celebrated the 15th anniversary of its first plenary session on May 12, 2014. It is not for me to say how the fledgling administration has impacted on the health service and economy, albeit the signs are not good. But when asked if devolution has delivered for Welsh education, regrettably, you would have to say no, it has not. True, the Assembly's youthfulness does not allow for a definite judgement on overall performance and with policies like the Foundation Phase – of which I remain cautiously incredulous – still not having impacted on external exam results, assessment is to a certain extent only provisional. The educational revolutions of countries like Cuba and Finland, let's not forget, were many years in the making. Davidson once professed that Wales' "groundbreaking education initiatives do indeed prove the effectiveness of devolution". Ultimately, it will be the success of those initiatives that determines how effective newfound freedom has been for Wales. It is important to note, however, that while evidence suggests standards have got progressively worse in Wales, Scotland has shown the way and proven devolution can be a success. Since the creation of a new Scottish Parliament in 1999, Scotland's education system has gone from strength to strength and there are no murmurings of discontent north of the border as there are here. There can be no more damning an indictment of the first 15 years of Wales' National Assembly.

Paradoxically, the results of four successive Assembly elections would suggest otherwise. Welsh Labour has won the largest share of the vote at every poll since 1999 and there is no sign of a landslide swing to the right. Wales is effectively a one-party state. Democratic it may be, but the reluctance of the electorate to even flirt with change puts little pressure on the ruling administration. For the most part, members are assured of their seats and ministers need only appease their leader. In spite of mounting disquiet over its handling of public services, Welsh Labour reigns supreme and the nation's political preference has created an unhelpful safety blanket. Sub-consciously, without the threat of usurpation you are surely less likely to perform consistently to your optimum. Failure to translate policy into results has not yet cost Welsh Labour its authority but the party's prominence is a slant on the opposition as a viable alternative.

Inevitably, critics are quick to apportion blame and each has their own theory on what went wrong for Welsh education and why. I have sought throughout these pages to paint a picture of collective responsibility, with no one person solely culpable for the situation in which Wales finds itself. But certain decisions stand out as being pivotal. In hindsight, removing SATs and league tables, albeit with support from within the sector, was regrettable. The promise of strengthened teacher assessments was not upheld and there appeared no way of gauging a school's relative performance. To pull two crucial layers of accountability without a tried and tested replacement was to commit educational suicide. It released the valve to complacency and created a situation in which practitioners did not know what "good" looked like, or indeed, where it could be found. The University of Bristol put forward a strong case with regards league tables and a recent report published by Estyn into standards of maths warned that "findings from school inspections do not support the strong increase in standards seen in teacher assessment outcomes".[2] The issue is almost certainly not exclusive to one subject. In conversation about the importance of accountability measures, Andreas Schleicher told me in summer 2014 that: "You can't improve what you can't see." The wiry German is as good a judge as any.

Andrews would reflect in 2014 that "banding, particularly in the first two years, made parents think about performance" and although it was never extended to primary schools, banding invariably raised the stakes. It was only ever designed to be a short, sharp shock to the system and, having served its purpose, there was little doubt it would be replaced. A new colour-coded national school categorisation system was officially unveiled in September 2014 and the promise of a moderated self-evaluation process was a defining factor in winning the support of unions. Unlike banding, categorisation would extend to primaries as well as secondaries and see schools in Wales clustered annually into one of four groups from January 2015.

The decision to do away with arm's-length qualifications body ACCAC and bring exam regulation in-house was also proven an error in judgement. The only real surprise is that it took so long for exam regulation to blow up, as it did spectacularly in 2012 and, to a lesser extent, two years later. Addressing a conference organised by the Central South Consortium, Lewis said in November 2014 that he did not think "that it is a mark of a good system... that a politician would have their mitts on the regulation of qualifications". But somewhere along the line, someone did.

With the launch of Qualifications Wales on the horizon, we will soon have a variation of SATs, league tables and ACCAC again in operation in Wales. The fact that all three have been resurrected in one way, shape or form suggests they should not have been ditched in the first place. In that respect, it could be said that Andrews spent much of his tenure unpicking the mistakes of his predecessors. One wonders how much easier it would have been for the Rhondda AM had Davidson, in particular, been a minister of a different colour. It is hard to imagine Andrews, so forthright in his convictions normally, being as tight-lipped about those he followed had they not been tainted by the same political party. If Davidson were a Tory or Liberal Democrat, she would doubtless have been subject to a more discernible diatribe. That is not to say Andrews himself got everything right. The Welsh Government's role in 2012's GCSE grading fiasco and a futile battle with Cardiff Met are testament to that. Look no further than the abject rolling out of CDAPs and the LNF as cause for more regret. But rest assured, Andrews achieved more than most and so particular was his planning, you felt heartened that there was at least some traction in the system.

As a politician, Andrews continues to polarise opinion. He could be extremely personable and open to dialogue. But so too could he change in an instant and Andrews was not averse to walking abruptly out of high-level meetings if things had not gone his way. The minister's fiery temper was most evident in media interviews and reporters would be under no illusions as to who was in charge. Perhaps the most infamous was Andrews' clash with BBC Wales presenter Aled ap Dafydd, who ran into the minister in an interview broadcast live on television early in 2011. In a bizarre row over Coco Pops and free school breakfasts, Andrews branded ap Dafydd a "disgrace" for name checking the popular cereal as he challenged the policy in light of poor levels of attainment. The unfortunate episode was a perfect example of Andrews' propensity to blow a fuse. The WJEC, most notably its board and chief executive, was one of the more hapless victims of Andrews' wrath and his conduct in the Senedd could at times be less than courteous. The level of vitriol he felt towards Gareth Pierce, Antony Chapman and, to a lesser extent, Scott, was borne largely out of their caution. The trio were not subservient and prevented Andrews from getting what he wanted. Never willing to let sleeping dogs lie, Andrews revelled in the power associated with being a government minister and was almost tyrannical in approach. The fact that neither Pierce, Chapman or Scott were named in Ministering to Education spoke volumes.

Towards the end of his tenure, Andrews became a victim of his own hype and media attention. There was a time when he would feature regularly on both lunchtime and evening television bulletins and he became increasingly conscious of his image. Andrews knew what made a headline and when to be provocative. The irony is that away from the spotlight of the media, Andrews was far more reserved and of a shy and retiring disposition. The minister played a character and like a hardened actor, came to life on stage. His bullish and dour demeanour was, for the most part, a façade. I accept that some will find that hard to believe. But there was a different side to Andrews of which many will be unable to familiarise. In the glare of the public eye, the minister was scowling, abrasive and almost deliberately argumentative. Away from the chamber, he was both humorous and humble. This was a man who drove half way across Wales to speak at clashing teacher conferences; a man who called his elderly mother on the afternoon of his sacking so as to prepare her for the evening's headlines; and a man who put aside any bitterness and self-pity to prepare the best he could the nation's next Education Minister.

Andrews was obsessive and a minister well and truly on top of his brief. He was well informed, rarely caught off guard and as an operator, well ahead of his time. It will not take long walking the corridors of Tŷ Hywel to establish that the calibre of AM and indeed Cabinet member that befalls the Welsh Assembly is somewhat lacking. Angela Burns, an underrated politician and extremely competent shadow minister, spoke for many in the sector when she said in January 2013 that, Andrews aside, Wales had been subject to a "succession of fairly feeble Education Ministers"[3]. As well as being a blatant attack on Messrs Hutt and Davidson, Burns had acknowledged Andrews' determination to roll up his sleeves. It is most unusual for a member of the opposition to be quite so forthcoming in their praise. As a journalist, Andrews had an answer for everything during interview and you could well imagine him burning the midnight oil in preparation. In fact, Andrews' life away from the chamber was conducive to his time spent in meticulous planning. With two grown up children and a wife pre-occupied directing British Telecom in Wales, the minister had the freedom others did not. Improved standards were everything under Andrews, but with no tangible results other than a streamlined university sector and improved school attendance, it may be some time before we can properly judge his legacy.

Comparisons are often drawn between Andrews and Davidson, given their extended run in the educational role. I have had the pleasure of interviewing both – and there are striking similarities. Andrews and Davidson were extremely confident in their own abilities and displayed an authority that commanded the respect of their staff. It is easy, therefore, to see why they did not see eye to eye. That said, neither spoke ill of each other's tenure – publicly, at least – and both retain a loyal following. What is certain, however, is that Andrews and Davidson took a very different approach to policy development that makes split allegiance impossible. Davidson will be best remembered as a curriculum innovator; a woman who caressed her way to the top and put faith in the profession to improve itself. A former teacher, she had a connection to the workforce and felt comfortable in the classroom environment. Andrews, on the other hand, did not have the same affinity toward the profession and his limited understanding of how the sector worked in practice would work against him. He was, by nature, more authoritarian and chose to challenge the sector from the top down. Andrews was an enabler and, quite literally, a shock to the system.

In the world of politics, one has to draw inferences by reading between the lines. Politicians have too much to lose by pinning their colours to the mast which, coincidentally, makes Lewis' accepting of guilt in December 2013 all the more remarkable. But there was enough of a chink in the armour of Welsh education's two key players to highlight that they too had conceded shortcomings in the nation's strategic direction. Consider first, during Davidson's headline interview with me in 2012, her reflection that "trying to turn around an education system" takes a huge amount of time. The fact ministers were attempting to turn around anything suggests errors had been made along the way. Coincidentally, her recollection of comparative funding and pupil attainment gaps appear somewhat blinkered when supporting figures are so pronounced. Andrews, meanwhile, readily acknowledged that the Welsh Government had taken its "eye off the ball" – the so-called "settled consensus" of Carwyn Jones' governments about the first decade of educational policy in Wales – in terms of accountability. His admission during interview in 2014 that his top 20 PISA target "was not as smart as it could have been" should not be overlooked, either.

Andrews was more explicit in his book, Ministering to Education, writing that: "The target was too ambitious, and it was naive." It is worth putting Andrews' grandiose goals into perspective. Ireland was the 20th ranked nation in the 2012 Pisa tests, with scores of 501 in maths, 522 in science and 523 in reading. To be in the top 20% in 2012, Wales would have had to better 13th-placed Canada, which scored 518 in maths, 523 in reading and 525 in science. The comparison with Wales' scores of 468 in maths, 480 in reading and 491 in science is startling and proves beyond all reasonable doubt that Andrews' targets were both irrational and reckless. You would not enter a Morris Minor into a Formula One race and expect a podium finish. Andrews can count himself lucky he was not still minister when the penny dropped and the goalposts unceremoniously shifted. A new aspiration of being in the "500 club" across all measures by PISA 2021 was akin to what Scotland achieved in 2012. It was ironic that both school banding and the top 20 PISA target – two of Andrews' headline pronouncements – would be ditched during his promotion of Ministering to Education.

Andrews' thoughts on his predecessors were none more prevalent than in the closing remarks of his 2014 muse, within which he said "since Carwyn Jones' election as First Minister, we have seen standards improve in Wales". Of course, Jones' election coincided with his own as appointment as Education Minister. Andrews' thinly-veiled attack appeared to support what others had said of those who came before him. He added: "The point of devolution was not to be different for the sake of it, but to deliver better for the people of Wales."[4]

From a personal perspective, I must of course declare an interest. Andrews was the minister I spent the most time working alongside, and indeed the minister I reported on the most. But that in itself means I am reasonably well-placed to pass judgement and having been employed to scrutinise his actions, I can testify there was a motivation and genuine will to improve Welsh education. Andrews was not afraid of taking tough decisions or upsetting people along the way. The sector was under-performing – and it needed telling; to sit and pretend otherwise would have cheated a nation. It is for that reason Andrews earned the respect of his peers and shortly after his departure from government, Colin Riordan – one of the most powerful men in Welsh higher education – told me that the former minister could have held his own at the top table of the UK Government. It was a significant commendation but Riordan was not alone and Andrews drew admiration from across the UK. For example, there is little doubt that while their politics were very different, Gove respected his adversary's valour when it came to defending his schools system. There was sure to have been a collective sigh of relief in England's Department for Education when news of Andrews' resignation broke and Gove's handwritten letter to the Welsh minister was symptomatic of their mutual respect for one another.

One of the biggest criticisms levelled at Andrews was that he failed to elicit the wholehearted support of teachers. While the majority of unions backed his drive for improvement, those at the chalk face resented his stinging criticism of a sector in "crisis". Somehow, they felt the finger of blame had fallen squarely on their shoulders and the minister was deflecting responsibility. Andrews, with no first-hand teaching experience of Wales' education system other than his visiting stint at Cardiff University, was to many the latest in a long line who professed to know what the sector needed better than the sector itself. His rallying call in February 2011 struck the wrong chord with large swathes of the profession, who found it difficult to forgive and forget. The tone would soften over time and despite his new mantra – that "there is world-class teaching in Wales" – irreparable damage had been done. In fact, any possibility of Andrews' one day becoming Welsh Labour leader and with it, First Minister, appears highly unlikely given his failure to win over education's strongest ally. Teachers, along with county councillors – with whom he was also at war – are the bedrock of local Labour parties and it is hard to imagine a leadership challenge being fought and won without their allegiance. Andrews was first touted as a successor to Rhodri Morgan in the late 2000s and speculation surfaced again in 2013, albeit he was never likely to stand against Jones. Nevertheless, if the First Minister were to step aside, on the face of it there are none more capable than Andrews.

A winner of multiple Politician of the Year awards, Andrews was both capable and hard-working. His dogged determination to see things through would be sorely missed and education's loss would almost certainly be local government's gain. But for all his work, the situation in which Wales finds itself with regards education remains perilous. PISA has shone a light on our inadequacies and the world is all too aware of our lowly position. In researching for this book, I stumbled across "turbo paralysis", a word coined by American writer Michael Lind, which I believe is easily applicable to the Welsh Government's record in education. Lind describes turbo paralysis as:

> "A prolonged condition of furious motion without movement in any particular direction, a situation in which the engine roars and the wheels spin but the vehicle refuses to move."[5] (Michael Lind, 2012)

The description encapsulates perfectly the Department for Education's desire to effect change, without it having impacted significantly on standards. The propensity of officials to throw more and more at the sector in the faint hope that some of it will stick has been proven to be ineffective. Despite a newfound and intense focus on outcomes and the quality of Wales' offer, there has been no significant narrowing of the performance gap. Modest improvements at both GCSE and A-level in August 2014 were to be welcomed, but as long as Wales remains so far behind England and Northern Ireland, there is still much to be done. Wales' shortcomings in GCSE maths were a stark reminder of the challenge in hand, with the proportion of Welsh pupils achieving A*-C grades in the subject a full 12.4% below that across the border. Indeed, improving maths is considered vital moving forward and Andrews himself acknowledged in Ministering to Education that "if we could get maths to the levels of English or Welsh then our overall performance would compare happily with other parts of the UK at GCSE level".[6]

So where do we go from here? The fear is that, under a relatively new and inexperienced minister and senior leadership team, the drive for improvement has lost impetus. There is concern over Lewis' grasp of the education portfolio and the sense of urgency stimulated by Andrews has long since dissipated. Jones' retention of Lewis following his September 2014 cabinet reshuffle was considered more an indictment on the perceived capabilities of other AMs than it was a clear commendation of his first 15 months as minister. When asked a year after his appointment how Lewis compared to his predecessor, an extremely prominent figure in Welsh education told me the new minister was "easier to talk to". Their foremost observation was telling. As with Davidson, Andrews would doubtless fall short in a popularity contest with Lewis. But the Rhondda AM's enabling qualities were far more prevalent and while every minister brings with them their own inimitable style, I firmly believe that Andrews made best use of his time in office. That said, his combative approach would have jarred completely had Welsh education been thriving at the time of his appointment. Andrews was a minister in the right place, at the right time.

Looking to the future, I fear the short-term outlook for Welsh education remains decidedly bleak. The vast majority of corrective policies will not have had time to bite by the time teenagers sit the next tranche of PISA tests in November 2015 and I would envisage it taking at least another three years after that before Wales can hope realistically to see meaningful improvement. The successful development of new Wales-specific qualifications will be crucial if Welsh pupils are to compete effectively on the world stage and the nation can ill afford the sort of institutional in-fighting that has plagued exam reform in the not so distant past. There is every chance that Welsh further education will continue to perform well in the face of severe funding cuts, though I anticipate a further streamlining of Wales' universities. Regardless of its chosen interventions, if standards continue to stagnate the Welsh Government will have nowhere to hide. Two decades is plenty long enough to direct improvement and Scotland, which assumed similar powers in 1999, is a useful yardstick in that respect.

It is not for want of trying that Wales has yet to emerge from the depths of the educational sphere and there is one thing working in our favour above all else: there is a hunger to improve and restore Welsh education to its former glory. There *is* room for improvement and the message is well understood. Wales needs a rise in consistency and far greater collaboration between providers; collective responsibility to put right what has gone wrong is essential and denial will get us nowhere. There must be an onus on quality not quantity, and we must strive to get the basics right. Most of all, we must learn from past mistakes and re-instil a culture of pride in our education system.

The *Financial Times* once highlighted Wales' education policy, both radical and distinctive, as "proof that the Welsh Assembly can affect its citizens in a big way". That much is certainly true, albeit a shame that the affect is not indisputably positive.

# Notes

1.   Andrews, Leighton. (2014). Ministering to Education. p 33.
2.   Estyn. (2014). Numeracy in Key Stages 2 and 3: An Interim Report. p 6.
3.   Burns, Angela. (2013). Western Mail. January 24.
4.   Andrews, Leighton. (2014). Ministering to Education. p 109, 114, 377.
5.   Lind, Michael. (2012). The Spectator, The Age of Turboparalysis. December 15.
6.   Andrews, Leighton. (2014). Ministering to Education. p 97.

# Index